★ AN UNCERTAIN TRADITION

AN
UNCERTAIN

TRADITI★N

U.S. Senators from Illinois, 1818–2003

★ David Kenney and Robert E. Hartley

Southern Illinois University Pr

Library of Congress Cataloging-in-Publication Data
Kenney, David, 1922–
    An uncertain tradition : U.S. senators from Illinois, 1818–2003 / David Kenney
and Robert E. Hartley.
        p. cm.
    Includes bibliographical references (p.) and index.
    1. Legislators—United States—Biography. 2. United States. Congress. Senate—
Biography. 3. Illinois—Biography. 4. United States—Politics and government.
5. Illinois—Politics and government. I. Hartley, Robert E. II. Title.
    E176.K39 2003
    328.73'092'2772—dc21
    ISBN 0-8093-2549-7 (alk. paper)   2003004553

Printed on recycled paper.♻

The paper used in this publication meets the minimum requirements of American National
Standard for Information Sciences—Permanence of Paper for Printed Library Materials,
ANSI Z39.48-1992. ∞

To Wanda Carter Kenney, with love
And in fond remembrance of Earl M. Hartley and Alva B. Geesling

CONTENTS

ILLUSTRATIONS

Figures

Plates

PREFACE

The state of Illinois cannot claim, as Ohio and Virginia can, to be "the mother of presidents." Even Abraham Lincoln, who moved to Illinois as a young man, was born in Kentucky and spent most of his growing up years in Indiana.

Ronald Reagan, it is true, was a native son of the Prairie State, born in Texico. He spent his boyhood in Dixon and was educated at nearby Eureka College. However, he wasted little time in going on to greener pastures, first across the Mississippi to Iowa, then on to California, where the glitter of Hollywood caught his fancy. After a successful career in motion pictures, he became governor of California and then president of the United States.

Ulysses S. Grant hardly counts, given that he lived in our state for only a few months. And even though the "Grant home" is proudly preserved in Galena, Illinois, Ohio, his birth state, rightfully claims him as one of its own.

That is about all Illinois can boast, so far as occupants of the White House are concerned. We are proud to claim Adlai E. Stevenson as a native son, even though he never became president of the United States. Twice, however, once in 1952 and again in 1956, he was the standard bearer of the Democratic Party in the presidential contest.

As to number, Illinois has had its full share of U.S. senators. As with each of the fifty states, it is entitled to a representation of two at all times. To the year 2003, there have been a total of forty-seven persons chosen for the Senate from Illinois, including one who was elected but never allowed by the Senate to be seated and another who was expelled.

That is a large enough number to afford a basis for generalizations. At the same time, it is not so large as to defy study. We hope we can offer a broad portrait of all those persons chosen to go to the Senate from Illinois, all white males except one of the most recent, a black woman. In the concluding chapter, we hope to offer certain generalizations we have discerned.

We make no pretense at original research, but we *have* plumbed the substantial historical literature. The standard sources of political history and biography have been employed. Our goal is to take a fresh look at the collective lives of persons who share only one characteristic: qualification for a seat in the U.S. Senate, representing the people of the state of Illinois.

We have attempted to integrate the lives of our subjects with the currents of Illinois and national politics upon which they have gone voyaging. Those currents have dashed some individuals upon the rocks of political defeat but have taken others into the harbors of success and acclaim. In one sense, this is a study of a set of political issues occurring over time and illuminated by the lives of participants in the politics of choice and service in the Senate.

Each of the forty-seven persons who have been selected or elected to serve in the Senate from Illinois falls into one of two sequences; thus, there have been two distinct sets of senators from Illinois (see figs. 1 and 2).

With terms of six years, the general practice since 1914 has been for the voters of Illinois to choose their senators at alternating intervals of two and four years. However, when Illinois became a state, the choice was in the hands of the state's General Assembly. Both positions were open and were filled at the same time. Since then, except once in each of four years due to the necessity of filling a vacancy, the rule has been the selection of only one senator at a time in a given year.

Treating two sets of officeholders, serving terms of six years, has made it necessary to move forward and backward in time. It seemed advantageous to deal with the entire tenure of one senator, whether that amounted to less than a year or a great many more, without interruption.

The alternative would have meant the constant interruption of each narrative to begin another account, only in turn to interrupt the latter in order to return to the former or to a newcomer on the scene. Our procedure has created a certain amount of repetition,

Sequence 1

Sequence 2

*v = vacant (Lorimer expelled).

Fig. 1. Illinois Senators Selected by the General Assembly, by Year

Sequence 1

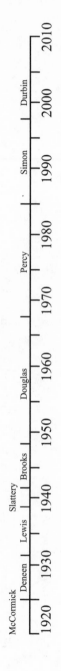

Sequence 2

*v = vacant (Smith elected but never seated).

Fig. 2. Illinois Senators Elected by the Public, by Year

but always from a changed perspective. It is hoped that these devices will not prove to be distracting.

We hope with this explanation of our procedure the reader can cope with the repetitive shuffling to and fro in time as we integrate the two separate sequences of senators that have taken form with passage of the years from 1818 to the present. At the beginning of each biographical sketch in this book, the year or years following the name of the senator are those of Senate service.

Work of this sort cannot successfully be done in isolation. It requires repeated interaction with other minds. Toward that end this has been a happy collaboration between a mature journalist and writer of biography and an even more aged, if not more mature, political scientist, also a writer of biography. The attention of both has in the past been turned toward other noted figures in Illinois politics.

Discussions with others from the worlds of journalism and academe have added a priceless dimension. A number of others have been recruited on the basis of their expertise to assist us in the evaluation of our subjects of study. The group includes former U.S. Senator Paul Simon, now director of Southern Illinois University's Public Policy Institute; Professor John S. Jackson, a political scientist, former interim chancellor of SIU Carbondale, and currently a member of the Public Policy Institute; Professor John Y. Simon, director of the U. S. Grant Papers project at SIUC; Professor Sam Gove, the longtime director of the Institute of Government and Public Affairs at the University of Illinois at Champaign-Urbana; Kenneth Buzbee, former state senator and currently a highly placed employee of the Illinois secretary of state; and SIUC professors Howard Allen, Kay Carr, and David Conrad of the history department, Bart Trescott of the economics department, H. Eugene Dybvig of the radio-television department, and John Baker and Barbara Brown of the political science department. Professor Gordon White of the educational psychology and special education department assisted in a statistical calculation.

Fortunately for the us, the authors, our ways of expression have been similar. As a result, our endeavors have fitted comfortably together. We are in full agreement that responsibility for any shortcomings this book may have is ours alone.

★ AN UNCERTAIN TRADITION

1 ★ The Founding Fathers

By 1809, when Illinois became a territory of the United States, settlers were flooding into its southern portions from Tennessee and Kentucky, guided there by the northward flowing Tennessee and Cumberland Rivers, and were coming down the Ohio. It was not a slave-owning society, by virtue of the prohibition in the Northwest Ordinance of 1787. Most of the early arrivals were poor whites in search of land and fortune, and escape from a culture dominated by the owners and managers of slave-worked plantations.

Mainly, the early settlers were agrarians, living for the most part in isolation on farms, and displaying the traditional values representative of the rural southern regions from which they came. They treasured family ties; male dominance; in case of a few, the role of the frontier Protestant church; freedom; and to a large extent, reliance on kin and neighbors instead of government.

The dominant national strains among early settlers of the Illinois country were English, Scotch-Irish, and German. Emphasis was on action and experience, and little stock was put in education, except for the most basic "readin', 'ritin', and 'rithmetic." Attention to politics was built upon personal acquaintance and loyalty and not upon issues.

Settlers coming from the forested hills of the south favored the southern portions of the Illinois country. It had trees for housing, fencing, and fuel, while the prairies further north did not. Land that would not grow trees could not be very fertile, they reasoned. What was more, the tough prairie sod was difficult to break.

There was little money on the Illinois country frontier. Markets for grain or pork were few and distant. The sale of whiskey was often the preferred way to market corn. Whiskey's bulk was far less than that of the corn used in its making, and thus it was easier to transport. The typical way of life was subsistence farming. The typical home was a small log cabin, with a dirt floor and few furnishings.

Elections saw most adult, male residents taking part as voters, but seldom as candidates for office. The candidates' role was usually filled by better educated, more experienced men recently arrived from some eastern region. The goals they sought were usually power, business advantage, and the income of public office, rather than public service.

According to Richard J. Jensen, when Illinois was a territory and early in its statehood, politicians built their coalitions on the basis of friendship and favors with kin groups and local elites. Before the 1830s, issues rarely concerned the pioneer. He expected few favors, much whiskey, and an acknowledgment from the candidate that the people in this land were the salt of the earth, God's most noble creation. The politicians in turn were after government contracts, land, personal glory, and the power that patronage would give them (27).

During the period prior to Illinois becoming officially a "territory" in 1809, loyalty or opposition to William Henry Harrison, the young soldier who was the appointed governor of Indiana Territory, which included the Illinois country, was almost the rule for those participating in the political process. That such loyalty was long lasting is illustrated by the fact that Harrison became president of the United States in 1841, an office his grandson Benjamin gained half a century later.

When Illinois became a state in 1818, it had fewer residents than in any earlier case of new statehood and perhaps any later one. The census that established its dubious eligibility for statehood was filled with fraud. Illinois's admission to the Union was driven by free-state versus slave-state politics and by the personal ambitions of certain of its early citizens.

In 1818, almost all of Illinois's non-Indian occupants were found in its southern one-third. Villages such as Cahokia, Prairie du Rocher, and Kaskaskia were established early in the French period (1673–1763), and Shawneetown, Edwardsville, and Vandalia were thriving communities long before there was any thought of Chicago or Springfield. Thus, the early politics of the territory and state of Illinois were of necessity conducted in southern Illinois, which soon became known as "Egypt," with its villages of Cairo, Thebes, and Karnak.

Expecting little from government, and probably receiving even less, early settlers felt little connection to the distant government in Washington, D.C. There was never a viable Federalist Party in Illinois, thus no need for a Jeffersonian Republican group to contest it.

It was not until the 1820s, when Andrew Jackson became an aspirant for the presidency, that much attention was paid to such contests. As a product of the frontier, and a famed Indian fighter, Jackson was able to appeal to other frontiersmen. That connection placed Illinois firmly in the grasp of the emerging Democratic Party during the 1830s.

In his introduction to the 1967 edition of Solon J. Buck's book *Illinois in 1818,* Allan Nevins wrote:

> The settlement of the raw new country was a rough, dirty, dangerous undertaking that required courage and endless hard work. But, as . . . Buck shows, it bred character. And the Americans who flocked to settle there had three great advantages. First, they entered a rich, empty, challenging new land where they had to fight savages and wild beasts, but could do so with hope of success. Second, they created a new people to do the work of conquering this land, an amalgamation of numerous national stocks: English, Scots, Irish, Dutch, Germans, Huguenot French, Swedes, Jews from eastern Europe. This new society had traits all its own, and prized social equality and tolerance. Third, the settlers insisted on a common language and institutions—English—and so kept their unity. They remained one nation. America, as Crevecoeur wrote, became a new nation, quite unlike any in the Old World. (xii)

If Nevins were alive and writing that introduction today, it is probable that he would include "Africans" in his listing of the ethnic stocks that contributed to the making of the Prairie State. Certainly their participation has been a significant one.

The vast inland empire that fell under the scope of the Ordinance of 1787—the Northwest Ordinance—was bound to attract adventurers in the realm of politics as settlers arrived in numbers sufficient to make statehood for the "Illinois country" an apparent possibility. Starting from near nothing, as the people of such areas did, so far as training, skill, and experience in the art of government were concerned, the making of new states in the Great Valley was dependent on the arrival of persons with such assets, from longer settled states and territories.

The first two U.S. senators from Illinois serve well as illustrations. One came from Indiana Territory after playing a role in its establishment, to do the same for Illinois. Awaiting statehood there, he served as a federal judge. The other came from an active political life in the state of Kentucky to serve for nine years as the only territorial governor of Illinois before becoming a U.S. senator. Factional rivals, not party leaders, they competed for the political prizes of early statehood.

Jesse Burgess Thomas (1818–29)

When Jesse B. Thomas was selected to be one of the first two U.S. senators from the state of Illinois in 1818, he already was a veteran warrior of territorial politics and, importantly, a survivor of frontier factionalism. Moreover, Thomas had firsthand experience with the two most nettlesome regional issues of the early nineteenth century. He fought successfully on the front lines of the effort to separate Illinois Territory from Indiana Territory, and to bring his adopted home ground to statehood. Along the way, he became an unapologetic booster of slavery for the new state.

In some respects, his two terms in the Senate were an anticlimax to the fractious experiences of 1805–18. But he had successes, too, at the federal level before concluding his service in 1829 in political ignominy.

Born in 1777, in Shepherdstown, Virginia, now a part of West Virginia, Thomas and his family left for Bracken County, Kentucky, where he grew to manhood. He worked on his parents' farm and attended school, such as it was in those years. He left home for Washington, Kentucky, where he served for a time in the county clerk's office, and studied law with an older brother. After admission to the bar, Thomas began practicing law in Brookville, the county seat of Bracken County.

Following the death of his wife of a short time, Thomas left Kentucky for Lawrenceburg, the county seat of Dearborn County in Indiana Territory, where he settled in 1799. There he practiced law and began a successful venture into territorial politics.

By 1805, the Illinois country was part of Indiana Territory, and the region had its first experience with self-government. In that year, eight members of a territorial House of Representatives were elected, and five councilors—they might be thought of as senators—were appointed. Together with the appointed governor, William Henry Harrison, they had authority to make laws for and administer Indiana Territory.

Thomas was among the first elected members of the territorial legislature, representing Dearborn County, in the eastern part of the territory. In terms of important public office, 1805 was doubly significant for Thomas, for he was also in that year appointed deputy attorney general of Indiana Territory. He already had a strong reputation for leadership and was chosen by his fellow legislators to be Speaker of the House. He served in that capacity for three years.

These positions threw Thomas into the thick of territorial politics. Already the region was divided over slavery, although most early residents of the Illinois country were supportive of it.

The clamor for more self-government and separation from Indiana had arisen in the Illinois country regions along the Mississippi River. This brought about two political factions, one supportive of Governor Harrison, mostly Indiana-based, and one opposed to him, led by Illinoisans. Thomas became an advocate of separation and, in 1808, aligned himself with the anti-Harrison, pro-slavery faction in the Illinois country. In a showdown with Harrison, legislators named Thomas territorial delegate to the U.S. Congress in 1808, with explicit instructions to bring about approval of separation of the Illinois country from Indiana Territory, as a territory in its own right.

In what must be termed a near-miracle of legislative agility, Thomas engineered passage of an act of Congress establishing the Illinois Territory in little more than four months of service that ended March 3, 1809. This achievement made him a hero in Illinois but was greeted in eastern parts of Indiana Territory as betrayal, and Thomas could see that his political career there had ended. Again showing political foresight, he arranged to be named a judge of the U.S. court for the northwestern judicial district, Illinois Territory, a position in which he served until statehood came for Illinois in 1818.

In 1809, Thomas became a resident of Illinois Territory. He built a home in the vicinity of Prairie du Rocher, mid-point between the present-day cities of Waterloo and Chester. His home was just a short distance from that built by Ninian Edwards, who was named governor of Illinois Territory in 1809. That closeness of residence did not necessarily make for a lasting friendship, as the two became determined political enemies. Later Thomas moved to Cahokia, then to Edwardsville.

Biographers of Thomas have noted that while he served satisfactorily as territorial judge, his temperament was more inclined to politics than judicial scholarship. It was this tendency to work the political angles of preparation for statehood that brought him into conflict with territorial Governor Edwards. Their quarrel was among the earliest high-tension battles between top-ranking Illinois officeholders.

Edwards was a well-educated aristocrat whose vanity and arrogance were apparent in his approach to governing. His personality affected his relationship with others who held high office in the territory. He was sharply critical of Thomas's performance as a judge.

Thomas was a rough-cut frontier politician, a self-made man. This was in the days before political parties were significant in Illinois, and political differences were more personal than ideological. Thomas, already familiar with the politics of personality during the days of Harrison, became the stalwart of the anti-Edwards faction as Illinois headed toward statehood. Patronage became the major issue between factions.

John Reynolds, who practiced law in Cahokia at the time and later was elected governor, wrote of the two that "Governor Edwards had the aged and sedate leaders of the people friendly to him, but Judge Thomas had the young, ardent, and energetic men, supporting him, who were mixing every day with the people" (134).

Despite this animosity, they continued to agree on two central issues: slavery for Illinois and statehood as soon as possible. Because of a prohibition of slavery in Illinois found in the Ordinance of 1787, the practice of it was subtle, but real. Both Edwards and Thomas owned slaves within the state.

Thomas added another political achievement when he was chosen as president of the Illinois constitutional convention of 1818 by its thirty-three members. He had been elected to the convention from St. Clair County. His selection as convention leader, too, was a sign of factional politics. Governor Edwards's supporters were in the minority at the convention.

Without a vote of the people, the constitution was adopted by the convention in twenty-one days and was approved by Congress on December 3, 1818. Earlier, in September, Shadrach Bond was elected governor without opposition, and the first legislature was chosen. It had the responsibility of selecting the state's first two U.S. senators and did so in October. On one of the few occasions when Edwards and Thomas agreed, they split the two Senate positions between themselves. In a drawing of straws, Thomas won the longer term of the two.

He headed for Washington, D.C., and quickly aligned himself with southern senators, primarily because of their similar positions on slavery and Thomas's background in Virginia and Kentucky. Thomas believed slavery was morally right, and he maintained his support of its permanent establishment in Illinois throughout his political career.

His quiet manner and attention to business played well in the Senate and gained him top committee assignments, as well as choice patronage in Illinois. From the beginning, he served as chairman of the Public Lands Committee, a policy area of vital concern to Illinoisans.

His success in the Senate was due in large part to his friendship with Secretary of the Treasury William Crawford, whom Thomas had known since 1815. The two became fast friends after Thomas entered the Senate, and he supported Crawford's run for the presidency in 1824.

Perhaps Thomas's most significant involvement during his Senate terms was the leadership he exhibited in passage of the Missouri Compromise, which allowed the admission of Missouri as a slave state. During congressional debate in what has been described as a constitutional dilemma that nearly caused the breakup of the Union, Thomas introduced a key compromise amendment. He then was named chairman of the Joint Conference Committee, which worked out the final agreement.

Thomas successfully stood for reelection in 1823 in a close vote in the state legislature. That body, angry over the antislavery stand of Governor Edward Coles, approved a constitutional amendment that would have established the institution of slavery in Illinois, then sought public adoption of it in an 1824 election. Thomas returned from Washington to lead the campaign for the proposal in a bitter political battle throughout the state. It was thrashed at the polls, with 6,640 in opposition and 4,972 in favor.

Thomas's second Senate term was uneventful and a political disappointment, and he soon found himself outside the power structure in Washington. When Secretary Crawford lost the 1824 presidential election, and John Quincy Adams won in a vote in the House of Representatives, which was necessary when no candidate had a majority of the electoral vote, Thomas switched his allegiance to the new president. In part, this was because of his long-standing opposition to General Andrew Jackson, and it alienated Thomas from Jackson supporters in Illinois. When Jackson swept into the presidency in 1829, it meant the end of Thomas's political standing in the Senate. He decided not to run for reelection and moved his home to Mount Vernon, Ohio.

Thomas participated in community affairs and pursued the accumulation of real estate in the Mount Vernon vicinity for more than two decades. He departed those routines momentarily in 1840 and attended the Whig Party national convention. There he supported the nomination of William Henry Harrison for president. After the death of his wife, Rebecca, in 1851, Thomas was disconsolate and suffered from bouts of depression. In 1853, he committed suicide and was buried in Mound View Cemetery near Mount Vernon.

Ninian Edwards (1818–24)

Ninian Edwards was the most prominent of the early players in the drama of Illinois politics. After serving as the appointed territorial governor from 1809 to 1818, he was chosen by the first state legislature, called the General Assembly, along with his political rival Judge Jesse B. Thomas, to represent Illinois in the U.S. Senate. The two drew straws to see who would have the longer term. Edwards lost and had to struggle to win reelection four months later.

Ninian Edwards was an aristocrat. He was born in Montgomery County, Maryland, on March 7, 1775, into a political family. His father, Benjamin, who came from Virginia, was a member of the Maryland convention that ratified the U.S. Constitution. Later Benjamin served in the Congress. His brother John Edwards, Ninian's uncle, was for a time a U.S. senator from Kentucky.

The young Ninian Edwards was educated privately by tutors and at Dickinson College, where he graduated in 1792. He had studied both law and medicine. He went to Kentucky to represent his father in business when he was only twenty. Like many young men when they are first freed from home or other supervision, he lived a dissolute life, drinking, gambling, and indulging other bad habits, to the alarm of his friends.

However, Edwards soon righted himself and began the practice of law. He won election to the state legislature before he was twenty-one years of age. He was appointed a judge at twenty-eight and four years later was named chief justice of Kentucky's court of appeals, the state supreme court.

Two years after that, in 1809, President James Madison appointed him governor of the newly created Illinois Territory. His political sponsors were Congressman Henry Clay and Senator John Pope, who was his uncle, both from Kentucky. From that point forward, his career was played out on Illinois and national stages.

We can assume that Edwards was a Jeffersonian Republican in politics from the fact that President Madison sent him to Illinois as territorial governor. There were few Federalists in the territory, and politics took on a factional, rather than a two-party, hue. Edwards clearly was the leader of one of the principal factions. He was looked on as the territory's leading statesman. His salary as governor was two thousand dollars a year, quite a sum for the time, and he was given his choice of a thousand acres of the public domain. He selected land near Kaskaskia and named the holding Elvirade, after his wife.

As territorial governor, Edwards was superintendent of the "saline," the important salt works near the Saline River; it supplied most of the salt used on the frontier. He was also superintendent of Indian affairs and devoted much time to that office. A major goal of his Indian policy was to prevent Indians from trading their furs with the British.

During the War of 1812, he personally led a military force in the field in guarding the Illinois frontier against attack by Indians allied with the British. His undisciplined troops committed a number of atrocities among the Indians and even treated some of the

9

inhabitants of French extraction less than politely. To Edwards's regret, more professional soldiers were placed in charge of the defense of the frontier, while the decisive battles of the war were being fought elsewhere.

Edwards is credited with helping to extend the vote in the Illinois Territory to all tax-paying white males with at least a year's residence. These voting qualifications were more liberal than those of any other territory.

The town of Edwardsville, named after the governor, was laid out in 1816, and he made his home there. According to records, at the time, he owned four slaves.

Governor Edwards, while not a prominent leader in the movement for Illinois statehood, facilitated its accomplishment late in 1818. The young man who was the driving force in the statehood movement, Daniel Pope Cook, had been appointed auditor of public accounts by the governor in 1816 and, two years later, became his son-in-law. Solon Buck speaks of the political situation on the eve of statehood:

> When in November, 1817, the question of advance to statehood was suddenly thrust before the people of Illinois, the political situation may be summed up as follows: two coteries of politicians, the one led by Edwards and the other by Thomas and [Elias Kent] Kane, were opposing each other in a contest of several years' standing over the patronage and the judiciary; [Pierre] Menard, [Shadrach] Bond, and others of the old established politicians, relying on their personal popularity, refused to align themselves with either of the factions; while the people, a simple people concerned principally with local interests and the advancement of material prosperity, readily gave their votes to any man who had won their personal liking. Besides these there were a small band of anti-slavery men watching and waiting for the opportune moment in which to free Illinois from any semblence [*sic*] of slavery. (206)

In the convention of 1818, during which the first state constitution was written, the Edwards faction was in the minority; Judge Thomas chaired the convention. The two had differed over the proper role of the territorial legislature in assigning duties to judges placed on the bench by Congress under authority of the Northwest Ordinance. Selection by the new legislature of both Edwards and Thomas to the U.S. Senate soon followed.

Edwards was elected on the first ballot, with thirty-two of the forty votes that were cast. That margin suggests the high regard in which he was held. It was not until a fourth ballot that the choice of a second senator was made, and then with only twenty-one votes, the necessary minimum.

Theodore C. Pease characterized Edwards in this way:

> Kindly, charitable, generous, and at the same time pompous, overbearing and affected, he had many warm friends, many enemies too, and perhaps many associates who humored his foibles so long as doing so would promote their own advantage. The quality of mental balance was almost completely lacking in Edwards. By turns he was bold and overcautious, headstrong and vacillating, now plunging rashly into an enterprise . . . now hesitating between two courses and striving to follow both when an irrevocable decision between them had to be made. A mental shiftiness sometimes led him into equivocal positions which he could justify only by elaborate explanations. (*Frontier* 92)

While in the Senate, Edwards favored liberalization of the terms of land grants to settlers and the admission of Missouri as a slave state. He was publicly charged with owning twenty-two slaves who were hired out to work in Missouri. He did not play a significant role in the struggle over slavery, which marked the first years of statehood for Illinois. He claimed to see slavery as an "abomination" but continued to own slaves and to buy and sell contracts of indenture. He lacked the courage of conviction.

The movement to legalize a form of slavery in Illinois came to a climax in 1824, in a referendum on constitutional change. There was a mixed array of feeling on both sides. Some opposed slavery on moral and humanitarian grounds. Others wished to prevent the development of a slaveholding elite. Some feared the presence of blacks, slave or free, in the state. In the end, the pro-slavery proposition was beaten by a ratio of approximately twelve to nine.

Edwards was given a full second term in the Senate in 1819, but only by a narrow margin. Howard feels that his "career as a U.S. senator was a disappointment" (*Mostly* 36). He and Senator Thomas joined forces in 1819 to secure from Congress a grant of land on the Kaskaskia River, some eighty miles above the village of Kaskaskia, as the site for the state capital. The new location was named Vandalia. The name came about as the result of the work of practical jokers, who sang the praises of a fictional tribe of Indians called the "Vandals."

In 1824, Edwards resigned from the Senate in order to accept a diplomatic post in Mexico offered to him by President Adams. He was en route to Mexico when he was called back by Congress to testify in hearings concerning charges that he had brought against Treasury Secretary Crawford. Discrediting circumstances kept Edwards from filling the post in Mexico. As a result, he sought reelection to the Senate seat he had vacated by resigning! Failing that, he sought to repair his political fortunes by running for governor in 1826.

Though he was still the principal factional leader in Illinois politics, he won election as governor by only a narrow margin over two insignificant opponents who had backing from the supporters of Andrew Jackson. Aristocratic by nature and inclination, Edwards could never have voluntarily been a true Jacksonian. He campaigned from a carriage driven by a black slave and was pompous and overbearing in his public appearances. He won with slightly less than half the vote. The factional system of politics that had long been in operation was in decline.

As governor, Edwards advocated the complete removal of Indians from Illinois, and control of public lands by the state rather than by federal authority. He had grown wealthy through the ownership of mills, stores, banks, and land. He alienated several legislators by charging them with corruption in connection with the state bank at Edwardsville. It became increasingly difficult for him to explain his shifting positions, no matter how much verbosity he brought to the task.

Edwards's political star was setting. He seemed sometimes to act rashly and without the good judgment necessary in one at his level of authority. The constitution of Illinois did not allow him to run for a second term as governor in 1830. When he sought election to the national House of Representatives two years later, he was not successful. Factionalism was being replaced in Illinois by Jacksonian party structures. Though Edwards attempted to reconcile himself with Old Hickory and his legions, he was not successful in the attempt.

With all his faults, Edwards was often a benefactor of his friends and neighbors. For example, in 1833, when cholera struck, he refused to leave his home in Belleville, a community he had been instrumental in forming and his place of residence since 1825. Like many frontier leaders, he had some medical training, and he remained in the village, giving aid and comfort to his neighbors until 1824, when the dreaded illness ended his life.

Ninian Edwards was buried at Belleville; in 1855, he was reburied in Hutchinson's Cemetery in Springfield. In 1866, his body was removed to Oak Ridge Cemetery, where he joined Abraham Lincoln in their final resting places. His grave lies on a hillside separated from Lincoln's tomb by a small valley.

Both Jesse Thomas and Ninian Edwards were factional leaders in the world of early statehood politics in Illinois. In that they were successful. Neither, however, had the good fortune to move successfully from that role into one of party leader. Edwards's senatorial career foundered on his vendetta against Secretary of the Treasury Crawford and a constitutional inability on his part to become a dedicated follower of Andrew Jackson.

Thomas, in contrast, backed Crawford for the presidency in 1824 and with that failure went over to support President John Quincy Adams. When Jackson was elected president in 1828, Thomas was finished as a force in the Senate.

It was a time for new players on the Senate stage for the infant state of Illinois.

2 ★ The Appearance of Political Parties

After Jesse Thomas and Ninian Edwards, Illinois was represented in the U.S. Senate for a decade and a half by individuals who on the whole were not distinguished and who left no lasting imprint on national policy.

Gradually factional politics in Illinois gave way during the late 1820s and 1830s to the same sort of Democrat versus Whig alignments that were apparent on the national scene. As in other frontier states, an inherent Jeffersonian Republicanism was transmuted into Jacksonian Democracy.

With the development of mercantile and industrial interests and antislavery feelings, a degree of backing for the Whig ideology appeared in Illinois. Settlers newly arriving in the state often came from other parts of the nation, different from those of the first wave of southerners. A distinctly Yankee element, with all of the characteristics that term implied, began to make an impression on the cultural life of the state.

In the words of Richard J. Jensen, the new arrivals

> took a poor outpost of traditionalism and transformed it into one of the richest, most progressive areas anywhere. In their ceaseless search

for new ways to improve themselves, their neighbors, their community and the nation, the modernizers had to overpower the resistance
of the traditionalists. Their success was never complete, though it was
enough to establish values, institutions, and a way of life that to this
day dominates Illinois.

Jensen calls the new arrivals from Yankeedom "modernizers,"
and says of them:

> Modernizers replaced fatalism with rationality. They repudiated super-
> stitions, folk remedies, waste, predestination, and quiet submission to
> fate. Reason, analysis, logical decision making were their guides, edu-
> cation their remedy, efficiency their ideal. Old fashioned ways of doing
> things were automatically suspect, unless they could be tested and
> proven efficient. (34)

After Thomas and Edwards and until the election of Stephen
A. Douglas in 1847, most of the individuals who served Illinois in
the Senate had much in common. They typically were born in a
more eastern state during the latter part of the eighteenth century,
educated elsewhere, usually in the law, and came to Illinois seeking the opportunities in government, politics, and business that a
new state offered.

One of their number, Elias Kent Kane, was a gifted individual
who played a leading role in Illinois becoming a state and in the
first years of its statehood. His performance in the Senate was
mediocre, however, and he died prematurely. Others who served in
the Senate at least until the appearance of Sidney Breeze in 1843
were a rather ordinary lot.

John McLean (1824–25, 1829–30)

In 1824, Ninian Edwards was succeeded in the Senate by John
McLean of Shawneetown. Edwards had resigned his position and
then had sought reelection. On the third ballot in the legislature,
McLean got thirty-one votes of the fifty-two that were cast. That
number was sufficient to make the office his, but only for the brief
balance of the term that his rival Edwards had vacated. One week
later Edwards challenged one of his own faction, his close friend
Elias Kent Kane, for the following full term in the Senate, but was
not successful.

McLean, who was born in Guilford County, North Carolina, in 1791, was a longtime member of the anti-Edwards faction. His family had moved to Kentucky in 1795. He arrived in Shawneetown in 1815, studied law, and was admitted to the bar a year later. He became the first representative in Congress from the new state of Illinois, chosen by the voters rather than the General Assembly. In 1819, he was defeated for the congressional seat by the young champion of Illinois statehood, Daniel Pope Cook, whom he had beaten for that office the year before.

McLean won election to the Illinois House of Representatives in 1820 and to the state Senate in 1822. He was chosen to replace the resigned Edwards in the U.S. Senate in 1824. His tenure in the Senate was almost as brief as his service in the U.S. House had been. He was replaced by Kane in 1825. He returned to the state House in 1826 for two terms, serving as Speaker in each. Again, in 1829, he was chosen by the legislature to go to the U.S. Senate, this time to succeed Jesse Thomas.

He died in office on October 14, 1830, and was buried in the Westwood Cemetery near Shawneetown. Pease evaluates him as "a man of considerable ability but with an irascible temper which led him to bitter and vindictive outbursts against enemies or false friends" (*Frontier* 94).

Elias Kent Kane (1825–35)

Elias Kent Kane, who after John McLean gained the Senate seat that Ninian Edwards relinquished in 1824, was a young man who had many similarities to McLean, his friendly rival. For more than fifteen years, Kane was the leader of the anti-Edwards faction whenever he chose to be. Much about him is an enigmatic puzzle.

Kane, who was born in New York City in 1794, was educated at Yale, graduating in 1813. He came to Kaskaskia from Tennessee in 1818 as a young attorney seeking his fortune. One account was that he came from an aristocratic New York family that had fallen on hard times. According to Pease, apparently Kane, at the time of his greatest power and influence, seemed to have no interest in the "Yale band" that was forming Illinois College in Jacksonville.

Also, according to Pease, even though certain historical evidence concerning Kane's political career is available, none of it serves to give a rounded picture of the man. None of it supplies "one human touch, not one phrase that can endow the man with a living personality." Pease refers to Kane as "a man in a mask" (*Frontier* 94).

When the statehood pot began to boil in Illinois Territory in 1818, Kane was engaged in the practice of law at Kaskaskia. He had been appointed to a judicial position. Apparently he was already of such stature in Randolph County that he could take his election to the first state constitutional convention for granted. He served as chair of the convention's Committee on the Census, which found the population of Illinois Territory to be "upwards of 40,000," a highly suspect figure. He might have questioned the legitimacy of that count but apparently did not.

The convention consisted of thirty-three white males representing the fifteen counties then in existence. After it decided to proceed with the quest for statehood, a process in which Kane had taken a leading part, the next decision was to draft a constitution. That task was given to a committee of fifteen, one member from each county. "According to all the evidence, the directing spirit [of the committee] was Elias Kent Kane" (Buck 266). One view, not well substantiated, is that the constitution was in fact largely drafted in Kane's law office some time before the convention met.

As the work of the convention went on, Kane played a significant role in each of its stages. With two other members, he comprised the final "committee on revision," which was responsible for final shaping of the new constitution.

From the fact that he gave the committee's report to the convention, we can assume that he was formally its chairman or played a dominant part in its work, or both. The work of the convention was finished in twenty-one days. Most of the content of the new constitution had been taken in part or in whole from those of the older states.

The first governor elected under the new charter was Shadrach Bond, a farmer and slave owner who had been the first representative of the Illinois Territory in Congress. His uncle, called Shadrach Sr., had been a "civilian scout" for George Rogers Clark's campaign to take and hold the Illinois country during the American Revolution. He must have liked what he saw around Kaskaskia, for he chose to settle in nearby St. Clair County. He became a judge.

The younger Bond held a series of public offices, siding more often with Thomas than with Edwards, but often standing aloof from the factional struggles of the time. As the first governor of the state, Bond was no sooner in office than he appointed Elias Kent Kane, subject to the approval of the Senate, to be secretary of state. Bond was not a learned man; perhaps he felt the need of having someone of Kane's ability at his side. According to Buck, Kane was qualified for the post:

> Although Kane was a leader of one of the political factions, his selection was probably due to a recognition of his qualifications for the office. In the convention Kane had demonstrated his ability to do the sort of work that would be required of him as secretary of state. He had been especially useful in proposing changes to bring the various sections of the constitution into harmony with each other and to improve the English of the document. Just such a man was needed by Governor Bond. . . . His state papers were believed to be Kane's work. . . . Kane was soon in a position to dominate the administration. (303)

Given his prominence in the writing of Illinois's first constitution and the part he played in the administration of the first governor, it is not surprising that Kane was able in 1824 to win election in the legislature to the U.S. Senate. He went there as a Jacksonian Democrat, supporting the policies favored by Jackson so far as the removal of Indians from the frontier, the national bank, and the distribution of public lands were concerned. He continued to be pro-slavery, even though Illinois in 1824 had turned its back on that institution by refusing to hold another constitutional convention.

When Kane's first term in the Senate ended in 1830, the factional alliances that had prevailed were giving way to the formation of the party allegiances that became known as Jacksonian or Democratic, and Whig. Again he used his considerable influence with associates such as John McLean to be returned by the legislature to his Senate seat. By 1832, it was becoming necessary for those wishing to win election in Illinois to show attachment to both the personality of Andrew Jackson and the policies that he favored.

Apparently Elias Kent Kane did not cut so large a figure in the U.S. Senate as he had in the politics of early Illinois statehood. He chaired a minor committee of the Senate, the Committee To Audit and Contain the Contingent Expenses, and was a member of the Committee on Public Lands and the Committee on Private Land Claims. Those two assignments probably reflect his interest in the public domain and its distribution. Historians pay little attention to his service in Washington and even less to his death in office in 1835.

Kane was buried in the family cemetery on the Kane farm near Fort Gage, now Fort Kaskaskia State Park.

David J. Baker (1830)

David J. Baker barely kept an Illinois seat in the U.S. Senate warm between the death of John McLean in 1830 and the election of John M. Robinson to complete McLean's term.

After McLean's death just a year into his term succeeding Jesse Thomas, Governor Ninian Edwards appointed Baker to serve until a successor to McLean could be chosen. Officially, Baker served from November 12 until December 11, 1830. He was not then a candidate for election to the seat, and the legislature chose Robinson. One wonders why such an appointment for such a brief period was made. The seat could have been left open.

Notable during Baker's brief tenure was the beginning of the winter of 1830, famous for the deep snow it brought to Illinois. He avoided the worst of it by remaining in Washington, D.C., until the winter was almost over.

Baker had a modest public service career in Illinois, in addition to his short sojourn in Washington. Born in East Haddam, Connecticut, on September 7, 1792, he was admitted to the Illinois bar in 1819 and practiced law and served as probate judge in Randolph County. After returning to Illinois in 1830, following his brief tenure in the Senate, he was appointed U.S. attorney for Illinois and served in that capacity from 1833 to 1841. He then resumed the practice of law and died in Alton on August 6, 1869.

William Lee Davidson Ewing (1835–37)

Elias Kent Kane was succeeded in the Senate, following his death in 1835, for the balance of his unexpired term, by William L. D. Ewing, whose service extended only through the following year. Ewing had had prior experience with brevity of tenure in office, since he had acted as governor of Illinois for five days late in 1834.

His experience as governor came about when John Reynolds, very near the end of his term, resigned that office so he could go to Washington as a member of Congress. The lieutenant governor had departed earlier, for the same reason, and Ewing became governor ex officio by virtue of his being the president pro tem of the state Senate.

Ewing was an interesting figure. His given names commemorated his maternal grandfather, a general who was killed in the American Revolution. He was born at Paris, Kentucky, on August 31, 1795. His father, a Presbyterian minister, was one of the four founders of the Cumberland Presbyterian Church.

Ewing arrived in Shawneetown in 1818 and began the practice of law. He was appointed by President Monroe as receiver of the land office at Vandalia in 1820. He gained credentials as a military figure, served as a brigadier general of the Illinois militia, and was colonel in command of the "Spy [scout] Battalion" during the Black Hawk War. The census report for 1830 shows that he owned two slaves. Three times he was chosen to be Speaker of the state House of Representatives, after having served as clerk of the House.

After his first term as Speaker, he was elected to the state Senate and became its president pro tem. His two weeks and a day as governor followed. That allowed him time for a message to the legislature. In it, he recommended the establishment of a state bank. Such action by the lawmakers followed, with results that were not always pleasing. From the governor's chair, Ewing went back to the state Senate and then was chosen for the U.S. Senate to complete the brief portion of Kane's term.

Ewing's service in the U.S. Senate was not distinguished. He followed the goals and ideas of Andrew Jackson. He was beaten in a bid for reelection in 1836 and again became a member of the state House, where twice more he was chosen to be Speaker. Each time he defeated Abraham Lincoln for that position. In the campaign for the speakership, he called Lincoln "a coarse and vulgar fellow" (Howard, *Mostly* 58). At that time, probably he was.

Later, Ewing again became clerk of the House. When he died on March 25, 1846, in Springfield, at fifty years of age, he was serving as the state auditor, by appointment of the legislature, in which he had so long served. The *Congressional Directory* states that "probably" he was buried in Oak Ridge Cemetery, though the date of his death makes one doubt that that was the case, at least at the time of his first interment. Perhaps later.

John McCracken Robinson (1830–41)

John M. Robinson's service of eleven years in the U.S. Senate equaled the longest tenure of any senator from Illinois from the beginning of statehood in 1818 until his longevity was exceeded by that of Stephen A. Douglas, who first went to the Senate in 1848.

Robinson assumed his Senate seat in 1830, after the death of John McLean. During his Senate years, he was a dependable vote for the programs of Presidents Andrew Jackson and Martin Van Buren, although he did not distinguish himself in leadership. He was named chairman of the Committee on Engrossed Bills for one session, and served on the Post Office and Post Roads Committees.

Like many officials of early Illinois, Robinson was a Kentuckian. He was born near Georgetown, in Scott County, Kentucky, on April 10, 1794, and graduated from Transylvania University in Lexington. He was admitted to the Illinois bar and began practice in Carmi in 1818, where he served as prosecuting attorney. Active and interested in military affairs, he rose to the rank of major general in the state militia.

After completing McLean's term in the Senate, Robinson was elected to a full term of his own in 1835. The issue that created the greatest controversy during his Senate years was President Jackson's proposal of an independent treasury. Robinson believed the idea was widely supported by the public in Illinois, but he was informed that both houses of the state legislature opposed it. In this matter, he opposed Jackson and voted against the bill.

In a letter to the public on March 3, 1840, in which he announced that he would not seek reelection to the Senate, Robinson went to great lengths to explain his official opposition to the treasury bill, and his personal approval of the measure. The letter read, in part:

> In giving the vote I did against this bill, it was done under the imperative instructions of a majority (not large to be sure) of the members of each House of our State Legislature. . . . My political tenets lead me to believe that the representative is bound by the will of his constituents, and that so far as it relates to a Senator in Congress, the Legislature is presumed to be the true exponent of that will. (Berry 79)

Robinson made it clear that his personal choice was to support the independent treasury bill. The letter added that he was "anxious for the success of the bill; believing, as I then did and yet do, its adoption to be demanded by the good of the country."

After leaving the Senate, Robinson was appointed to the state supreme court in 1843. Two months later he died in Ottawa, Illinois.

Richard Montgomery Young (1837–43)

William L. D. Ewing was followed to the Senate in 1837 by Richard M. Young, a Jacksonian Democrat who served for six years. Young was born in Fayette County, Kentucky, in 1798. He was admitted to the bar in that state at eighteen and began the practice of law in Jonesboro, Illinois, a year later. In 1820, he was elected to the Illinois legislature.

Young became a circuit judge in 1825 and continued on the bench until 1837. He was chosen in 1836 to go to the U.S. Senate, defeating the incumbent Ewing. He served in the Senate for a six-year term. For two sessions, he chaired the Committee on Roads and Canals. In 1839, he was one of a mission of three who went to England to negotiate a loan for the Illinois state bank. That venture turned out less than well for the state. Young went to the state supreme court in 1843, rather than attempting to be reelected.

Apparently, he was a durable politician, for in 1847, he was appointed by President James K. Polk to be Commissioner of the General Land Office. When he left that post, he became clerk of the U.S. House of Representatives for two years. In the tradition of more recent senators, he had remained in Washington, practicing law, after his period of government service ended. He died there in November 1861 and was buried in the congressional cemetery.

Prior to Young's time, U.S. senators from Illinois, dying in office or soon after leaving office, were buried near their homes. Apparently, Richard M. Young took a somewhat different view of his place in the political world.

Young's service in the Senate marks the end of an era. He was one of the last of the first group of Illinois senators born in one of the older states during the last quarter of the eighteenth century who were a part of the movement that ended in statehood. Generally, they were educated elsewhere, for Illinois had little to offer in that regard. They were educated usually in the law and came to one of the frontier settlements in southern Illinois in search of political and professional opportunity.

There were hardly any settlements in the central or northern parts of the state to which they could go. The paths of migration down the Ohio River, and out of the Appalachian highlands and Kentucky by way of the Tennessee and Cumberland Rivers, led to southern Illinois.

They became lawyers, judges, legislators, governors, senators. Without their presence, the new state would have been hard pressed to find the talent that the achievement and management of statehood required.

By the 1840s, an era quite distinct from the early years of territorial status and statehood had begun. Many politicians still came from other states, but after two decades or more of statehood, Illinoisans had developed a political culture less dependent on the history and culture of the East and the South. Factional politics and a fascination with Jacksonian ideals were running their course, giving way to the beginnings of a two-party system.

Gradually, the Jeffersonians came to be identified with Andrew Jackson and, with his followers, were called the Democratic Party. With the demise of Federalist groups in the East, those opposing the Democrats became known as the Whig Party. With the coming of the 1840s, there had been a sufficient development of commercial, industrial, and financial interests in Illinois for elements of the Whig Party to contest elections with Democrats.

Subsistence farmers were strongly Democratic, while the more affluent business and professional groups were strongly Whig. German and Irish immigrants tended to become Democrats, at least until the Civil War, and the urban Irish continued strongly in the Democratic fold.

Whigs had little success in electing state and local officials in Illinois in the 1840s and 1850s and during the latter decade gave way to the new Republican Party. Political struggle between the traditionalists, strongest in the southern portion of the state, and the more modern Yankees in the north, continued without clearcut victory on either side, throughout the nineteenth century.

It was an era that became quite distinct from the early years of territorial status and statehood. Illinois, directly through its representation in the U.S. Senate, was about to enter debates to decide the nation's future.

3 ★ The Calm Before the Storm

A short period of relative calm settled over Illinois politics during the latter part of the 1830s. The early formative period of achieving statehood, determining the issue of slave or free, and the appearance of two distinct political parties lay in the past. Ahead were the gathering storms of secession and civil war.

During that interval of calm, no one of the three persons who on the whole represented the state of Illinois in the U.S. Senate from 1841 to 1849 gained any distinction through that service. One disliked his experience there and did not seek reelection. Another became distinguished in a judicial career after his Senate service of a single term. The third died after only two years in Senate office.

Samuel McRoberts (1841–43)

Samuel McRoberts, the first U.S. senator born on what became Illinois state soil, was in the thick of factional politics and the battle over slavery in the earliest years of statehood. His service in the Senate was brief, compared to his activity on the state level and in federal appointive positions beginning in the early 1820s. A Democrat, he began his term in the Senate on March 4, 1841.

McRoberts was born near Maeystown, in a portion of the "Territory Northwest of the River Ohio," in what became Monroe

County, Illinois, on April 12, 1799. He was educated by private tutors and graduated from the law department of Transylvania University in Lexington, Kentucky. He was admitted to the Illinois bar in 1821 and began practice in Monroe County.

McRoberts was named a state circuit judge in 1825 and served two years, then was elected to the state Senate from Clinton County. During this time, he lost a bid to become state attorney general. Two years later, in 1830, President Andrew Jackson appointed him U.S. attorney, and he remained in that position until 1832.

He held the position of receiver of the land office at Danville, Illinois, from 1832 until he was appointed solicitor of the General Land Office in Washington, D.C., in 1839. He resigned from that position in 1841 when he was elected by the Illinois legislature to the U.S. Senate. He followed Senator John M. Robinson, who had chosen not to seek reelection, in that position.

McRoberts's baptism in state politics had come shortly after he was admitted to the bar in 1821. He quickly joined forces with pro-slavery officials, such as Jesse Thomas, Elias Kent Kane, and Judge Thomas Reynolds, in support of the constitutional change that would have legalized slavery in the state. The proposal failed at the polls, but McRoberts had cast his lot in opposition to antislavery interests. In factional politics, he opposed policies of Governors Edward Coles and Ninian Edwards during the 1820s.

Two years after taking his seat in the Senate, McRoberts died in Cincinnati, Ohio, on March 27, 1843, at forty-four years of age. He was buried in the Moore Cemetery in Waterloo, Illinois.

James Semple (1843–47)

James Semple moved in and out of careers at the state, national, and international levels, fought in the Black Hawk War, and tried grand business ventures before spending four years in the U.S. Senate from 1843 to 1847. By most measurements, his time in Congress was just another entry in his employment record.

And as one historian observed, if Semple had not grown disenchanted with Senate life, he probably would have been reelected in 1847 and might have changed the course of history by delaying the appearance of Stephen A. Douglas upon the Senate scene.

A lifelong Democrat, Semple was born on January 5, 1798, in Green County, Kentucky. He never stayed long in one place. He moved to Edwardsville, Illinois, in 1818, then to Missouri, and back to Kentucky, where he was admitted to the practice of law. He returned to Edwardsville in 1828. He was a brigadier general during the Black Hawk War and, riding on that distinction, served as state attorney general in 1833 and 1834. He had also been elected to the Illinois House of Representatives in 1832. During six years in the House, he was the Speaker for four.

During Semple's legislative career, he was an unsuccessful candidate for the U.S. Senate in 1836. Meanwhile, he had joined Congressman A. W. Snyder and others in a land speculation scheme involving promotion of a new town in southern Illinois, on the future route of the Illinois Central railroad, called Tamaroa. Just as this venture was getting off the ground, the national "panic," or recession, of 1837 occurred, and Semple lost everything he had.

In need of a paying job, Semple sought a federal appointment through friends in government. President Martin Van Buren solved the problem by appointing him chargé d'affaires in Bogotá, Colombia. The Senate confirmed him without a dissenting vote. He remained in that position until 1842, when he was named a judge of the Illinois Supreme Court.

With the support of his friend Douglas and others in the state, Semple was elected by the legislature in 1843 to succeed the deceased Senator McRoberts. In his few years as a senator, Semple sought a resolution of the dispute with the British over the Oregon country. He favored the annexation of Texas and entry into the Mexican War. He never liked being in the Senate and decided in 1846 not to seek reelection.

Upon his retirement, Semple said, "I was never so sick of politics in all my life. I have seen enough of it. Henceforward, I will keep myself in the cool sequestered vale of life."

William L. Burton, in writing of Semple, said:

> [H]is multifaceted career in law, state and national government and land speculation provides a virtual model of Jacksonian America. . . . He was representative of the class of men who moved in and out of public office and who capitalized on experience and personal contacts to promote business enterprise. (67)

After his time in the Senate, Semple returned to Alton, where he entered the real estate business, promoted ideas for locomotive transportation, and wrote about family genealogy. He moved to

Jersey County in 1853 and later founded the town of Elsah over-looking the Mississippi River. Perhaps there he found the "cool sequestered vale" he had been seeking.

During the 1850s and 1860s, Semple stayed away from active participation and debate in political matters. However, his letters reflect a strong sympathy with the Southern cause. When war came, he remained loyal to the Union.

Semple died on December 20, 1866, in Elsah, and was buried in Bellefontaine Cemetery in St. Louis.

Sidney Breeze (1843–49)

Richard Young was followed to the Senate in 1843 by Sidney Breeze, who was distinctively of another sort than those from the state who had preceded him. Rather than playing a central role in the achievement of statehood for Illinois, he was a student reading law in the office of Elias Kent Kane during the summer of 1818, where, some believe, Kane in that year assembled much of what was to become the first Illinois constitution.

Like Kane, Sidney Breeze was the scion of an aristocratic New York family. Arthur, his father, had an honorary degree from Yale and was the clerk of the New York Supreme Court for seven years. In his large home in Utica, he entertained such notables as the Marquis de Lafayette during his visit to the United States. Such a home environment doubtless made a deep impression on young Sidney.

The second son among nine children, born July 15, 1800, he was educated privately by a Presbyterian clergyman, attended Hamilton College, and graduated from Union College at eighteen. Just as his father had trekked westward from New York City in search of professional opportunity, so Sidney went out to the Illinois Territory with the same purpose, in 1818, at the invitation of Kane, a family friend. Breeze read law in Kane's office in Kaskaskia.

There Breeze later claimed to have witnessed Kane writing much of the Illinois constitution before the convention had ever met. It must have been an exciting time for an eighteen year old seeking his fortune in political affairs in the new state of Illinois.

When the state capitol was moved from Kaskaskia to Vandalia in 1820, Sidney Breeze, a twenty-year-old stripling from an aristocratic New York family, earned twenty-five dollars by bringing the state archives from Kaskaskia in a small wagon. Breeze, who was

Secretary of State Kane's friend and one-man office staff, spent a week on the journey. Underbrush in many places had to be chopped away so that the trail could be widened.

Breeze was admitted to the bar in 1820. Suffering stage fright, he lost his first case and came near giving up the profession. He was rescued from despair by an appointment as postmaster at Kaskaskia. Apparently, he stood in well with President James Monroe. He also became the first official reporter for the Illinois Supreme Court and served in that capacity for eleven years.

In 1826, President Adams appointed Breeze U.S. attorney for the region. When the spoilsman Andrew Jackson was elected president, however, Breeze lost that position. There resulted a continuing feud between Breeze and allies of his among the Adams supporters in Illinois, on the one side, and those who were becoming Jacksonians, on the other.

Breeze exercised his political ambitions by seeking a seat in Congress in 1830. He did not succeed. One of his platform planks was state control of all public lands within its borders. This was a common view among Illinois politicians of the time. Pease speaks of him as "constructively a Jacksonian if his land-bill past were forgotten, but otherwise with a whiggish tendency" (*Frontier* 139). He supported both internal improvements by the federal authority and the protective tariff.

He won election as a circuit judge in 1835 and, several years later, gained a seat on the Illinois Supreme Court, along with another rising political star of the time, Stephen A. Douglas. The lives of the two were often intertwined in the years that followed, usually in an adversarial mode.

In 1838, Breeze sought the Democratic nomination for governor but failed to win it. Four years later he had a similar inclination, and greater strength. However, in bargaining with the eventual winner, his fellow-partisan Thomas Ford, Breeze settled for selection by the Democratic General Assembly to the U.S. Senate. This led to a falling out with Douglas, who wanted the seat for himself.

In the Senate, Breeze's accomplishments were modest, but creditable. He gained a slight reputation for learning and scholarship. During five of his six years, he chaired the important Committee on Public Lands. He was a "hawk" on the Oregon country, demanding with others "54-40 or fight." He supported President Polk in the war with Mexico and the annexation of Texas.

In keeping with his Jacksonian leanings, by this time in his career he generally opposed federal expenditures for internal improvements. An example is a proposed public land donation for the development of the Cumberland Road. As a politician in Illinois of his time, however, he grudgingly accepted the idea of federal aid in the building of railroads and canals. Any other posture would have been politically hurtful to him.

He proposed the building of a rail line that would parallel the Mississippi River, a concept that eventually took shape as the Illinois Central. Breeze and other politicians invested in the Cairo City and Canal Company, knowing that any north-south rail line would necessarily end at the city of Cairo, at the junction of the two great rivers. Breeze advanced the idea in the Senate of granting land to the Illinois Central to offset rail line construction costs, and to allow a profit in the enterprise, but without success.

Douglas, who had captured the other Senate seat in 1846, was also interested in the north-south rail line in Illinois. He preferred to have the federal government grant land to the state of Illinois, which would then build the railroad with the revenue from land sales.

During the time Breeze was in the Senate, the Illinois Literary and Historical Society made an appeal for the writing of manuscripts that would record Illinois history. He was one of those who responded, with a history of the state until 1763. Pease states that "Sidney Breeze, William H. Brown, Thomas Ford, and John Reynolds all have left their interpretation of the state's past; to an amazing degree they have shaped the tradition of Illinois history" (*Frontier* 412).

When Breeze sought reelection in 1848, he was beaten by a military hero of the war with Mexico, James Shields. His career in the Senate was over. He was not content, however, to pass quietly from the political scene.

Resilient as ever, two years later he was elected to the Illinois House and became its Speaker. A quarrel with Senator Douglas over whose idea the Illinois Central truly was ended badly for Breeze. After he left the Senate in 1849, Douglas, still a senator, revived the idea of the Illinois Central.

A heavy investor in Chicago real estate, Douglas sought to have the northern terminal placed at that city rather than Galena. In order to secure greater support in the Senate for the innovation of land grants for railroad building, he extended the proposed line into the southern states through which the Illinois Central might pass.

Thus it seems that both Breeze and Douglas contributed to the conceptual bundle that became the Illinois Central Railroad. Each was motivated by personal profit through land investment, and, no doubt, by the great public good that would result. Douglas was equally skillful in melding regional and sectional interests in support of the project.

Sidney Breeze's career did not end here, although his Senate days were over. In fact, he went on to an illustrious career as a jurist.

Breeze continued to interest himself in national issues. He sought the Democratic nomination for Congress in 1852 but failed to get it. In 1854, he joined other Democrats such as Lyman Trumbull, John A. McClernand, and John Reynolds and publicly sided with Abraham Lincoln in opposing Douglas's Kansas-Nebraska bill, which would have allowed the spread of slavery into Kansas and other territories. In Springfield, at the state fair, the issue was debated at length during two successive days, with Douglas standing alone against the others, led by Lincoln.

In 1857, Breeze was elected to a partial term on the Illinois Supreme Court. At last he had found a public stage suited to his taste and talents. He flourished. Still he could not resist making a run for the U.S. Senate seat in 1858. He failed again. In 1860 and again nine years later, he was reelected to full terms on the supreme court. He became one of the most respected jurists in the nation at a time of great change in its industrial and economic organization.

In 1870, Judge Breeze wrote the majority opinion in the case *Munn v. Illinois,* upholding the right of the state to regulate grain elevators. This decision was upheld by the U.S. Supreme Court and became one of the landmarks of the nation's economic and regulatory history. According to Howard, the case "brought national attention to the elderly Sidney Breeze, chief justice of the state's Supreme Court, who wrote a landmark opinion . . . asserting that . . . a business could be regulated if it was in the public interest" (*Illinois* 364).

Weak-voiced, and never a star performer in debate, Judge Breeze found his true intellectual home in the traditions and performance of a high court of appeals. His logic was sound in the writing of opinions, and his literary skills were adequate. He may not have approached the level of early U.S. jurists John Marshall and Joseph Story in those respects, but the quality of his work was high. His place in the history of American jurisprudence is secure.

4 ★ "The Little Giant" and "Lincoln's Duelist"

During the first thirty years of Illinois statehood, no individual senator had served two full terms or made much of an impact on the life of the nation. Early senators adequately represented Illinois, but before 1847, the state had no special ranking or position of influence in the Senate. Stephen A. Douglas changed all that during his fourteen years of service there.

Stephen A. Douglas (1847–61)

Douglas blew into the U.S. Senate in 1847, stirring the issues, creating havoc in his wake, and serving during one of the nation's most tumultuous times. His career calls to mind the fury of a prairie windstorm. No matter how hard the winds of change and crisis blew, he remained upright in the middle of the storm. He became a lightning rod for such momentous national issues as western expansion, slavery, and civil war. His debates with Abraham Lincoln remain one of the state's most dramatic episodes.

Early historians held divided opinions about Douglas's place in Illinois history. Accordingly, he was often characterized as both statesman and hero or as clumsy bumpkin and inept political hack. They agreed that his volatile personality could have abetted either assessment.

Scholars now believe that Douglas, much as with other major players in American history, was a man of good intentions and high ambitions; a victim of sectional hatreds he could not control; a passionate, impetuous, and eloquent promoter of often ill-conceived public policy; and an officeholder much maligned in life and death. All agree he represents an unforgettable chapter in Illinois history.

Douglas arrived in central Illinois in 1833 at age twenty, already a committed Jacksonian politically and determined to make a mark quickly on the Illinois frontier. A native of Brandon, Vermont, he was rough cut.

Historian Allen Nevins described the young Douglas in this way: "Essentially uncultivated in everything except politics, he was also essentially an unreflective, unphilosophical man, who thought only of propulsive forces" ("Douglas" 390). Before he was twenty-one, Douglas's diminutive physical stature and blustery, often belligerent approach to every phase of life resulted in the nickname "the Little Giant." His speed of action attracted friends, allies, and enemies equally.

Douglas, in his first decade in Illinois, can be described as peripatetic. He taught, read law, and acted as register of the U.S. land office in Springfield, was state's attorney of Morgan County for a year, served as Illinois's secretary of state for three months, was elected to a term in the state House of Representatives, ran political campaigns, and developed a gambler's instinct for public office.

He made a bold run for Congress in 1838 and lost by only thirty-six votes. He served briefly as a state supreme court justice and was forever after known as "Judge." In 1843, just thirty years old, he was elected to Congress. He attacked work and fellow members in the House just as he attacked life: unrepentant and unforgiving. John Quincy Adams, the former president then serving as a congressman, wrote in his diary after hearing Douglas speak for the first time:

> His face was convulsed, his gesticulation frantic, and he lashed himself into such a heat that if his body had been made of combustible matter it would have burnt out. In the midst of his roaring, to save himself from choking, he stripped and cast aside his cravat, unbuttoned his waistcoat, and had the air and aspect of a half-naked pugilist. (Nevins, *Adams* 566)

Douglas served two terms in the House before the Illinois legislature chose him, when he was thirty-four, to go to the U.S. Senate in 1847. He took the place of James Semple, who had chosen not to seek reelection. Douglas became a member of the Senate during the period that the biographer Robert Caro has called its "Golden Age" (15). It was a time when the Senate's brightest stars were John C. Calhoun, Noah Webster, and Henry Clay, and great issues of national expansion and preservation of the Union were vigorously debated and resolved.

The nation was on the eve of emotional debates over slavery and the accompanying issues of sectionalism and westward expansion when Douglas took his seat. He remained in the Senate, always seeking higher public office, until he died in 1861. In 1852, he ran for president as a Democrat and failed. He successfully sought reelection to the Senate in 1853 and 1859. In 1860, he again sought the presidency, this time against his Illinois friend Abraham Lincoln, who had contested with him for the Senate seat in 1858. It was that campaign that produced the famous Lincoln-Douglas debates.

Douglas entered the Senate in time to lead the Congress in its pursuit of continental expansion, carrying forward the programs of Presidents Andrew Jackson and James K. Polk. In his first term, he had been named chairman of the Committee on Territories, a Senate hot seat in the 1850s. He used the position to leave his impression on frontier America. He shaped the laws under which five territories were organized and five states admitted to the Union. Senate politics forced him to give up the chairmanship in 1859.

Douglas realized that Illinois could benefit from trade with the West Coast and championed the idea of a rail line to the Pacific. He believed strongly in national growth and was in the front line of argument for the admission of Texas, California, and Oregon as territories and then as states. He supported U.S. objectives in its war with Mexico.

Of all the issues Douglas confronted, none shook the Union to its core as did the Kansas-Nebraska Act of 1854, and the debates and conflicts that accompanied it. In the wake of that statute, the nation was irrevocably divided and finally went to civil war in 1861. He wanted desperately to avoid the conflict, and just as strongly to be president. Those goals led him into a central role in national affairs that branded him more as provocateur than compromiser.

Slavery had been a national issue almost from the first day of the Republic. In a pair of hotly debated pieces of legislation—the Missouri Compromise of 1820 and the Compromise of 1850—the agreements that were made by the Congress retained slavery but limited its spread. Southerners on the slavery side never favored those laws. By the 1850s, extreme elements clamored for their repeal. Northerners wished to retain compromises that limited slavery in the main to the southern states. Northern extremists were just as unmovable as their counterparts in the South.

Douglas could not resist the temptation to take center stage in this conflict. He thrust himself between extremists in the North and the South. Some said he fashioned the Kansas-Nebraska Act to appease southerners so they would help nominate him for the presidency. Others said that he wanted only to find a lasting peace between the two factions and that his motives were to shape a law that would heal national wounds.

To facilitate a compromise position between the "ultras," as extremists on both sides were called, he fashioned a bill advancing his theory of "popular sovereignty." Under this plan people in the new territories would create their own constitutions and resolve the question of slavery as a local issue, as long as it did not collide with the federal constitution. If the people of a territory and state wanted slavery, they could vote it in. He argued against the federal government making decisions about the expansion of slavery.

Southern extremists pushed Douglas further and further in rewriting his proposal. He also allowed language that encouraged fraud and deceit in the territorial process of deciding on slavery. In 1854, the bill passed Congress and was signed by President Franklin Pierce. The law opened the door to the shameful episode of "Bloody Kansas," in which the territory became a violent battleground pitting proponents of "slave" and "free."

Strangely, the border war between Kansas and Missouri—North versus South—presented Douglas with an opportunity for statesmanship. The event occurred in 1857 when delegates gathered in LeCompton, the territorial capital of Kansas, to debate and approve a constitution for the state. A majority of the delegates favored slavery, and several owned slaves. However, sentiment in the territory made it clear that its citizens would defeat a pro-slavery document. Angered by that reality, the convention voted to send such a constitution directly to Congress without a popular referendum. This created a national furor.

In desperation, the convention chairman proposed submitting just the issue of slavery to the citizens and sending the rest of the constitution directly to Congress. The delegates accepted that compromise, and the convention leadership hoped Douglas would support that solution to the problem.

The LeCompton matter put Douglas at another crossroads in his winding political career. If he supported the compromise or the original idea of no public referendum, he would be turning his back on the Kansas-Nebraska Act, which called for submitting the entire constitution to a vote of the people of Kansas Territory. If he argued for submitting the entire constitution to a referendum, he would lose all support from the South, and from the administration of President James Buchanan.

Buchanan, who favored slavery in Kansas, and the southerners stood ready to cut Douglas adrift if he stood his ground for the Kansas-Nebraska principle of a popular vote. The *Chicago Tribune* asked in an editorial:

> [Will Douglas] redeem his pledges . . . that the people of Kansas should be left free to regulate their own domestic institutions in their own way? Or will he, when he reaches Washington, stand coldly back while the South crams slavery down the throats of the people of that Territory?

Douglas conferred with his friends and advisers before taking a public position on Kansas. In the end, he stood for the faithful execution of the Kansas-Nebraska Act. He condemned the LeCompton movement and took his fight to Congress, where he hoped for a bill that would overturn it and preserve the principle of Kansas-Nebraska. In Washington, the conflict expanded to the White House and what has become a famous exchange between President Buchanan and Douglas, both Democrats.

Buchanan recalled the fate of those senators who had flouted Andrew Jackson's will and said, "Mr. Douglas, I desire you to remember that no Democrat ever yet differed from the Administration of his own choice without being crushed." To which Douglas replied, "Mr. President, I wish you to remember that General Jackson is dead, sir." Both houses of Congress debated the issue furiously, with the administration working to save its position in favor of LeCompton. In the end, Congress accepted a proposal that led to a vote on slavery in Kansas. It was rejected by an overwhelming majority.

While that outcome appeared to put the Kansas issue to rest, it destroyed Douglas's standing in the South and split his party along sectional lines. Douglas's biographer Robert W. Johannsen said of the Kansas matter: "The LeCompton crisis left a legacy of party disruption and sectional hatred from which the nation could not recover, and Douglas was the chief inheritor of that legacy."

The Kansas-Nebraska Act determined the focus of Douglas's tenure in the Senate and occupied him until he died in 1861. The issues of slavery and the 1854 law became the foundation of the famous Lincoln-Douglas debates, which actually began informally in 1854. They came to a climax in 1858 when the two men contested for the Senate seat.

In seven confrontations of classic stump campaigning on stages across the state—at Freeport, Ottawa, Galesburg, Quincy, Alton, Jonesboro, and Charleston—Lincoln rose as the man opposed to slavery. Douglas, forced to refine his arguments for popular sovereignty, denied that he favored slavery.

Douglas technically won the debates because he won reelection in the legislature to his Senate seat, but he gained no advantage on the national stage and failed to renew his standing with southern partisans. On the other hand, Lincoln's star began its ascendancy.

Commenting on the Lincoln-Douglas rivalry, historian Allen Nevins put this light on the senator's dilemma: "It is a great misfortune, as Aaron Burr found out in Jefferson's time, and Calhoun in Jackson's, to be the opponent of a president who becomes a national hero" (*Adams* 402).

Embattled in Illinois and the nation, Douglas's career went into steep decline. Although stripped of his power in the Senate and increasingly fatigued, he never gave up on the passions of his life. In the midst of national anguish and personal disappointment, one more opportunity for statesmanship arose.

Douglas hated to lose the 1860 presidential election, although he had known his chances of winning were remote. After the election, he became a supporter of Lincoln on the issue of union, while still maintaining opposition to the politics and positions of the Republican Party. He accepted Lincoln as president and privately told his friends that Lincoln would make the right decisions if war came. At a personal meeting of the two, the president said he intended to call for seventy-five thousand volunteers to fight the rebels. Douglas said that he would favor calling two hundred thousand.

It did come to war in 1861. Douglas considered it a personal defeat, and a terrible setback for the Republic. He wanted to believe, and wanted others to believe, that he had fought valiantly to hold the Union together. As the crisis deepened, he denounced southern interests and actions and stood squarely for the Union. After Fort Sumter, Douglas made what turned out to be his final trip to Springfield. In a much-anticipated speech before the legislature, he turned up the heat on his patriotism, declaring:

> The first duty of an American citizen is obedience to the constitution and laws of the country. . . . Do not allow the mortification growing out of defeat in a partisan struggle and the elevation of a party to power that we firmly believed to be dangerous to the country—do not let that convert you from patriots to traitors to your native land.

Before the chamber erupted in cheers and applause, Douglas concluded:

> To discuss these topics is the most painful duty of my life. It is with a sad heart—with a grief that I have never before experienced—that I have to contemplate this fearful struggle; but I believe in my conscience that it is a duty we owe ourselves, and our children, and our God, to protect this government and that flag from every assailant, be he who he may.

At the request of President Lincoln, in 1861 Douglas began a tour of Illinois, urging support of the Union. He fell ill at Tremont House in Chicago and died of typhoid fever on June 3. His final words, preserved by historians for generations of Illinoisans, were "Tell my children to obey the laws and uphold the Constitution" (Milton 347).

Compromises wrought in the Senate time after time, during the forty some years since Illinois became a state, had averted civil war and a dissolution of the Union. With southern states seceding and Fort Sumter fired upon and surrendering, the death of Stephen Douglas marked a close to the period known as the Senate's Golden Age.

James Shields (1849–55)

The man, James Shields, who had won out over Sidney Breeze in the contest for the Senate in 1848, was a different sort of person from Breeze in many significant ways, yet strangely similar in others. He had returned from service in the war with Mexico a certi-

37

fied military hero. He had earlier seen action in the Black Hawk War and was commissioned a brigadier general of Illinois volunteers when hostilities threatened south of the border in 1846.

Seriously wounded at Cerro Gordo, he was promoted to major general. Later at Churubusco he led a charge of New York Irish and South Carolina troops that was considered sufficiently heroic and important to be immortalized in mural form on the wall of the national Capitol.

Shields returned to civilian life and his law practice in Kaskaskia and Belleville in mid-1848. He must have enjoyed a favorable reputation in Washington, for almost at once he was appointed governor of Oregon Territory.

Rewarding military service with public office was also common in Illinois, and soon thereafter, the legislature elected Shields to the seat in the U.S. Senate that had been Breeze's. He preferred the eastern journey over one to the west, and foregoing Oregon, served in the Senate until 1855. A technicality raised by Whigs as to his length of residence in Illinois kept him for a year from beginning his term in office.

James Shields was born on May 12, 1806, in Altmore, County Tyrone, Ireland. At the insistence of his mother, it is said, he gained a good classical education for the time and place, in a "hedge" or country school, an academy, and from his uncle, who was a retired Catholic priest.

When he was only sixteen, Shields set out in a sailing ship for Quebec. His trip was short, as he and two companions, the only survivors of a shipwreck, were cast up on the coast of Scotland.

He earned his living as a tutor in Scotland until he had managed to save enough to fund passage to the United States. He arrived in New York City in 1826. For whatever reason, he went to Kaskaskia, where he taught French, read law, and was a participant in Democratic politics. Eventually, he was licensed to practice law and in 1836 was elected to the legislature.

Shields became state auditor, a position filled by appointment by the General Assembly, and helped to restore stability to the disordered finances that had come upon the state in the 1830s, when it went deeply in debt for internal improvements such as canals and railroads. A fiery individual, he was not reluctant to declare himself ever ready to take up arms for Irish independence if the time became right.

The Whig press was critical of Shields's conduct as auditor, and unflattering letters critical of him, both in a political sense and personally, were published. Thinking Abraham Lincoln to be responsible for some of the material that had appeared, Shields challenged him to a duel.

Knowing he hardly would be a match for Shields with the pistol or rapier, Lincoln chose broadswords as the weapons to be used, feeling that his greater height, strength, and reach would allow him a better chance with that sort of weapon. The matter went so far as to take the two and their seconds across the Mississippi River onto Missouri soil but was compromised before any blows were exchanged.

Eventually, it was learned that Lincoln's future wife, Mary Todd, and a friend of hers, Julia Jayne, later to be the wife of Senator Lyman Trumbull, himself to win in 1855 the Senate seat that Shields occupied, had written most of the letters in question. The whole matter ended without bloodshed, and Lincoln and Shields became good friends.

While dueling was illegal in Illinois in 1842, and punishable by a lifelong prohibition on public office holding, it was not an unusual way for affairs of an affront to honor to be settled. Shields had been involved in other dueling episodes, but no one was injured. One took place in his youth, after he had quarreled with a retired British army officer, who later became Shields's friend.

In 1850, while he was in the Senate, Shields stood as second to Senator Jefferson Davis in a potential duel with Illinois Congressman W. H. Bissell, over an argument concerning deeds of valor during the Mexican War. Fortunately, the matter was stopped short of bloodshed. Otherwise the Confederate states might eventually have had a different president or Illinois a new congressman, or both changes might necessarily have taken place.

Shields was allied in Democratic Party politics with Thomas Ford, who was elected governor of Illinois in 1842 in the political bargaining that saw Sidney Breeze go to the Senate. Later Shields edited and in 1854 published the *History of Illinois* that Ford wrote. It is generally regarded as an authentic and valuable work.

Ford rewarded Shields in 1843 by appointing him to a vacancy on the state supreme court. While Shields's service on the court was not lengthy, it generally was well regarded.

The General Assembly appointed Shields to a full term on the court in 1845. But soon thereafter, President Polk named him commissioner of the general land office in Washington, D.C. This appointment was followed by his service in the war with Mexico, his appointment as governor of Oregon Territory, and then his election as U.S. Senator from Illinois.

Shields's law partner Gustave Koerner, who was once lieutenant governor of the state, left this impression of the man:

> In stature Shields was of medium height, very broad-shouldered, and with rather long arms. His complexion was fair and healthy, his eyes grey and very sparkling. In a passion they seemed to shoot fire. His hair was dark brown and his features quite regular. In conversation he spoke rapidly and vivaciously, showing very little trace of the Irish brogue. He was not an orator, but a ready debater. His mind was discriminating. He succeeded better with the court than with the jury and on the stump. Indeed, he very seldom addressed large crowds in election times. He was exceedingly vain and very ambitious, and, like most ambitious men, on occasion quite egotistical. . . . Upon the whole his ideas were lofty. In his manner he was peculiar, not to say eccentric. Although he had not had a thorough classical education, he understood Latin pretty well, and had picked up enough French to read it and understand it. His knowledge of English literature was quite extensive, and so was his knowledge of history, particularly modern history. . . . He really did not seek popularity, but yet had a sort of winning way about him that made him friends quite readily. Fond himself of being flattered, he paid back what he received in the same coin. Yet when he could not persuade, he did not fail to show his displeasure and to become an open enemy. When attacked, he struck back. I knew all his weaknesses and his vanity amused me. When asked why I liked him and fought for him so much, I really had no particular answer to make. It was his enthusiasm, I believe, even his impulsiveness. (Myers 27)

In legislative matters, Senator Shields was a staunch Democrat, short of temper on occasion and arrogant in manner. He pursued a moderate course in regard to the slavery issue, which waxed hotter during his time in the Senate, but did side vigorously for a free California. In the Senate, he was also noted for favoring land grants for veterans of the war with Mexico; aid to railroad construction, as was the obligation of any senator from Illinois of his time; and assistance for education in agricultural methods. He assisted Douglas in finally gaining passage in 1850 of the proposal to grant land to the states to defray costs of railroad development.

With the coming of the 1850s, the extension of slavery had become the burning issue of the time. New players appeared on the political stage. The Whig politician Abraham Lincoln, now a member of the new Republican Party, wanted the Senate seat for himself in 1854. When he and the incumbent Shields appeared to be deadlocked in the legislature, Lincoln threw his influence on the side of Lyman Trumbull, who became the compromise choice on the tenth ballot. This was heralded as a victory by the "anti-Nebraska" press in all parts of the state.

As had been the case with Sidney Breeze six years before, Shields did not retire to some backwoods cabin and rock away his remaining years after his defeat in 1855. Senator Douglas had him appointed an Indian agent in Minnesota. There he organized several townships and encouraged Irish settlement in them. It was a time just following the great Irish emigration to Canada and the United States, which had been forced by the "potato famine" of 1845 to 1851.

Shields was elected to the U.S. Senate from Minnesota but only for a short term. When it ended in 1859, he was denied reelection by a Republican legislature. He journeyed then to California, and in San Francisco in 1861, he married the daughter of an old friend from Ireland. The couple settled in Mazatlan, Mexico, where Shields was manager of a mine that he owned in part.

With the Civil War coming on and President Lincoln and Illinois calling for volunteers, Shields was appointed a brigadier general in August 1861 and served until March 1863. He resigned his commission at that time and went again to San Francisco.

In California, Shields was appointed a state railroad commissioner. By 1866, he was living in Missouri. He lost in a bid for Congress on a technicality of counting votes. By 1872, he was supporting candidates of the Liberal Republican Party. He became a lecturer on religious, Irish, and charitable causes and gained election to the state legislature. Appointed to the state railroad commission, he was chosen U.S. Senator from Missouri in 1879, to fill a short-term vacancy. Poor health kept him from seeking the full term that followed, and he died later in the year while on a lecture tour in Iowa, active to the end. He was buried in Carrollton, Missouri.

James Shields, the only person ever to represent three separate states in the U.S. Senate, is immortalized by statues in both Missouri and Minnesota, and by one placed by Illinois in the Capitol in Washington, D.C.

5 ★ A Puritan Conscience

We have seen that early in its history, there was a significant group of men who came to Illinois seeking the opportunities that a frontier environment and an infant state might offer them. With roots in one of the more eastern states, usually well educated for the time before reaching Illinois, they filled the necessary public positions such as governor, senator, judge, secretary of state, and so on. Without them there would have been a dearth of talent to perform such tasks. Often they found business opportunities awaiting them as well as political ones. Without the help of their wives, they would have succeeded in little.

Illinois politics were dominated for almost three decades by the men who ushered in its statehood. James Shields represents a time of transition from new-state issues to the politics of dissension over slavery, secession, and civil conflict. He was a contemporary of the next great figures on the Illinois political scene—Stephen A. Douglas, Lyman Trumbull, and Abraham Lincoln.

Lyman Trumbull (1855–73)

Lyman Trumbull was one of the group who came to Illinois seeking political opportunity. He was born in Colchester, Connecticut, on October 12, 1813. After a stint at teaching school in Georgia, and reading law, he had made his way by 1836 to Belleville, Illinois, where he began a law practice and took part in Democratic politics. He was one of a small group of lawyers who brought suits, without hope of compensation, in behalf of the rights of blacks, both slave and free.

Trumbull became a member of the legislature in 1840 and a year later was appointed secretary of state by Governor Thomas Carlin. He nearly won the Democratic nomination for governor in 1846 but was out-maneuvered in the party convention. In 1848, he was elected to the state supreme court and four years later was reelected to a term of nine years.

In 1854, he was elected to the U.S. Senate, when Abraham Lincoln and the incumbent James Shields contested the seat. Lincoln, a Whig, could not gather the necessary number of votes to win. Since he preferred Trumbull's view on the expansion of slavery to Shields's, Lincoln threw his influence in that direction, and Trumbull was chosen on the tenth ballot. He had been one of the group that had debated the issue with Douglas at Springfield. No doubt that influenced Lincoln in his favor. This sacrifice on Lincoln's part strengthened his bid for Republican support in the contest with Douglas two years later.

Trumbull served three full terms in the Senate, substantially longer than any Illinois senator who had preceded him. His time in office spanned the Civil War and extended into the period of Radical Reconstruction. The several ideological and partisan changes that he experienced during and after service in the Senate can be better understood with a knowledge of the background that produced him.

Lyman Trumbull's paternal grandfather was Benjamin Trumbull. Until he was in his thirties, the family name was Trumble. His ancestors had been in New England at least since 1639. A graduate of Yale, he took training in theology and became licensed to preach.

The Reverend Trumbull was pastor of the Congregational church at New Haven, Connecticut, for sixty years. For six months during the American Revolution, he served as a military chaplain. Later, he was a captain of the militia in his community.

He was strongly motivated to perform service to the state, and at the urging of Governor Jonathan Trumbull, who was his first cousin once removed, and others, he undertook to write a history of Connecticut. Eventually, it was published in three volumes and proved to be a valuable historical guide. Later, he managed to complete one volume of a projected three volume history of the United States.

He also wrote and had published sixteen other books and pamphlets, all but three on theological subjects. With his writing, pastoral, and military duties, Benjamin Trumbull was a busy man. Apparently, he was conscience-driven, a trait that seemed to appear as well in his grandson Lyman.

There was a general impression among the Reverend Trumbull's contemporaries that he was a man of "great melancholy." This sentiment came through in his sermons and in his demeanor generally. It was said that those who heard his sermons felt that he was likely to burst into tears at any moment, so heavily did the cares of the world rest upon him. Attendance at the services he conducted depended more on his reputation as a patriot and historian than on their uplifting and inspiring nature.

No doubt the apple that was Lyman Trumbull fell not far from the grandfatherly tree. It is likely that he too had a strong compulsion to public service. He was in governmental office almost from the start of his adult life. He entered the U.S. Senate at a time when the controversy over "popular sovereignty"—the idea that on admission to the Union the citizens of a new state could decide for themselves between slave soil or free—was raging. He was one of a group of young Democrats who had taken issue with Douglas, champion of popular sovereignty in the Senate.

Trumbull, who began his political life in Illinois as a Democrat, became in the Senate a staunch Republican, because of the politics of slave or free. In 1856, he supported John Charles Fremont for the Republican nomination for president. Next he campaigned for Lincoln against Douglas for the other Senate seat, speaking in Chicago, Alton, Jacksonville, and other places.

He favored control by Congress of the question of whether newly admitted states should be slave or free, in opposition to Douglas and his idea of popular sovereignty. He campaigned actively in behalf of Lincoln for president in 1860 and was himself reelected to the Senate by a Republican legislature.

When civil war came, he raised the standard of the Constitution in issues of secession and extraordinary executive power, such as the suspension of habeas corpus. When General Ambrose Burnside halted publication of the *Chicago Times,* Trumbull protested on the ground of freedom of the press.

His thought generally was ahead of Lincoln's when it came to freeing the slaves. Early in the war, he advocated freeing slaves of all those in rebellion against the Union. When the war went badly in the early months, Senator Trumbull was not hesitant publicly to voice his criticisms of the Lincoln administration. According to one analyst:

> [T]his thoroughgoing champion of freedom . . . had now been transformed into a leader of the radical republican following in congress. Trumbull was a man whose austere talents had little of that warmth that attracts a large circle of friends, yet his intellectual leadership and honesty, backed by a puritan conscience, won for him a political following that was a silent but effective tribute to his genius. As the author of the first confiscation [of enemy property, including slaves] act and as a leading figure in every movement for the effective prosecution of the war, every suggestion of his carried weight with those who were shouting the battle cry of freedom. (Cole 298)

Trumbull supported a proposal of national conscription for raising troops and pressed for its adoption by the Congress. It became law early in 1863. Illinois had responded so readily with volunteers that no further claims on its manpower were made through conscription. That fact made his support of the draft law no political liability to him. The same condition continued throughout the war. When it ended, it was found that for all periods of service, more than a quarter of a million men from Illinois had been in uniform.

Trumbull joined with Governor Richard Yates in urging the use of blacks as soldiers. A black regiment was authorized for Illinois in 1863, and five hundred men were recruited for it the next year. Inequality of pay and other benefits limited the number of blacks serving from Illinois in the Union Army to fewer than three thousand.

In 1864, Senator Trumbull, as chairman of the Senate Judiciary Committee, introduced the bill that prohibited slavery and became the Thirteenth Amendment to the Constitution. That this action was in accord with public opinion in Illinois is suggested by the fact that the state became the first to ratify the amendment after it had been approved by Congress. Trumbull also acted as the president's agent for the plan that Lincoln had devised for the readmission of the Confederate states to the Union.

When the war ended, Trumbull took as hard a view as any so far as treatment of residents of the Confederate states was concerned. "We may treat them as traitors, and we may treat them as enemies, and we have the right to be both belligerent and sovereign as far as they are concerned," he declared (Keiser 81).

After Lincoln's assassination, Trumbull in time was at odds with President Johnson over the latter's vetoes of bills that Trumbull regarded as crucial steps in Reconstruction. Examples of two such bills that he had drafted are the bill strengthening the Freedmen's Bureau and a civil rights bill intended to implement the Thirteenth Amendment.

The Republican legislature had no reason not to reelect Lyman Trumbull to a third term in 1867. Even so, he was challenged by some with military records and more radical views. A contemporary newspaper held up "his lack of social qualities, his austerity of manners, his aristocratic sympathies and his natural tendency toward conservatism" (Cole 404) as reasons for him to be replaced. In the end he prevailed.

Trumbull came more and more during his third term to differ with the Radical Republicans in the Senate. He placed his faith in the Constitution as they, too often, he felt, did not.

Even though he disagreed with President Johnson on many matters, when it came to his impeachment, Trumbull was one of seven Republican senators who voted with the Democrats against Johnson's conviction and removal from office. In so doing, Trumbull lost much strength in Republican ranks and gave up any hope he might have had of winning a fourth term. Trumbull's vote in this matter was consistent with the course he had been following in Reconstruction.

In explaining his vote on conviction on charges of impeachment, he warned:

> Once set the example of impeaching a president for what, when the excitement of the hour shall have subsided, will be regarded as insufficient cause, and no future president will be safe who happens to differ with a majority of the House and two-thirds of the Senate on any measure deemed by them important. (Keiser 84)

This same argument was heard in 1999 when President Clinton was impeached. Like Johnson, he was not convicted in the Senate.

In his book *Profiles in Courage,* John F. Kennedy gives great credit to Senator Edmund O. Ross of Kansas for casting the deciding vote against the removal of President Johnson through the impeachment process. In fact, it was Ross's own actions of timing that made his vote seem crucial. There were six other Republicans who voted as

Ross did, and all are entitled to equal credit for the result. Kennedy explains the pressures on those seven Republicans in this way:

> Ross and his fellow doubtful Republicans were daily pestered, spied upon and subjected to every form of pressure. Their residences were carefully watched, their social circles suspiciously scrutinized, and their every move and companions secretly marked in special note-books. They were warned in the party press, harangued by their own constituents, and sent dire warnings threatening political ostracism and even assassination. (155)

We can assume that that kind of pressure was applied as much to Senator Trumbull as to the other Republicans who were not committed to vote for President Johnson's removal. While featuring Ross in *Profiles in Courage*, Kennedy recognizes the sacrifices made by the six other Republicans who voted "not guilty."

No one of them, he states, was ever again elected to the Senate. "I could not close the story of Edmund Ross," he wrote, "without some more adequate mention of those six courageous Republicans who stood with him." Kennedy reports that a leading Republican in Illinois warned Trumbull, who was one of those six, not to appear on Chicago's streets, for fear of being hanged from a lamppost. Kennedy quotes Trumbull as writing, after the vote had been taken, that if Johnson had been convicted and removed,

> what then becomes of the checks and balances of the Constitution so carefully devised and so vital to its perpetuity? They are all gone. . . . I cannot be an instrument to produce such a result, and at the hazard of the ties even of friendship and affection, till calmer times shall do justice to my motives, no alternative is left me but the inflexible discharge of duty. (168–69)

Republicans were enraged over Trumbull's vote in the Johnson impeachment trial. It was suggested in the *New York Tribune* that his son had bet heavily on the outcome and stood to win five thousand dollars when removal failed. The *Tribune* also charged that considerable vote buying had taken place in Johnson's behalf. Such criticism of Trumbull did not end with the Johnson presidency but continued after General Grant had replaced him.

The senator defended himself vigorously, declaring that he would stand on his record. The *Chicago Tribune* pointed out that in April 1868,

> while Senator of the United States, he . . . received out of the federal
> treasury $10,000 as a remuneration for an opinion, written at the
> request of President Johnson. . . . Anyone . . . will at once perceive
> the connection between the $10,000 and the singular acquittal.

Despite Trumbull's explanation that the legal work had been
originally commissioned by Secretary Stanton and was fully legitimate, his fee being unconnected with his work as a senator, critics
continued to allege wrongdoing. In 1880, a campaign pamphlet revived the charges, concluding that Trumbull's fee was "estimated
at the rate of one million dollars a year" (Keiser 85).

Aside from any question of bribery and corruption, Senator
Trumbull was ill advised to accept such a fee at the time in question, or, for that matter, at any time. His career had been no stranger
to controversy. One of his earliest public acts had been the suggestion of a plan for the repudiation of the state debt, which had
brought a storm of protest.

Trumbull and the six Republicans who voted as he did against
President Johnson's removal from office were able to see their view
prevail because such removal required the approval of two-thirds
of the Senate instead of a simple majority. One vote was lacking,
and the Senate stood as a bulwark in defense of the separation of
powers described by the Constitution.

Trumbull's gradual alienation from the Radical Reconstruc-
tionists, on matters of principle, and his refusal to vote conviction
on charges of impeachment for President Johnson, caused him to
be dropped from Republican leadership circles. Further disillusion-
ment caused by the nature of the Grant administration led him in
1872 into the ranks of the Liberal Republicans. He was given some
consideration for the presidential nomination of the Liberal group,
as was David Davis of Illinois, whom Lincoln had appointed to the
U.S. Supreme Court. Trumbull ended up unselfishly campaigning in
behalf of the eventual party convention choice, New York editor
Horace Greeley, probably the weakest one of the serious contenders
for the nomination. The Liberal Republican movement failed.

Trumbull ended his Senate term the following year and went
to live and practice law in Chicago. Like Breeze and Shields before
him, however, his political life was not ended with his retirement
from the Senate. He acted as counsel to the Tilden side of the controversy over the results of the presidential election of 1876.

By that time, he had resumed the cloak of the Democratic Party. Thus he completed a journey in seeking a political home that had taken him from that affiliation, through the ranks of the Republican and Liberal Republican parties, and back into the fold of the Democracy. In 1876, Trumbull explained his leaving the Republican Party, in a letter, in these words:

> I became satisfied in 1872 that the Republican Party had become as a body corrupt, and that the people were being plundered in almost all branches of the public service. . . . That General Grant is personally corrupt I would not intimate, but he has been singularly unfortunate in some of the men and influences that have surrounded him.
>
> I do not believe the Republican organization or General Grant which is really in most cases but its instrument, will allow the Secretary to approve even this whiskey business, to say nothing of the corruption in other branches of government.
>
> You see I have no hope of reform and purification through the Republican organization. Its power must be broken. Public sentiment in the west . . . is unsettled. The public are dissatisfied but know not what to do. (Keiser 85–86)

When Trumbull sought to win election as a Democrat to the governor's chair in 1880, he was ridiculed for his frequent changes of party loyalty and charged with being an opportunist. Although he was not successful, his reputation as one who put conscience above party has come down to us relatively unblemished.

In 1887, Trumbull was associated with Edward Dunne, Clarence Darrow, and others in petitioning for amnesty for the surviving members of the group that had been convicted in the aftermath of the Haymarket "riot." Years later, Governor Altgeld pardoned them.

Trumbull's last political involvement was with the Populist movement. In 1894, he proposed a platform that members of that party from Chicago took to its national conference in St. Louis. In the same year, he joined Darrow in defending Eugene Debs against a charge of conspiring to violate a court injunction issued in the Pullman labor dispute. Debs was found guilty and sentenced to six months in jail. During that time, he formed the views on which he ran, time and time again, for president of the United States on the Socialist ticket.

To say the least, Lyman Trumbull was involved in the passions of his time. According to one view of his political career:

His death [in 1896] removed one of the ablest statesmen of his generation, an unpretentious, scholarly constitutionalist, who failed to scale political heights because of a conscience and a lack of popular appeal. The conscience drove him from party to party seeking a place where he could abide, and his colorless public personality denied him the kind of support on which spectacular careers are built. (*D.A.B.* X, 20)

Trumbull died on June 25, 1896.

6 ★ Civil War and Reconstruction

Throughout Lyman Trumbull's service in the Senate, Illinois was also represented there by another person. It is timely here to give consideration to the several senators who filled that other chair. There is no better example of the impact of Civil War and slavery politics on Illinois than the combined stories of the U.S. senators who were in office from 1847 to 1876, through nearly thirty years of continuous tumult in the state and in Washington, D.C. They spanned the political landscape from frontier days through Reconstruction.

Aside from Trumbull, of those serving in the Senate, Senator Stephen A. Douglas had by far the greatest impact on national and state agendas during those three decades. On the other hand, the four persons who occupied the "Douglas seat" from 1861 to 1876 reflected the years of the "Little Giant," Abraham Lincoln, the Kansas-Nebraska Act, and Civil War and Reconstruction.

The four whose tenure in the Senate following Douglas occupied the second half of those thirty years are Orville H. Browning, William A. Richardson, Richard Yates, and John A. Logan. Their political roots plus those of Douglas and Lincoln go back to the state legislature of the 1830s and 1840s, when they framed opinions that shaped political discourse in Illinois throughout the Civil War and the years that followed.

That their lives and careers were intertwined for so many years and at such a critical time in the state's history is a matter of wonder. From those state legislative times in Vandalia and then Springfield through the war years and reconstruction, they contested on the political stump, on the floor of Congress, and in head-to-head presidential elections. They carved out the enduring images of Illinois and its Civil War-time politics.

While their service in the Senate ties them together, except for Lincoln, they had distinguished careers at all levels of public service and in the private practice of law. And, incredibly, their personal relationships survived, in spite of the victories, defeats, and passions of partisanship. At one time or another, each of them supported the Union in its darkest hour.

Orville Hickman Browning (1861–63)

Orville H. Browning made it to the U.S. Senate in spite of his long-time association with Abraham Lincoln, who failed in that endeavor in 1854 and 1858. The two had worked shoulder to shoulder through travails of the Whig Party, in opposition to the Democrats, and in the beginning of Republicanism.

Browning, one of the many Kentuckians who migrated to Illinois politics, was born on February 10, 1806, in Harrison County, Kentucky. He attended college, studied law, and in 1831 moved to Quincy, Illinois, where he opened a law practice. He served in the Illinois volunteers in the Black Hawk War of 1832, as Lincoln did.

Browning was elected to the state Senate in 1836 and remained there for two terms. He tried for a congressional seat in 1842 but lost to Douglas. Until Douglas's death in 1861, Browning never won office against him or his Democratic Party faithful, despite several attempts. Running as a Whig, he tried unsuccessfully for Congress in 1850 and 1852 against Douglas loyalist William A. Richardson, who also was from Quincy.

During the 1850s, Browning worked tirelessly to build the Republican Party in Illinois. This brought him in frequent close contact with Lincoln. One might assume that that contact would have put Browning at the forefront of Lincoln's candidacy for president in 1860. Strangely, Browning did not support Lincoln for the Republican nomination, and that short-circuited a political alliance and possibly a friendship.

Historians believe that Browning felt superior to Lincoln both politically and intellectually, and thought that since he could not be nominated for president, Lincoln should not be. While Illinois Republicans enthusiastically rallied for Lincoln, Browning supported Missourian Edward Bates for the nomination, and only reluctantly decided to support Lincoln after the nominating convention had adjourned. Upon Lincoln's election, Browning violated one of the cardinal rules of politics when it comes to asking for favors: Do not ask if you did not support.

Browning lobbied hard for a significant position in the Lincoln administration. When nothing materialized, he turned to pleading for an appointment to the U.S. Supreme Court. These frantic requests in correspondence were accompanied by ongoing criticism of Lincoln and his policies. The president politely responded to those jabs by continuing to ask for Browning's help and ignoring his requests for appointment.

Through a turn of fate in Illinois politics, Browning finally got an opportunity to serve in Congress. When Douglas died in 1861, the governor, Richard Yates, was a Republican. He had the right to appoint a successor to Douglas to serve until after the next general election in 1862, when legislators would select a senator for the balance of the Douglas term. He appointed Browning.

Closer then to Lincoln geographically, Browning occasionally saw him socially and discussed policy matters with him. On the great bulk of issues, Browning supported the administration, but when it came to acts of the president relating to policy toward slavery, the relationship became less than harmonious. Browning feared that Lincoln had fallen into the hands of the Radical Republicans, and he told the president so.

More specifically, Browning and the president split over the Emancipation Proclamation. Browning felt it would only prolong the Confederacy's resistance and drag out the war. That was the last straw for the patient Lincoln, and he rebuked Browning for sticking his nose where it was not wanted. After that, the two never again were close politically.

When Browning's brief term neared its end in 1863, the fortunes of state politics briefly had turned against the Republicans. Although Yates remained governor, the Democrats had taken control of the legislature in the 1862 election. Recognizing that he did not have any chance of being retained, Browning stepped aside. The legislature selected his longtime Quincy nemesis, William A. Richardson, to fill the Senate seat.

Browning had one last fling at public service from 1866 to 1869 as President Andrew Johnson's secretary of interior. He returned then to Quincy, where he died on August 10, 1881.

William Alexander Richardson (1863–65)

In the practice of legislative politics, there are those of vision and those who accomplish the visions of others. Sometimes there are persons capable of both. When it came to the vision of Stephen A. Douglas for the state and nation, the agenda was so huge it required many helpers. One who devoted much of his public life to Douglas was William A. Richardson.

Richardson did not spend all his life laboring anonymously for Douglas. He enjoyed an extended career in elective office at the state and federal level, before being chosen to go to the U.S. Senate in 1863. That alone would rank him among the state's political achievers. The fact is that in the end he had little to show of his own creation. He must be measured in the image of Douglas.

Like many of his contemporaries, Richardson came to Illinois from Kentucky. He was born in Lexington on January 16, 1811. He attended an academy in Kentucky and Transylvania University. After teaching school, he studied law and was admitted to the Illinois bar in 1831. He began his practice of law in Shelbyville.

Youth was not a drawback to a state legislative career in those times, and that applied to Richardson as well as to Douglas and others. At twenty-six, Richardson, a Jackson Democrat, entered the state House of Representatives for a single term. He served there with Lincoln, Douglas, James Shields, James Semple, and John A. Logan, among others who wrote their names in history. From 1838 to 1842, he was a member of the state Senate. He returned to the House from 1844 to 1846, when he served as Speaker, a recognition of his leadership and parliamentary skill.

Richardson took time from his political ventures to serve with distinction as a lieutenant colonel in the Mexican War. Coming off that adventure and with favorable publicity of his war record, he sought and won the chair in Congress that Douglas vacated when he decided to seek a Senate seat in 1847.

On the stump, Richardson, except for his physical stature, might have been a political double for Douglas. He had a frontier spirit about him, a robust demeanor that sometimes bordered on outrage, to make his point. Robert D. Holt describes him this way: "Richardson loved the rough and rugged life of the pioneer politician. His huge body shook emotionally as his deep voice roared forth his arguments. In his mannerisms he was unguardedly rough, almost crude at times" (272).

From the beginning of his political career, Richardson took Douglas's agenda as his personal goal. He became chairman of the House Territories Committee, the counterpart to Douglas's assignment in the Senate. They worked Douglas's Kansas-Nebraska bill in both chambers and finally got it enacted into law. In Illinois, both men took heat from unhappy constituents who believed the two had sold out to slavery interests. Richardson immediately tested his popularity in the 1854 congressional election and won.

He resigned his seat in Congress in 1856 to seek the governor's chair. He lost, in his first and only election defeat, to William H. Bissell, a Republican from Monroe County. Douglas had campaigned at length across the state for Richardson.

Out of office and out of work, but always a loyal Democrat, Richardson had the expectation of some kind of political job. President James Buchanan appointed him governor of Nebraska Territory, where he lasted only a few months.

Richardson returned to Illinois to help his mentor Douglas run for president in 1860. Like Douglas, he opposed the LeCompton constitution in Kansas. For that stand, both men were castigated by President Buchanan and southern extremists in his party.

Failing to get Douglas elected president, Richardson himself was returned to Congress in 1861, just in time to take the point for Democrats in the House in regard to Lincoln's war policies. Again following Douglas's lead, Richardson became a stalwart unionist. He opposed secession and struggled to prevent civil war, always standing firm for the Constitution.

Republican Governor Richard Yates had appointed Richardson's Quincy neighbor Orville Browning to succeed Douglas in the Senate, following the latter's death in 1861, but that was only a temporary tenure, lasting until the legislature had been formed after the election of 1862. Democrats, in control, looked to Richardson for the Senate seat. He was chosen over Governor Yates.

In the Senate, though still a unionist, Richardson remained fiercely loyal to the Democratic Party and went on the offensive against Lincoln's war policies. He spoke openly as a "peace Democrat" and, during a party debate in Springfield, stated his position clearly:

> I regard every man who is opposed to the [party] resolutions, as an enemy of the Democratic party. . . . I have only to say to every fellow citizen that the whole Democratic party are for peace. The road to peace is plain. Beat at the ballot box the Republican party—a party without wisdom enough to carry on war or make peace.

To the end of his Senate term in 1865, Richardson bitterly opposed Lincoln's antislavery policies and pleaded for a compromise that would allow slavery to exist in the South. Republicans regained control of the legislature in 1864, elected Yates to the Senate, and sent Richardson into retirement. For the next ten years, he lived in Quincy and practiced law. He died on December 27, 1875.

Richard Yates (1865–71)

Richard Yates is best known in Illinois history as the "soldiers' friend" governor, from 1861 to 1865, but his full public career includes more than twice that many years in Congress and a lengthy battle against slavery.

Another of the Kentucky migrants to Illinois who climbed to the top of the political ladder early in life, Yates was born on January 18, 1818, in Gallatin County, Kentucky. A student and scholar, he earned the first diploma presented at Illinois College in Jacksonville. He next returned to Kentucky to Transylvania University in Lexington, for a degree in law. In 1837, he began the practice of law in Jacksonville.

Yates's baptism in political work came with his support and campaign effort for William Henry Harrison, the Whig candidate for president in 1840. Two years later, he was elected to the state House of Representatives from the Democratic stronghold of Morgan County. At twenty-four, he was one of the youngest members of that body. He served there from 1842 to 1846, and again in 1849 and 1850. During that time, he developed a strong sense of outrage at the treatment given Negroes.

During 1849, Yates spoke against Illinois laws that discriminated against Negroes, calling the statutes "tyrannical, iniquitous, and oppressive upon the weak, harmless, and unfortunate class."

He added, "Any law thus placing any man, white or black, in the power of a purchaser, for money, is utterly inconsistent with the humanity of the age and the spirit of our free constitutions" (Kimball). Yates was a rare antislavery voice in the Whig Party and was to be a call to conscience for all of his public life.

In 1850, Yates took the next step in his political career with election to the U.S. House of Representatives, where he was its youngest member. He served two terms, until 1855, and took positions on the momentous issues of the time, but not always on the most popular side. He was against repeal of the Missouri Compromise and passage of the Kansas-Nebraska Act, in opposition to the efforts of Douglas and Richardson. His aggressive stance gained him a national reputation among those opposed to extending slavery to the western territories.

His outspoken opposition to slavery and support of total suffrage for Negroes cost Yates a seat in Congress, as citizens of his district were not as ready to embrace such then radical positions. His opponent accused Yates of being an abolitionist, which was a dangerous label to carry in Illinois politics at that time. Yates lost the election by two hundred votes and returned to Jacksonville to practice law. In 1860, by then a staunch Republican and supporter of Lincoln, he staged a political comeback, was elected governor, and served as such throughout the Civil War.

Yates earned his reputation as the "soldiers' friend" by working tirelessly to promote the Union cause, seeing that soldiers were well cared for in Illinois and visiting the battlefields of the West. As one biographer wrote, "Yates was a fiery denunciator of nullification, disunion, and secession, and felt that all of them belonged to the same category of despicable doctrines" (Krenkel 97). Robert Howard wrote that "no governor worked harder in behalf of the war effort than Richard Yates of Illinois" (*Illinois* 307).

Although a Lincoln man, he openly criticized the president for not moving sooner to emancipate the slaves. Yates adopted the Radical Republican position in opposing any compromise with the Confederacy.

The governor's name was offered as a candidate for the U.S. Senate in 1863 for the balance of the term to which Douglas, who died in 1861, had been elected, but it was more a courtesy than a serious nomination. Democrats controlled the legislature and named Richardson to fill the seat. Yates's time would come in 1865 with a Republican majority in the legislature and with him at the height of his popularity in his party. The legislature chose him for the Senate just weeks before the assassination of President Lincoln.

As historians have observed, Yates earned the Senate term by means of his no-compromise Republican positions and strong gubernatorial leadership. Unfortunately, his six years in Washington were an anticlimax and diminished his ranking in the state's history. In large part, his poor showing resulted from a drinking problem that reduced his effectiveness.

The postwar period was troublesome for Congress as it wrestled with reconstruction issues, Radical Republican attitudes, and the aftermath of sectional conflict. Yates was among those calling for severe punishment of the rebels. On other issues, he found opportunities to encourage western growth with service on committees for a railroad to the Pacific and territorial expansion.

In the early part of his term, Yates had a seat at one of the most dramatic episodes in U.S. history, the Senate impeachment trial of President Andrew Johnson in 1868. In announcing to the Senate his vote to convict Johnson of impeachment charges, Yates said:

> Standing here in my place in this mighty temple of the nation, and as a Senator of a great Republic, with all history of men and nations behind me and all progress and human happiness before me, I falter not on this occasion in duty to my country and to my State. . . . As a juror, sitting on this great cause of my country, I wish it to go to history and to stand upon the imperishable records of the Republic, that in the fear of God, but fearless of man, I voted for the conviction of Andrew Johnson, President of the United States, for the commission of high crimes and misdemeanors. (Krenkel 261)

By the time Yates completed six years in the Senate, drinking and poor performance had greatly damaged his reputation. In 1871, the state legislature rejected him for another term and elected war hero John A. Logan to the seat. Yates took the defeat hard and recognized that alcoholism had caused his downfall. He wrote Governor John M. Palmer, saying, "I think I will never drink again. I have been a good member of the Senate; done a great deal of work and made a great many speeches but they are buried because I drank."

Desperate to restore his reputation, and for his livelihood, Yates pursued President Grant and his aides for a federal appointment. None materialized, and he returned to Jacksonville.

Finally, in 1873, he was appointed to a short-term commission to inspect a land grant railroad in Arkansas. Returning from the completed task, Yates became ill and stopped in St. Louis to recover. There on November 27, 1873, he died of a heart attack.

John Alexander Logan (1871–77)

John A. Logan enjoyed a long, high-profile public career in Illinois as a legislator, military hero, man of the people, and player on the national political stage. A tireless politician from southern Illinois, he waged constant political war within his party—Democrat and Republican in turn—and bounded back repeatedly from threatened oblivion. He carried his causes to the public and, at various times, basked in enormous outpourings of public acclaim. His early political history and first term in the Senate is the focus here because of their close connection with politics of the war years.

Younger than those who followed the line of succession after Douglas during the 1860s, Logan had entered state politics in the 1850s and was elected to the U.S. House of Representatives just prior to the Civil War. Still, his political upbringing shares a time period and career influences with his predecessors in the Senate.

Born on February 9, 1826, in what became Murphysboro, Logan entered the Illinois House of Representatives in 1853 as a Democrat for one two-year term and again for one term in 1857. He followed Douglas's guidance on the Kansas-Nebraska issue and opposition to the LeCompton constitution in Kansas Territory, although the Illinois legislature had no direct involvement in either matter. He earned early on a reputation as one with a fiery temperament and a booming voice from the House floor.

In 1859, Logan moved to Congress following his election to the House of Representatives. Immediately, he argued for a compromise between northern and southern interests and expressed sympathy for retention of slavery in the South. As war clouds gathered, he declared against secession, but he worked hard to gain compromises from the federal administration to avert the conflict.

After a lackluster first term in Congress so far as achievements were concerned, southern Illinois voters nonetheless returned Logan to the House in 1860 by a large margin. They liked what he had to say. He campaigned hard for Douglas for president and shared the disappointment of many Illinois Democrats at his defeat. Logan picked up on the Douglas rhetoric after Lincoln's victory, saying that "the Union must and should be preserved." The question that plagued Democrats, Logan among them, was how to achieve that preservation.

Following Lincoln's election and near the brink of civil war, no one could have predicted the sharp turn Logan's politics would take through the war years. At that moment it appeared he would be a Democrat forever. He looked and sounded like a carbon copy of Douglas and others in Illinois who rejected everything Republicans stood for. On the floor of the House in 1859, he had declared:

> I came here as a Democrat, and I expect to support a Democrat. I may have differed with gentlemen on this side of the House in reference to issues that are passed; but God knows that I have differed with the other side from my childhood, and with that side I will never affiliate so long as I have breath in my body. (Jones, *Freshman* 286)

As Lincoln took office and war seemed inevitable, Logan planted his feet firmly in the Douglas-unionist camp. "The election of Mr. Lincoln, deplorable as it may be, affords no justification or excuse for overthrowing the republic," he said (Jones, *Stalwart* 52). Logan put his energy behind efforts at compromise with the South. He brought that case to Lincoln personally, although with no visible evidence of success.

The Civil War made heroes of many civilians, and none was more prominent than Logan. However, as the conflict began, he was no shining star of defense for the Union. He was assailed by Republicans as a compromiser and was criticized by many Democrats as a warmonger. With the war heating up in 1861, he announced plans to join the army to demonstrate his loyalty to the Republic.

Logan not only took a commission as a colonel, he organized and recruited soldiers in southern Illinois for the Thirty-first Infantry Regiment. Men came to serve with Logan from all over the region. Observers from other parts of Illinois watched with astonishment as Logan challenged southern sympathizers and the area's youth signed up.

Logan established a reputation from the start as a courageous warrior, and the Thirty-first took its place among the storied units from Illinois. In battle under the command of General Ulysses Grant, Logan rapidly moved up in the officer ranks. He was cited for battlefield bravery during the hard-fought contest at Fort Donelson, Tennessee, in February 1862. Commanding the Thirty-first from the front lines, he was wounded by a rifle shot in the shoulder and one in the thigh. Bleeding badly, he continued to direct his regiment during some of the most intense fighting, until he could no longer stay in the saddle. In time he healed, with nursing care from his wife in the field. He returned to battle, again under the command of General Grant.

Logan was promoted to brigadier general on March 21, 1862, after the battles of Fort Henry and Fort Donelson. He made major general on November 29, 1862, and served as commanding general of the Fifteenth Corps at the siege of Vicksburg, the victory that catapulted Grant to the rank of general of the armies. At the end of the war, Logan commanded the Army of the Tennessee.

Grant and other regular army officers, many of whom had graduated from the U.S. military academy at West Point, honored Logan as the epitome of the citizen soldier. In his memoirs, written many years later, Grant gave Logan special praise for his loyalty to the Union, his courage in organizing an infantry unit in southern Illinois, where southern sympathizers abounded, and his personal service in action.

Along with Logan's military service came certain changes of mind. He turned away from his prewar political positions and anti-Republican rhetoric. When on leave, he returned to Illinois and spread the gospel of unionism and patriotism across the state. While citizens hailed him as a hero, Democrats worried that he had become a believer in Lincoln's policies. In any case, his wartime experiences must have changed his political mind. It is likely that he realized who the winners were going to be and the probable political strength of Union veterans.

At war's end, Logan did what was to many Democrats the unthinkable. After vacillating for months, he finally declared himself a Republican candidate for the U.S. House. More importantly, he postured as a Radical Republican, dedicated to punishing the rebels. On the political stump, he became one of the Radicals who waved the "bloody shirt" of unionism to remind everyone of the transgressions of the South. He returned to the Congress in 1867 and served two terms there before finding an opportunity to become a U.S. senator.

In 1870, Logan worked unceasingly on two fronts. First, he wanted to be reelected to the House in November. Second, he wanted the legislature to send him to the Senate. Longtime Republicans did all they could to deny him that second ambition. They did not trust him. He canvassed the state to make sure that he had enough votes in the legislature to succeed Yates in the Senate. Logan defeated fellow Republicans Richard Oglesby and John Palmer for the party caucus nomination, then won easily in the legislature against the Democratic candidate.

During his first term in the Senate, Logan spent much time avoiding contamination from the scandals of the Grant administration. He successfully dodged suggestions of impropriety on his part and maintained his distance from Grant's appointments and policies. He did, however, support the war hero for reelection in 1872.

During those six years, Logan created a storm within his own party and among Independent Republicans by firmly standing his ground against patronage reform. He owed his political success in large part to loyalists whom he had provided with jobs. Logan knew that if Congress passed a civil service law, his political base would shrink. He never supported reform throughout his political career, although that stance probably cost him reelection in 1876.

Through much of Logan's six year term, he sat silently during Senate debates, and he did not offer any significant legislative proposals. As that term neared its end, he fretted openly about his chances of reelection. Republicans won more state legislative seats than Democrats did in the 1876 elections, but as many as fifteen members declared themselves Independent Republicans, enough to swing the election. Logan's fears of how the Independents would vote were well founded. They rejected his brand of politics and voted for David Davis, a longtime political associate of Lincoln, a member of the U.S. Supreme Court, and an Independent.

For the first time since he entered government service in 1853, John A. Logan had no visible means of support and faced life on the outside of the political system. His ambitions were by no means fulfilled nor his energies exhausted, however, and the voting public was destined to hear from him again.

7 ★ "Uncle Dick" and "Black Jack"

Richard James Oglesby (1873–79)

One of the most durable political figures of his time in Illinois, Richard J. Oglesby survived a chest wound suffered in the Civil War at Corinth and was elected governor three times nonconsecutively, and to the U.S. Senate once. He replaced Lyman Trumbull in the Senate in 1873. Trumbull had fallen out of favor with the Republican Party, largely because of his vote against the removal of President Johnson on charges of impeachment.

In common with most other nineteenth-century political leaders in Illinois, Oglesby was born in another state, in Oldham County, Kentucky, on July 25, 1824. His father was a slaveholder and a one-time member of the Kentucky legislature.

Richard lived the first ten years of his life in Kentucky, losing both of his parents to cholera when he was eight. Two brothers and a sister also perished in the same epidemic. The trauma that he endured from that massive loss must have been cruel and lasting.

He went to live with an itinerate uncle, and for several years the two experienced an almost nomadic life. In 1836, when Richard was ten, they came to the vicinity of Decatur, Illinois, where there were relatives. They worked a farm for a season, spent some time in Decatur, and then went to Indiana.

A year later, Richard came back alone to Decatur. Two of his aunts then sent him to Kentucky to learn the carpenter trade. After two years at that endeavor, he came back once more to Decatur and, for the first time in his life, attended school. Apparently, he had come to the conclusion that there might be better ways to earn a living than those he had been pursuing.

After a school term of three months, he spent the summer growing hemp, an activity that in this modern age might land him in jail, and making rope from the fibers. He became a familiar sight on the streets of Decatur, driving a team of oxen that pulled a farm cart.

The young Oglesby read law in the office of Silas Robbins in Springfield and was admitted to the bar in 1845. He practiced law for a time in Sullivan, Illinois. The case of wanderlust that he had contracted in his youthful travels was still with him, however, and instead of working the family farm or continuing his law practice, he joined a Decatur army company and fought in the Mexican War. As a first lieutenant in the Fourth Illinois Volunteer Regiment, he took part in the siege of Vera Cruz and the battle of Cerro Gordo. He was back at home in Illinois in time to campaign in 1848 as a Whig for General Zachary Taylor for president of the United States.

With that campaign successfully over, he practiced law for a time and attended a series of lectures on the law in Louisville. Wanderlust returned, however, and he set out in 1849 for the California gold fields. He aimed to score not as a miner but as one who supplied miners with their necessities. He borrowed two hundred fifty dollars to stake his enterprise and set off with eight other men and eighteen mules. The latter made up three six-mule hitches, and in ninety-five days, the party and its mule-drawn wagons filled with merchandise traveled from St. Joseph, Missouri, to Sacramento, California.

Oglesby turned his hand in the gold fields to whatever promised to make him a profit. He kept store, mined a bit, dabbled in banking. Within twenty months, he was back in Decatur with his debts paid and five thousand dollars in gold to his credit. Skillful investments in real estate allowed him to double those dollars, which became the basis of his later wealth. Five thousand dollars would be the equivalent of at least twenty times that much today.

It is said that one of his first ventures after returning from the West was a trip to Kentucky to buy the freedom of "Uncle Tim," who had been his father's slave. We have to credit Oglesby with a long memory, for his father had been dead for eighteen years, since

was also a seat in the U.S. Senate to be filled, however. The method of choice was still election by the legislature, and Oglesby had taken care to campaign for candidates for the state House and Senate who would cast a vote for him for senator. He was chosen to replace Lyman Trumbull. His term as governor the second time around lasted only two days. Duties of the office were taken over by the lieutenant governor, John L. Beveridge.

Though he may have been the star of the Republican national convention in 1872, Oglesby proved to be a dud in the Senate. His colleagues there were less than impressed by his flamboyant oratory. Eastern audiences were not so easily enthralled as were G.A.R. lodges back home in Illinois. The first Adlai Stevenson, a Democrat who was a contemporary of Oglesby and later vice president of the United States, believed him to be out of his intellectual depth in matters of the tariff and revenue. There is no great national issue of his time in the Senate with which Oglesby's name is associated.

He chaired the Committee on Public Lands, a perennial favorite of Illinoisans, and served on the Committees on Indian Affairs, Pensions, and Civil Service. Safeguarding and enhancing the pension benefits of Union army veterans was a special interest of Senator Oglesby.

When his term neared its end in 1878, he faced a formidable foe in the person of John A. Logan, who had previously served six years in the Senate. Logan had had two years without public office to solidify his political following, and as a former national commander of the G.A.R., he had strength in that quarter. The result was easily predictable—with almost a four-to-one advantage in the Republican caucus, Logan went back to the Senate in Oglesby's place.

Business, law, and politics occupied Oglesby's time until he was nominated for governor by acclamation of the Republican state convention in 1884 and elected to that office for the third time. He was the only person to be so honored until Jim Thompson turned the "hat trick" in 1982. Oglesby won over Carter Harrison, the Democratic candidate and mayor of Chicago, by only fifteen thousand votes. The Democrat Grover Cleveland was elected president of the United States, but Oglesby managed to hold the governor's chair for his party.

The most noted action of Oglesby's third term as governor was the extension of executive clemency to two of the "Haymarket anarchists," thus saving them from execution by hanging. Four others went to the gallows. And maintaining veteran pensions continued to be a special interest.

Joseph W. Fifer, the Republican who succeeded Oglesby in 1889, spoke of his "endurance, his bubbling humor, his eloquence, sometimes on the most homely subjects, the twinkle in his eye that never seemed to dim, his faculty for remembering names and faces, and the spontaneity of the crowds in their response to his presence" (Howard, *Mostly* 133–34). Shelby Cullom, who served for thirty years in the U.S. Senate and heard all the great speakers of his time, believed that only the noted Robert G. Ingersoll was more effective than Oglesby.

Oglesby's final years were active ones. He made another effort at election to the U.S. Senate in 1890 but was passed over in favor of the Democrats' choice, former Republican Governor John M. Palmer. In 1896, Oglesby joined four other former Republican governors in campaigning for the party's candidate for that office, John R. Tanner, who was elected.

Oglesby's first wife had died during his first term as governor, leaving two children for him to bring up. During his first year as a U.S. senator—1873—he married the widowed daughter of a Mr. Gillett, the largest landowner in Logan County. With her he had four more children.

Together they built in Decatur an Italianate mansion that boasted seven fireplaces. It is preserved to the present as a historic site. When Oglesby left the governor's chair in 1889, he and his wife built a home on the site and around the remains of the first Logan County settler's cabin. In the following year, they built the palatial place they called Oglehurst, on Elkhart hill, a prominent feature of the stretch of prairie between Springfield and Bloomington. Long unoccupied, it was burned at the request of its owner in 1984.

Richard J. Oglesby continued in his declining years to be a speaker much in demand for inspirational and entertaining presentations. He died April 24, 1899, at Oglehurst. Funeral services were held in the Gillett family private Episcopal chapel on Elkhart hill. He had come a long way from his days as a wandering, unschooled orphan boy from Kentucky. One observer sums up Oglesby's personality in this fashion:

> He was a fine looking man with a bluff, friendly manner that appealed to the people. This, added to his wit and good humor, his sincerity

and enthusiasm, and his ability to speak to the people in the vernacular, made him an excellent stump speaker, and as such he acquired considerable fame. He believed in the people and in their ability to govern themselves; in return, he was dearly beloved by them, to whom he was known as Uncle Dick. (*D.A.B.* VII, 648)

John Alexander Logan (1879–86)

Richard J. Oglesby was followed to the U.S. Senate in 1879 by John A. Logan (whose first term, 1871 to 1877, in the Senate is dealt with in chapter 6). Logan had had two years out of public office to fine-tune his political machinery and strengthen his relationships with chapters of the G.A.R., in which he had earlier served as national commander. His military record had more glitter about it than Oglesby's did, and Logan's edge in the legislature proved to be decisive.

Returning to the Senate was important to Logan in more ways than one. He was remarkably ambitious politically, but he also was dependent upon office for his livelihood. He had no established law practice or other business to fall back on.

In the Senate, Logan behaved as a conventional Republican as far as his vote was concerned. He was given to flights of oratory of the sort that had discredited Richard Oglesby. One of his speeches was said by an observer to be "the oddest performance I ever saw. Such ghastly rubbish . . . would disgrace a freshman in a Western College" (Keiser 96). It is probable that his critic was both a Democrat and from the East.

Senator Logan was always attentive to benefits for veterans of the Union army and navy. The dislike that he harbored for graduates of West Point, which had been fostered in him when he had been relieved of command of the Army of the Tennessee in favor of a West Pointer, often colored his views.

In 1880, Logan campaigned actively for Grant for the Republican nomination for president of the United States, for a third term. When Grant was not favored, Logan was sturdy in his support of James A. Garfield, a compromise choice in the convention.

Four years later, Logan sought the presidential nomination for himself but had to settle for second place on the ticket as a running mate for James G. Blaine. He was not highly regarded in the East, however. *The Nation* editorialized that "nature made him a soldier and a politician, but neither nature nor art ever designed him to be a statesman" (Keiser 96).

Unfortunately for both Blaine and Logan in 1884, the Democrats succeeded in electing the president for the first time since before the Civil War, in the person of Grover Cleveland. Logan had the meager consolation of seeing Illinois support him and Blaine.

In 1885, Logan's second term in the Senate ended. He ardently wished for reelection not only to keep the wolf from the family door but also to maintain his viability as a prospect for the presidential nomination in 1888.

The Illinois legislature was so evenly divided between the two major parties in 1885 that a month was required to elect a Speaker and deadlock was broken only by selection of the lone independent, Elijah Haines. Business could then go forward, but the balloting for senator dragged on for months, from February until May.

Finally, a member of the legislature from a solidly Democratic district died. A special election was set to choose a replacement. The Republicans did not put forward a candidate, lulling their opposition into the secure feeling that victory would be a matter of course.

The Republicans of the district had other ideas, however. In a ploy managed from Springfield and no doubt orchestrated by Logan, they sent agents posing as cattle buyers and lightning rod salesmen—some said insurance agents and vendors of sewing machines—throughout the district. Their presence excited no suspicion. Instead of buying beef and retailing rods, however, they were providing Republicans with ballots inscribed and marked for a certain Republican candidate.

Instructions were given for the Republican faithful, so armed, to lie low until late in the day before going to the polls. By the time the Democrats realized what was happening, the polls were closed and the Republican candidate had the most votes. The even balance of power in the legislature was ended, and Logan, on the 120th ballot, at last was given a third term in the Senate.

Two years later, he was dead, at the age of sixty, from wounds and illnesses that had been contracted during the Civil War. If he had lived, he might well have been the Republican standard bearer in 1888 and have become president of the United States. He was eulogized mightily, but Robert Todd Lincoln declined an invitation to be a pallbearer. Roscoe Conkling, a notorious patronage politician and former senator from New York, was one of those who accepted.

There is no doubt that John A. "Black Jack" Logan was the outstanding volunteer soldier of the Civil War. Although never governor of Illinois, he was sent to the Senate three times by that state. He was charismatic in actions, speech, and appearance. No one doubted his bravery in battle. He could stir audiences and win elections. He was one of the first of Illinois's prominent leaders to be born in the state. With his generation, at last the mantle of leadership lay on the shoulders of men who were native to Illinois.

His wife, who once stood by with a loaded shotgun so that he could finish a speech to a hostile audience, was a person of charm and intelligence who was of great help to her politician husband. With all of that, it would be gratifying to record that his service in the Senate was statesmanlike and of a high order. Unfortunately, that is not the case.

8 ★ Lincoln's Campaign Manager

David Davis (1877–83)

Illinois can claim its share of maverick U.S. senators, but *independent* senators—those who eschew traditional party designation—have been rare. David Davis was one who set a standard for independence and broke the mold.

Davis took an unusual route to the Senate—for legislative experience he had served only one term in the state legislature—but his whole public service was extraordinary. He managed Abraham Lincoln's campaigns for the U.S. Senate and for president, and he gave up a seat on the U.S. Supreme Court to serve in the Senate. He differed with Democrats and Republicans alike.

Davis was unusual in other ways. He weighed three hundred pounds or more much of his adult life and cut an imposing figure wherever he was, and especially so on horseback, riding the eighth Illinois judicial circuit. Among his accomplishments, Davis made a fortune in merchandising and real estate. That may have contributed to his streak of independence.

Born near Cecilton, in Cecil County, Maryland, on March 9, 1815, Davis attended Kenyon College in Ohio and studied law in Lenox, Massachusetts, and at Yale University. He arrived in Illinois in 1835 and, a year later, moved to Bloomington, where he maintained a residence until his death in 1886. Davis left an indelible mark on Illinois legal affairs during his fourteen years as a judge of the Eighth Circuit.

Shrewd and smart, Davis commanded respect on the bench and received attention in any meeting. He could exchange political gossip with the best of the attorneys who appeared before his court and who often frequented the same inns and eating places of the county seats making up the circuit. Gustave Koerner said of Davis, "He had a big head, and a big body, a big brain and a big heart." Another friend from the time said, "[H]e was the central presiding officer of every company, social or otherwise, in which he happened to find himself" (King xi).

He met Lincoln, Douglas, and many of the other political players of the Civil War era while they practiced law in the courthouses of such places as Decatur, Champaign, Bloomington, Jacksonville, and Springfield. Taking court to the far reaches of frontier Illinois was no picnic. With his writings, Davis provided vivid descriptions of life and hardships on the roads leading to the fourteen counties in his circuit. He told of the bedbugs, dirty and smoky taverns, food of questionable origin and substantial grease, political discussions around hotel fireplaces, and lonely Sundays.

From their meetings on the circuit and at Davis's home in Bloomington, he and Lincoln became more than legal acquaintances. Davis saw in the other the potential of a national leader, and Lincoln recognized the political skill and organizational ability of his large friend. They first worked together during the Senate contest in 1854. Davis and his Whig friends courted votes for Lincoln in the legislature, only to see Lyman Trumbull win the seat. Davis lamented, "Lincoln ought to have been elected."

They were on the stump across the state during 1858 against Douglas for the seat he occupied in the Senate. For more than four grueling months, Davis and his lawyer friends campaigned for Lincoln, only to see him lose again. Their next test came in the 1860 presidential campaign.

Historians agree that without Davis as his campaign manager Lincoln might not have been elected president. The campaign began with Davis engineering Lincoln's selection by the Illinois Republicans as their "favorite son." Then, in the insufferable heat of "the Wigwam" during the party's national convention in Chicago, Davis brought in hundreds of volunteers to create enthusiasm for Lincoln.

When the time came to cut deals with political leaders of other states to get the votes necessary for nomination, Lincoln often hesitated. But at the center of events, Davis charged ahead, knowing instinctively that deals were necessary. His involvement continued after Lincoln was nominated by the convention and in the campaign that followed.

Always the manager, Davis steered Lincoln toward a middle course, whether during a campaign or while in office. He tried to keep Lincoln in a moderate position on the emancipation of slaves and feared the president sounded too much like an abolitionist.

After being named to the Supreme Court, Davis continued his coaching and urged the president to modify the Emancipation Proclamation to prevent further sectional disorder. Davis feared that the coalition that put Lincoln in office would fail if the president became too radical.

The opportunity for Lincoln to reward Davis for his loyalty and devotion came in late 1861, when an associate justice of the U.S. Supreme Court died. Friends of Davis, especially from the old Eighth Circuit in Illinois, urged Davis's appointment to the position. They made it clear they felt that Lincoln owed Davis the seat. Lincoln hesitated for months—angering Davis in the process—before making the nomination to the Senate in October 1862. Upon seeing Lincoln in Washington for the first time, Davis told friends, "Mr. Lincoln is very kind, but care worn" (Sandburg, II, 66).

Davis served for fifteen years on the Court, by all assessments with dignity and high standards of intellect and scholarship. Through the presidential terms of Lincoln, Johnson, and Grant, he observed the actions of both political parties with increasing concern. He was displeased by the Republican use of power and, by the 1870s, believed the party had held the presidency too long and that government reforms were needed.

This attitude, combined with his widespread popularity in Illinois and the national political community, plunged Davis into presidential politics during the election campaign of 1872. Reacting mainly to the corrupt administration of President Grant, Republicans seeking a different direction in government formed the Liberal Republican movement. Davis encouraged the effort and became potentially a prospect for the splinter group's nomination for president in 1872. In his biography of Grant, William McFeely described the Liberal Republicans in this way:

> Liberal Republicans wanted government not of the rich and the well born, but of the intellectually well endowed and the well bred. They favored civil service reform, free trade, hard currency and civility. They held in disfavor political patronage, inflationary monetary policies, and the militarism they associated with a national constabulary necessary to police a national citizenry. (70)

Also contending for the Liberal Republican nomination for president in 1872 were Senator Trumbull and Governor John Palmer. The three deadlocked with other aspirants, and the party compromised on Horace Greeley, a New York City newspaper editor—probably not the best choice for party success. Mainstream Republicans nominated Grant for a second term. Democrats liked Greeley's prospects and embraced him as their party's candidate. Grant crushed Greeley in the general election and thus ended the Liberal Republican movement.

Disappointed in the outcome, Davis continued as a Supreme Court associate justice. If anything, the loss reinforced his independent tendency. An opportunity to serve in another political office as an independent arose during deliberations of the state legislature in 1876.

John A. Logan, completing his first term as a U.S. senator, wanted reelection but saw his chances dimmed by an unusual partisan lineup in the state legislature. Republicans outnumbered Democrats, but neither of the parties had a clear majority. Fifteen members declared as independents and held the balance of power. For forty-four ballots, during which Logan led but could not get a majority, the contest labored on, with Davis receiving just enough votes to stay in the running. Finally, Democrats and independents compromised on Davis and voted unanimously for him. The man who did much to put the first Republican president in the White House became a U.S. senator on the vote of Democrats and independents!

If anyone thought that would end Davis's independence or turn him again toward Republicanism, they were mistaken. He openly criticized Republican leadership, including the man who became president in 1877, Rutherford B. Hayes. Davis had predicted that Republican arrogance toward the South would backfire, and in the election of 1876, it did. The presidential contest was very close, with many believing Samuel Tilden had beaten Hayes in a disputed outcome. In addition, the Democrats gained control of both houses of Congress. As Illinoisans openly wondered which way Davis would lean, a defining issue arose in 1879 that harked back to Lincoln's time.

In that year, the Senate debated at length a bill to eliminate the government's authority to use troops in the polls at election time in the South. Democrats believed troops were not needed so long after the war had ended, and Republicans argued that without troops there would be widespread abuse and Negroes would be prevented from voting. Troops first had been used for such a purpose during Lincoln's presidency. Davis always had disliked the idea of using troops at the polls. After lengthy arguments, Davis told the Senate:

> No man loved Mr. Lincoln better or honors his memory more than I do, nor had anyone greater opportunities to learn the constitution of his mind and character and his habits of thought. . . . Such a man hating all forms of oppression . . . would never have willingly entrusted power to anyone, unless war was flagrant, to send troops to oversee an election. (McFeely 381)

The troops were withdrawn, ushering in almost a century of repression of the right of blacks in the South to vote. The world around Davis erupted. Democrats hailed him as the party's next nominee for president. Republicans denounced him in the strongest terms. Said the *Chicago Tribune:* "Davis is an imposter and a fraud. He has been nothing but a Democrat of the meanest type ever since he entered into the senate." Continuing, the *Tribune* said Davis dishonored "the memory of Lincoln" (McFeely 383). Davis appeared unmoved by either criticism or praise.

He did not seek the presidency in 1880. Republican James A. Garfield won the general election over Democrat General Winfield Scott. Davis did not think much of Garfield and supported Scott, in the hope that his election might lessen sectional strife. The Senate was split evenly between the parties after the election, and Davis voted with the Democrats in organizing it.

Then his streak of independence surfaced again. The Democrats offered him the chairmanship of the prestigious Judiciary Committee, but he refused the offer. Davis explained, "I have never acted distinctively with the Democratic party and unless its methods change and its wisdom is broadened there is little prospect of my revising opinions calmly formed" (King 296).

As Garfield put together his administration, Davis weighed in with the recommendation of Robert Todd Lincoln, the president's son, as secretary of war. Garfield accepted the suggestion, and Lincoln received the appointment.

The assassination of Garfield in 1881 brought Chester A. Arthur to the presidency and opened the door to one of the highest honors of the federal government for Davis. The vice president was next in line for the presidency and also sat as president pro tem of the Senate. The law in 1881 stated that in the absence of a vice president, the president pro tem selected by the Senate should succeed to the presidency if the president should die or in any other way become disqualified for the office.

Concerned about succession, Arthur called a special session of the Senate to elect a presiding officer—its president pro tem—to put someone next in line for the presidency. The Democrats temporarily controlled the Senate and named Senator Thomas Francis Bayard Sr. of Delaware.

With the addition of three new Republicans early in the session, however, that party gained control and unanimously chose Davis to be president pro tem. Thus, for almost four years, he stood next in line to Arthur for the duties of the presidency. Historians have pointed out the paradox that Davis was elected to the Senate by Democrats and was elected to be its president pro tem by Republicans.

Senator Davis appreciated the honor and became a popular presiding officer. His biographer, Willard King, wrote: "Decisive, dignified, benign, he treated the senators as he had the Eighth Circuit bar, frequently writing personal letters while they wrangled among themselves. The newspapers usually referred to him as Vice President" (302).

In analyzing Davis's contribution to the Senate, King wrote:

Although Davis became influential in the Senate, although the press mentioned him perhaps more frequently than any other senator, his career there was not significant in American history. No important law bore his name; he defeated no notable measures. His independence removed him from the main currents of political action. His position was secure and he felt no need to establish himself. (303)

True to a pledge he made when chosen to be president pro tem of the Senate, Davis stepped down as senator in 1883 and returned to Bloomington, Illinois, with his second wife, Addie, whom he had married a year earlier. They made their home in the large, Italianate Victorian style mansion that can be visited today as a state historic site. It has been judged as one of the five best surviving examples of its type of building in the United States.

Until the state acquired the house several decades ago, it had been continuously owned and occupied by members of the Davis family. One descendant, David Davis IV, served the district in which Bloomington is located as a state senator for sixteen years. Later he was an elected member of the Sixth Illinois Constitutional Convention. Like his illustrious great-grandfather, he was a large man and, also like him, a leader in the deliberations of the legislative bodies he graced with his presence. Members of the convention enjoyed his friendship during the months in which it met. They were told that he resembled the first David Davis in many ways.

Following his retirement in 1883, David Davis kept busy with books, farms, and family and gave help to longtime friends from the judicial and political worlds and their families. Although both Grover Cleveland and James G. Blaine, nominees for president in 1884, sought his support, he remained true to character—neutral.

David Davis died of the effects of diabetes on June 26, 1886. His funeral drew a huge throng to the relatively small community of Bloomington. The crowd was estimated at twenty thousand. It is probable that then, as now, such an estimate was overstated. Still it was a large crowd.

Among the pallbearers were Robert Todd Lincoln and Vice President Adlai E. Stevenson. Stevenson, like Davis, was a resident of Bloomington. Thus, within a decade, Bloomington had been able to boast of producing a virtual and an actual vice president of the United States.

9 ★ From Generals to Journeymen

It was inevitable that the time would come when the Illinois political system would exhaust its supply of Civil War generals. Those who had come to prominence in public life on the basis of service in the Mexican and Civil Wars and who dominated political discourse for a generation were fading from view as the nineteenth century moved toward a close.

Another type of politician was appearing—one with a career in law or business, or both, and steady advancement up the civic and commercial ladder until at last the legislature rewarded long service with selection to the U.S. Senate. As the frontier culture gave way to expanding industrial and urban significance after the Civil War it was inevitable that the type of person sent to Washington to represent the state in the Senate would change.

The impact of the Civil War had contributed much to the growth and maturity of the state of Illinois. Weak state banks were largely replaced by those chartered by authority of the United States. Twenty-eight hundred miles of railroad track in the state in 1860 was increased to ten thousand by 1890. The movement of farm products by rail greatly enhanced the state's agriculture, and coal burning locomotives caused coal mining to expand. Chicago grew in population from 100,000 in 1860 to 1,700,000 in 1900.

Skills of command and administration learned in warfare during the 1860s were put to good use in business and commerce. By 1890, Illinois ranked third in the nation in industry, employing a quarter of the Illinois labor force. With these changes, the balance of political power in Illinois passed from the Jackson Democrats, strong in the rural south, to the Yankee Republicans of the northern part of the state. First among the new breed of U.S. senators was Shelby M. Cullom.

Shelby Morris Cullom (1883–1901)

Shelby M. Cullom served for thirty years in the U.S. Senate, more than any other senator from Illinois either before or since. Incredibly, his tenure in public office—counting service at local, state, and federal levels—reached half a century. Still, Cullom is a perfect example of how length of service does not automatically insure history's blessing.

Cullom is one of the forgotten men of Illinois when it comes to Senate service, in spite of his long tenure in office. At the end of his career, Cullom wondered why he had not received greater credit for service or more acclaim for achievements. An answer may be found in a comment by a biographer who described Cullom as "able, durable, rather colorless, and generally conservative" (Howard, *Mostly* 163).

Born in Wayne County, Kentucky, in 1829, Cullom moved with his family to Tazewell County, Illinois, in 1834. He was admitted to the bar in 1855 without a college degree or legal education. In 1857, he won a seat in the state House of Representatives, beginning a tenure in one sort of office or another that lasted with only a few interruptions until 1913.

His history of public office holding is breathtaking and deserves special notice: 1855, city attorney, Springfield; 1857–58, 1861–62, state House; 1865–71, U.S. House; 1873–76, state House; 1877–83, governor of Illinois; and 1883–1913, U.S. Senate. His Republican colleagues chose him to be Speaker of the state House of Representatives in 1861. During the few years he was out of office, he practiced law with one of Springfield's top firms and served as president of a Springfield bank.

Cullom did not win every election that he ran in prior to being elected governor in 1876. He failed reelection to the state House in 1858, as a delegate to the state constitutional convention in 1861, and to the state Senate in 1862. He sought but did not gain nomination for a seat in Congress in 1872. He did not lose again until 1912, when he failed to win nomination in a statewide primary for a sixth term in the U.S. Senate. It is apparent that he was not invincible at the polls, and also that he must have learned how to win elections through losing.

In spite of his impressive record of office holding and public service, historians have been of several minds about Cullom's accomplishments, and what the citizens of Illinois received in return for keeping him in office all those years.

If he lacked a single quality that might have lifted him above his peers in history, it was the image of a leader. Cullom was no match for Stephen A. Douglas, David Davis, Paul Douglas, or Everett Dirksen when it came to leadership and charisma. There was nothing wrong with Cullom; some have it and others do not. His biographer James W. Neilson wrote:

> Not that he had ever been a popular idol, for by his very nature the man was not the sort who could captivate the imagination of the public or the hero worshipers. He appeared colorless, sometimes taciturn, even self-effacing. Men of his type are not those who become public idols or the subject of heroic biographies. (V)

Biographer Robert Howard offered this description:

> A tall and spare man, Cullom was proud to think that he "looked like Lincoln," who had been a friend of Cullom's father and in whose office the young Cullom had hoped to begin the study of law. Cullom's hair was black, his forehead high and massive, and his clear-cut features expressive. His speeches were convincing rather than oratorical. He was at his persuasive best in face to-face explanations of his political and legislative plans. (*Mostly* 164)

Another biographer, Henry A. Converse, an advocate of Cullom as an accomplished legislator, listed the senator's attributes in this way:

> His hands were clean. His life beyond reproach. No one can read the record of noble things done and ever sneeringly refer to him as a time serving politician, a chronic office seeker, without hanging his head

in shame. He had his ideals and ambitions. He would do big and last-ing things. He knew the American people and he knew that political success was the science of second bests. (78)

These impressions, and others less flattering, left many people of Cullom's time and later to conclude that his conservative ap-proach to public office meant that he was behind the times, lack-ing in initiative, and essentially a do-nothing officeholder. His public record shows that he picked and chose carefully when it came to public positions. Citizens of Illinois apparently took comfort in the fact that he did not crusade, rant and rave, or shout on the floor of the Senate. Stability, conservatism, and loyalty to Illinois were quali-ties that paid off for Cullom.

Most of his contemporaries displayed leadership qualities that sustained them in the history books. In most cases, military or pub-lic service during the Civil War anchored their reputations. John A. Logan, Richard Oglesby, and John M. Palmer all served with distinc-tion in the army and led the patriotic struggle on the home front. Richard Yates had been the wartime governor, the "soldiers' friend."

For some inexplicable reason, Cullom chose not to serve in the military, and his public profile was modest during the war. No one seemed to doubt his loyalty or patriotism, and his lack of military service never seemed to haunt him at election time. He waved the "bloody shirt" of Republican radicalism as frequently as anyone and praised the memory of Union victories. Still, he did not carry the title of general as Palmer did, or a heroic war record like Logan's.

Evaluations of Cullom generally agree on praise of his politi-cal agility. If there were nothing else of consequence to his career, the skill with which he gained election, often against odds and en-trenched opponents, is recognized. In fact, much of Cullom's story deals with his electoral victories. He defeated opponents who had little by way of a public record, but he also turned back some of the state's biggest political names. At one time or another, he won over Oglesby, Trumbull, the younger Yates, and John Tanner.

The key to Cullom's success in elections was a finely tuned or-ganization, combined with skillful use of federal patronage. With Republicans in control of the state legislature throughout his time in the Senate, he was able to concentrate on keeping a majority in that branch on his side and did not waste time campaigning through-out the state. He employed some of the most efficient and thorough political handlers that were available to him to keep his name before the public and the legislature while he stayed in Washington. Those who labored for him served only Shelby Cullom and wasted no time campaigning for other persons. For Cullom to prevail was their only objective.

On the two occasions when he sought statewide election as governor, Cullom won with only 50.6 percent of the vote each time. In 1876, he defeated Lewis Steward for governor by 6,799 votes, the second smallest victory margin in Illinois history. (Jim Thompson's margin over Adlai E. Stevenson III in 1982 was 5,074.) Cullom won reelection as governor in 1880 by 37,003 votes over Lyman Trumbull, the independent U.S. senator. With those figures, Cullom viewed his chances of winning a third term as slim and turned his eye toward the Senate. When an opening came in 1883, he won in the legislative vote over five opponents.

During his gubernatorial years, Cullom saw himself as an administrator, not an innovator. After concluding his two terms in that office, he defined his approach to governing, saying, "I no more thought of influencing the legislature than I have thought of attempting to influence the judiciary" (Keiser 94).

But Cullom had to govern, even if he did not propose grand plans. In 1878, strikes by railroad employees in Chicago and downstate communities threatened civil order. He sent state militia to East St. Louis to quell a riot and, later, asked for federal troops to maintain order in Chicago. The threats ended with little property damage and minimum loss of life.

Much of the credit for Cullom's political success is given to John R. Tanner, a brilliant political tactician and Cullom loyalist who grew up on a farm near Carbondale. He enjoyed a successful career in politics himself, concluding with election as governor in 1896.

The story of Cullom and Tanner is not all harmony, however. Tanner assumed that as Cullom advanced in age, he would anoint his longtime associate as his successor. Instead, Cullom held on to office—he retired at age eighty-three—and showed no inclination to reward his friend. They engaged in a bitter contest for the Senate seat in 1901, with Cullom defeating Tanner after successfully gaining signed commitments from a majority of the state legislators.

With so much exposure to national politics in Washington, and his own record of success, it is not surprising that Cullom thought he would make a fine president of the United States. Three times he toyed with making a run for it. In 1888, 1892, and 1896, he went so far as to announce that he would not turn down the nomination if it were offered to him. No one offered.

Cullom's record as a legislator resulted almost totally from his relationship to one major subject: interstate commerce regulation. He had championed the regulation of railroads as Speaker of the Illinois House, in response to abuses of farmers, and devoted virtually his entire Senate career to creation of the Interstate Commerce Act and its implementation.

Cullom introduced an interstate commerce bill in 1883, during his first session in the Senate. Fellow senators greeted the freshman's overture with disinterest, if not outright hostility. That did not kill the bill, however, as the public took an interest in the idea, and Cullom refused to give up the fight. From the outset, the Senate was of three minds on the question. One group was for a law and a commission. A second was for legislation, but not a commission. A third was opposed to any new statute at all.

Old guard senators constituted the group that wanted no legislation. They hesitated to kill the bill outright or make a public issue of their opposition because of strong public support for the idea. Opposing senators tried every trick in the congressional book to stop the bill in committee and on the floor. They delayed, amended, and planted procedural roadblocks, but the bill moved relentlessly toward a vote. Opposition by the *Chicago Tribune,* the state's most influential newspaper, stunned Cullom but did not derail the proposal or change the senator's mind.

Cullom's original bill, which was somewhat changed before final adoption, called for a five-person commission with five-year terms to monitor interstate commerce. Members would have jurisdiction over all interstate commerce and the operations of companies engaged in it. The bill covered all rail and joint rail and water routes having the same management. A similar bill, without a commission, was introduced in the House and moved in parallel through that chamber.

Finally, in 1887, after changes and compromises, both bodies approved the final bill with large numbers of members abstaining. In relatively little time, Cullom had gained the one major achievement of his thirty years in the Senate. He became chairman of the Senate Committee on Interstate Commerce and watched over that regulatory process throughout his tenure.

During Cullom's lengthy service in the Senate, Illinois was, of course, represented by several other senators, in turn. They make interesting contrasts to Cullom and to one another.

Charles Benjamin Farwell (1887–91)

When Senator John A. Logan died in office in 1886, he was replaced by Charles B. Farwell of Chicago. Farwell was the first Illinois senator who had his home in Chicago at the time his service in the Senate began. Both Douglas and Trumbull had moved their residences to Chicago after going to the Senate.

Farwell was born at Meade Creek, near Painted Post, Steuben County, New York, on July 1, 1823. His ancestor, Henry Farwell, was living in Massachusetts Bay Colony as early as 1639. Farwell appeared with his family in Mount Morris, Illinois, in 1838. Until he became of age, he worked at surveying and farming.

In 1844, he moved to Chicago, clerked in several businesses, and became involved in real estate and banking. He served as the elected clerk of Cook County from 1853 to 1861.

With the opening of the Illinois and Michigan canal in 1848, Chicago grew apace, and there were many opportunities for a canny businessman. When the Civil War came, others sought glory on the battlefield. Farwell grew rich in business as Chicago's industrial and distribution facilities expanded under wartime conditions. He prospered in real estate and, after 1865, in sharing in his brother's wholesale dry goods business, one of the largest in the city. It was a new age of influence for those who controlled the ebb and flow of business and finance.

Farwell held several minor offices before going to Congress in 1871. As a Republican, he narrowly defeated "Long John" Wentworth for the congressional seat. He served until May of 1876, when he lost in the settlement of a disputed election of fourteen months earlier. He was elected again to Congress in 1880 and served a single two-year term.

Farwell became state chairman of the Republican Party and was seen by some as heading Chicago's "Tammany Hall." When Logan's Senate seat became vacant late in 1886, Farwell and Governor John M. Hamilton contested for it in the legislature. John Tanner went to Chicago to interview both so that he could give a recommendation to Senator Cullom.

Tanner did not like what he saw in either man. "The trouble with Charlie," he told Cullom, is "he seems to think that everybody is for sale." Even so, Farwell seemed to Tanner to be preferable to Hamilton. The legislature agreed.

In the Senate, Farwell chaired the Committee on Expenditures of Public Funds but otherwise did not distinguish himself. By one account, "in Congress he played no very active part. The only subjects in which apparently he took any interest were the currency and banking, but his speeches display no particular insight" (*D.A.B.* III, 294).

Farwell did not seek reelection in 1891. Popular dislike of the "McKinley tariff" and opposition from the grassroots organization called the Farmers' Alliance would have made his return to the Senate difficult. He went back to the business world in Chicago and his home in Lake Forest. There he was active in the formation of Lake Forest University.

Charles Farwell and his wife, Mary, had nine children. Four of them lived to adulthood. He died at his home on September 23, 1903. His career in both business and politics seems to represent fairly the time in which he lived.

John McAuley Palmer (1891–97)

When Charles B. Farwell left the Senate in 1891, there was a spirited contest to succeed him. Democrat John Peter Altgeld, later to be governor, was making his second bid for a Senate seat. This time he had the support of the noted attorney Clarence Darrow but fared no better than before. The voting went to the 154th ballot before the Democrat John M. Palmer, who had served as governor from 1869 to 1873 as a Republican, was chosen. Lyman Trumbull had not been alone in switching back to the ranks of the Democracy.

The Republican Party was suffering from general dissatisfaction (a phrase that might have made a good nickname for Palmer, in view of his military record and movement from party to party) in 1891. Of concern was the administration of President Benjamin Harrison and, in particular, unhappiness over a new tariff law, backed by Congressman William McKinley, that hurt the farm economy. That made Farwell less than a popular candidate to succeed himself. His party turned to its old standby, "Uncle Dick" Oglesby, then in the twilight of his political career.

Three legislators were also members of the Farmers' Alliance, which supported farm policies that would later become part of a broader populist program. The three backed a supposed radical named Alson J. Streeter for the Senate. As a result, neither Republicans nor Democrats had the clear majority of the total membership of the General Assembly necessary to elect a senator. John M. Palmer was the ultimate compromise choice.

Palmer, who was seventy-five years of age when he went to the Senate, was born in Scott County, Kentucky, near Eagle Creek, on September 13, 1817. His great-grandfather, Thomas Palmer, had come to Virginia from England early in the eighteenth century. When John was fourteen, he came with his family to the vicinity of Wood River, Illinois. Two years later, his mother died, and the family broke up soon after.

When John was seventeen, his father, a Baptist preacher with antislavery sentiments, gave him his freedom from any further filial work obligation, saying, "[A] healthy boy as you are needs no help, you may go tomorrow morning. . . . Don't disgrace me. May God bless you" (Howard, *Mostly* 46).

John, who had had little formal schooling, worked at odd jobs for a time and attended Alton, later Shurtleff, College. Then he went to the region northwest of the Illinois River to peddle clocks and became a schoolteacher in Canton. By age twenty-one, he was reading law in an office in Carlinville and was soon admitted to the bar.

Palmer was inclined to be a Democrat and was encouraged further in that direction by Stephen A. Douglas. After losing a race for county clerk, he was elected in turn to the positions of probate justice of the peace, delegate to the constitutional convention of 1848, county judge, and state senator.

Clearly, he was one who could appeal to the voters. His reputation for liberal thought and political courage grew. He broke with Douglas over the Nebraska question. When Illinois Democrats supported Douglas for president in 1856, Palmer became a Republican. He was one of that party's founders, in 1856, at a mass meeting, sometimes called by historians a convention, in Bloomington, which he chaired. The southern counties of the state had little representation there.

Palmer became a Republican leader in both civil and military affairs. After running for Congress in 1858, and failing, he backed Lincoln for the presidency and helped him win that office in 1860.

He became one of the first of the "political colonels," as leader in the Fourteenth Illinois Infantry Regiment, in the army that was being assembled, and before the end of 1861, he was promoted to brigadier general.

He took part in the Tennessee campaign and became a major general, leading troops of the First Division of the Army of the Mississippi in rigorous battle at Stone's River and Chickamauaga. Like John A. Logan, he developed a dislike for West Pointers, and this led him to leave the service in 1864. President Lincoln appointed him military governor of Kentucky, and he acquitted himself well in that role.

He was under indictment for helping slaves escape when the Thirteenth Amendment to the Constitution was adopted. The charges were dropped. When he took a black child back to Carlinville and made him a part of his household there, he was indicted and tried under the "black code," which a decade earlier Logan had taken the lead in having enacted by the legislature. A jury found him not guilty.

When the war ended, Palmer moved his family to Springfield and resumed the practice of law. He became a leader in the establishment of the Grand Army of the Republic (G.A.R.). The original idea for such a brotherhood had come from the two men who had been surgeon and chaplain in the regiment that Palmer had first led. After Governor Oglesby had taken the lead in the formation of the G.A.R., Palmer became its first state commander. Its national commanders for its first five years were all former generals from Illinois.

Palmer maintained a foothold in politics and began to be thought of as a candidate for governor in 1868. The constitutional provision against the governor succeeding himself prevented the incumbent from seeking to continue in office. But Palmer did not wish to be nominated for governor. The constitution limited the salary to fifteen hundred dollars a year, and he was making several times that amount in his law office. He had a large family, and two of his children were not well. He wrote to his son:

> I am pressed on all sides to be a candidate for governor, but my repugnance to the thing is definite. The emergencies of the party may make my nomination a necessity and the same necessity may compel me to accept it, but I don't want to do it. . . . My income for January was $1,186 and for February $1,602 which is for two months $788 more than a whole year's salary as governor. Now stop income and

our situation is mere gilded poverty. With six children at home and two sisters-in-law, can I wisely pay that enormous price for a very empty honor? (Keiser 87)

When the Republican state convention gave him a clear majority on the first ballot, Palmer gave in and agreed to run. He won easily, with almost as many votes as were cast in Illinois for Ulysses Grant for president, and proved to be a strong-minded and aggressive chief executive. His emphasis on the position of the states in the constitutional system made him unpopular with many Republicans. As a constitutional lawyer, he saw the right and wisdom of having a clear-cut reservoir of residual power in state hands, with the federal authority limited to the specific grants of power that the constitution bestowed. This was the familiar concept of states' rights.

He favored a state civil service system and, at one time, prohibition of the sale of intoxicating beverages. Certain reforms in the judicial system were among his recommendations. On the less liberal side, he once denied a license as notary public to a woman in Chicago, simply because she was female.

As governor, Palmer favored the calling of a constitutional convention in 1870. He wanted to curb the spate of private bills and laws that had plagued the years following the Civil War. There had been many abuses in connection with the railroads, both in their building and operation, and he favored a greater regulation of them. In his message to the legislature in 1871, he held

that to deny that the state had the power to regulate railroads is to assert that a power has grown up in the State greater than the State itself, and makes an issue that the representatives of a free people cannot, without the most palpable disregard of their duty, evade. (Keiser 161)

Two years later, in his final message to the legislature, Governor Palmer observed that "the people of the State, aware of the refusal of [the railroads] . . . to obey the laws, and of the mischiefs their contempt of authority of the State produces, look to the General Assembly to make further and efficient efforts to provide a remedy" (Keiser 163).

The next session of the legislature saw a large number of railroad bills introduced, and even a few of them passed into law. The governor also had foresight enough to warn against the use by corporations of labor spies, private police, and strike breakers, acts of authority rivaling that of the state that eventually were curbed by law.

The great Chicago fire of 1871 occurred on Palmer's watch, and he took decisive actions aimed at assisting the city and its people in recovering from the damage. When federal troops arrived to help keep order, uninvited by the governor, he objected, holding that the state was competent to preserve the peace.

The whole matter became quite controversial before it ended, with the fatal shooting of a prominent citizen, a former general, by a University of Illinois student who was a twenty-day volunteer in the federal service. Governor Palmer asked for indictments on a charge of murder for the militiaman, the mayor of Chicago, the military commander, and General Philip Sheridan but failed to get them.

By 1872, he found himself unable to support President Grant's campaign for reelection and abandoned Republican ranks for the Liberal Republican camp. He felt that he could not again seek the governor's chair as a Republican. He had some following in the Liberal Republican convention for its presidential nomination. Eventually, he supported Lyman Trumbull, but the less politically able Horace Greeley won out. Palmer backed Gustave Koerner as the Liberal Republican candidate for governor, and Koerner, like Greeley, went down in defeat.

Out of gubernatorial office, Palmer returned to his law practice in Springfield. He made the transition from Liberal Republican over to the Democratic fold and was sent by that party to Louisiana as chairman of a committee charged with observing the counting of the vote in the disputed Hayes-Tilden presidential contest of 1876.

In the following year, he was the choice, through twenty-one ballots, of the Democrats in the Illinois legislature for election to the U.S. Senate. When deadlock was obvious, he withdrew, and David Davis, as an independent, was the final choice.

In 1884, both Palmer, as chairman of the Democratic state convention, and the convention as a whole were for the eight-hour day and the right of labor to organize. He was a delegate in that year to the Democratic national convention, which nominated Grover Cleveland for the first time.

Four years later, he was nominated once more for governor, with the understanding that he need not campaign. Even so, he stumped 60 of the state's 102 counties and came within 12,547 votes of defeating the Republican Joseph W. Fifer—and that in a year in which President Cleveland was beaten by Republican Benjamin Harrison.

In 1890, Palmer actively sought election to the Senate. He urged the Democratic Party to campaign for candidates for the legislature pledged to vote for him on a platform stressing the rights of labor and other liberal ideas. The outcome was a legislature almost evenly divided between the two major parties but with neither having a majority. As reported previously, it took 154 ballots before Palmer prevailed.

While in the Senate, he stood in opposition to the protective tariff and favored direct election of senators, an idea that was beginning to gain popularity. He also suggested the establishment of retirement benefits for justices of the U.S. Supreme Court, in a time when pension plans for public servants were almost unheard of. He reasoned that retirement pay might be an inducement to aged justices to leave the Court, when without such benefit they might be inclined to hang on to office as long as possible. He served on the Committees on Military Affairs, Pensions, and Railroads and sought repeal of the Sherman Antitrust Act of 1890.

Palmer broke with the Democrats in 1894 over their plan for the free coinage of silver at the ratio of sixteen to one in its value to that of gold, by weight. He felt that overvalued silver would cause gold to disappear from circulation. He was in opposition in that regard to William Jennings Bryan, whose "Cross of Gold" speech at the Democratic national convention had won for himself the presidential nomination.

Palmer took the lead in organizing the National Gold Democratic Party and became its candidate for the presidency in 1894. He could not tolerate the strong tariff policies of the Republican candidate, William McKinley. His running mate was Simon Bolivar Buckner of Kentucky, who like Palmer had been a general in the Civil War. Buckner, however, had fought on the Confederate side. It was the last great "hurrah" for the long line of generals who had been so prominent in politics in the United States for the preceding thirty years.

Palmer and Buckner campaigned in the larger cities. Even though their rallies were well attended, the Gold Democratic ticket did not win. However, the votes it received may have made the difference between Bryan and McKinley, with the Republican candidate winning in a close contest. Palmer received only 130,000 votes nationwide.

It is understandable that neither major party would have wished in 1896 to give Palmer another term in the Senate. He returned to Springfield. His wife died in 1885; three years later, he married the city librarian, a widow named Hannah Kimball.

Perhaps it was with her help that he was able to put together two worthwhile books in the years left to him after 1896. One was his memoir, subtitled quite fittingly *The Story of an Earnest Life,* and the other a two volume work of biographical sketches of leading lawyers and judges of Illinois.

He spoke often at public gatherings and was able in 1900 to attend a reunion that marked the forty-fourth anniversary of the Bloomington meeting that had spawned the Republican Party. Only a handful of those who had made history that day were able to be present. On the night of September 24 of the same year, he died in his sleep.

John M. Palmer stands below only Abraham Lincoln in the ranks of eminent statesmen coming out of Illinois in the nineteenth century. Like Lincoln, he had little formal education but made of himself an educated and literate man. Also like Lincoln, he had humble beginnings. Palmer, like Lincoln, opposed slavery and acted politically to curb and abolish it. He was idealistic and, like Trumbull, went from one political party to another to another, seeking an ideological home. Of all the statesmen of the time, his values seem most suited to building a sound foundation for the century to come.

The contrasts between Palmer and Charles B. Farwell, who preceded him, and William E. Mason, who followed, are substantial.

William Ernest Mason (1897–1903)

By 1896, the Republican Party was firmly in the majority in Illinois, at least as far as the vote for president of the United States and members of the state legislature were concerned. That meant the appointment of a U.S. senator from the Republican ranks. The Yankee element that had been strengthening itself in the state, with its emphasis on education, efficiency, good government, and the credo of capitalism, had triumphed over the Jacksonian Democrats, who had their power center in rural southern Illinois.

To replace John M. Palmer in the Senate, the Illinois legislature chose a veteran Republican politician of quite a different sort. The day of the generals at last was over. William E. Mason had served in the Illinois General Assembly from 1879 to 1885 and in the Congress from 1887 to 1891 without distinction, before he was favored with elevation to the Senate.

Mason continued the nineteenth-century tradition of Illinois political figures having been born in one of the older states. In his case, it was in Franklinville, Cattaragus County, New York, on July 7, 1850. His family moved to Iowa when he was eight years old. He taught school for four years before he was old enough to vote and then went to Chicago to study law and gain admission to the bar.

As a legislator, Mason became a skilled public speaker and used his talents with evident effect in the Republican campaign for William McKinley and against William Jennings Bryan in 1896. That round of oratory helped him win the Senate seat in the year that followed. Of Mason's service in the Senate, Howard wrote that

> Mason, a rotund and jovial Chicagoan who had replaced Palmer . . . , became a leader of lost causes at Washington. With speeches and occasional filibusters, he denounced McKinley for executive inaction when the Cuban people needed help. Later he deplored a trend toward imperialism, which did not seem to concern the people of his home state. By protesting the acquisition of the Philippines and then working for their self-government, Mason established a reputation as an insurgent. (*Illinois* 414)

He chaired the Committee on Manufactures but otherwise was not distinguished.

Mason adopted the cause of the Cuban revolt against Spain and urged a reluctant President McKinley to take action in its aid. Republican groups in Illinois were angered by his criticism of the president. He had opposed the Republican leader William Lorimer, and that earned him some animosity.

The Old Tippecanoe Republican Club of Chicago asked for his resignation and expelled him from its ranks. The senator, learning of that action, stated that if he had known he was a member, he would have resigned. By one account,

> Mason's nemesis in this incident was a Colonel McWhorter, who had introduced the expulsion motion. Mason said he knew McWhorter as a "professional deadbeat" and "political toucher" who had once sent a representative to ask Mason for $25. Mason had replied that he would "chip in a dollar if the colonel would take a bath" but

McWhorter's representative, according to Mason, had replied that this was asking too much. Mason closed with the statement, "Meanwhile, I am for liberty and self-government in Cuba, the Philippine islands, South Africa, and Chicago, McWhorter or no McWhorter." The *Chicago Tribune* was nearly as bitter about Mason as McWhorter and the Old Tippecanoe Club but thought it was too much to hope that he would resign. The *Tribune* commented, "He will cling to his office like a child to the breast of his mother." (Tingley 8)

Senator Mason would have liked to have been returned to the Senate when his term expired in 1903. He began his campaign by opening a headquarters tent at the state fair in 1902. The fact that he had opposed President McKinley's goals in foreign relations doomed his chances. He retired to his law practice in Chicago.

A taste for high office remained with him, however, and he unsuccessfully sought the Senate seat when it became open in 1909. In 1916, he ran in another statewide race, this time for the position of congressman-at-large. Now his fate was in the hands of the voters, not the legislature, and he prevailed, though he had gone into the campaign with little money and less organization. One of his campaign remarks that became memorable was "the Democratic party has the brain of a canary. The peacock is a lovely bird but it takes a stork to deliver" (Tingley 187). After a fourteen-year absence, Mason was back in official Washington.

War with Germany was looming when Mason took his place in Congress in 1917. Soon he resumed the role of obstructionist, which had been his role years before in the Senate. In the company of four other Illinois congressmen, he opposed the resolution for a declaration of war when it came before the Congress. Donald Tingley sums up Mason's position in this way:

> Mason, consistently pacifist and libertarian, spoke vigorously against the resolution. Mason held that Germany had acted within the limits of international law [in sinking merchant ships carrying the U.S. flag] and had given no cause for war. He warned that the United States was unprepared for war and that the people of Illinois were not in favor of war. He insisted the war was wrong: "It is a dollar war. . . . It is a war between kings for money and for territory. It does not involve a single human life that interests a great republican democracy like the United States." Mason opposed the war because "it means an entrance on our part into European war and European politics,

the dangers of which were foreshadowed by Washington and are familiar to every student of the history of the United States." Mason closed with the warning: "We will be tied to a treaty that we can not break without dishonor to a hundred million people, and your peace and your war and the destiny of your Republic hangs in the balance and in the caprice of a few crowned heads in the Old World." (198)

It can be argued that there was much truth in Mason's views. Tingley characterizes him as "a pacifist of long standing" (207), although observers of his single term in the Senate two decades earlier did not evaluate him in that way.

Mason was associated in 1917 with a coalition of pacifist groups called the Peoples Council, which opposed the war. At this distance, its aims and proceedings seem reasonable, but many at the time viewed it as a treasonable organization. Denied the right to meet in Minneapolis, it came to Chicago, where Mayor William "Big Bill" Thompson, who was known for his anti-British views, was sympathetic. Mason addressed the group, saying, "No worse thing ever happened in the history of the United States than is happening now when people like you are branded as criminals and denied the right of free assembly" (Tingley 216).

The council adopted a set of reasonable war aims and hurried to adjourn before troops sent by Governor Lowden to break up the meeting could arrive. So bitter was Mason's hostility that the Senate once entertained the motion of a resolution to investigate him.

Mason was reelected to Congress in 1918 and again in 1920. He was reunited with his party in opposing entry of the United States into the League of Nations. He ended his legislative career in character, pleading for independence for Ireland. He did not live to complete his last term but died on November 7, 1922. His daughter, Winifred Huck, was appointed to serve until the term expired. She was the first woman to represent Illinois in Congress. She sought the Republican nomination for election to the position but was not successful and faded from the political scene.

It appears that William E. Mason was a promoter and defender of lost causes ranging from opposition to the imperialism of William McKinley to opposition to the internationalism of Woodrow Wilson. If his talents and energy had been directed toward positive ends rather than defensive ones, he might be credited with being a more effective and statesmanlike U.S. senator.

Shelby Morris Cullom (1901–13)

While Farwell, Palmer, and Mason came and went from the Senate scene, Shelby Cullom remained.

During Cullom's last two Senate terms, beginning in 1901, his popularity diminished. The battle with Governor Tanner for Republican votes in the legislature, over the Senate seat, turned ugly. Tanner, bitter toward his former friend, expressed dark thoughts about Cullom. He said of the senator's tenure:

> [H]e has cheated and deceived somewhere along the line almost every Republican who has befriended him. He is known from one end of the state to the other as a wire puller, a foxy trader, always standing ready to trade off his friends for personal success. He has never been true to any principle. (Tingley 161)

Even after the election, the two never reconciled their differences.

Cullom's opponent in the 1907 contest for a fifth term brought back memories of the post–Civil War period. Richard Yates, son of the Civil War governor, was elected governor in 1900 but lost his reelection bid in 1904. Many in the Republican Party considered him an attractive alternative to Cullom, and Yates believed he had the promise of the votes he needed in the state legislature. Cullom, still crafty and politically agile, called on congressional colleagues to pressure legislators. Yates realized he could not compete with the veteran on those terms and withdrew before the legislature voted.

Cullom's success against Yates resulted mainly from strong Cook County support provided by Congressman William Lorimer, and by allies of Governor Charles S. Deneen. The alliance with Lorimer led to the most embarrassing experience of Cullom's political career.

In 1909, Lorimer managed to pull off an upset victory in the legislature to win the U.S. Senate seat in tandem with Cullom. Soon reports surfaced that he had bribed legislators to get their votes. In 1911, after a report on the allegations, the Senate voted on whether or not to expel Lorimer. By a vote of forty-six to forty, the senators voted to let him retain his seat. Cullom voted on Lorimer's side, saying the evidence was not sufficient to expel him.

The issue did not die with that vote, however. More damaging evidence of the bribes developed, and the Senate took a second vote in 1913. This time, with Cullom switching his position, Lorimer lost fifty-five to twenty-eight and was expelled. Cullom said additional evidence convinced him to vote against Lorimer. Throughout the episode, Cullom took a beating from the newspapers and his political opponents for backing, then abandoning, the controversial Lorimer.

Cullom wanted a sixth term. But the rules of election had changed in Illinois. Before the legislature voted to fill the Senate seat, it was necessary for an advisory statewide primary to be held. Cullom entered the primary and stated that he would abide by the voters' preference, even though the results were not binding on the legislature. His opponent was Lawrence Y. Sherman, a former Speaker of the Illinois House, who also, like Cullom, thought he "looked something like Lincoln." Cullom lost the advisory primary vote and, true to his promise, did not ask the legislature for reelection.

Shelby M. Cullom retired from the Senate in 1913 after a record setting thirty years. He died a year later and was buried near Lincoln in Springfield's Oak Ridge Cemetery. Perhaps the best that can be said of him is that he was a durable politician.

10 ★ A System in Transition

The new century brought with it a new sort of figure to the White House and changes in the way that U.S. senators were chosen. Theodore Roosevelt, vice president when President William McKinley was assassinated in 1901, was the first chief executive in many years whose thinking and emotions were not shaped by the Civil War. Soon a new kind of politician began to appear in the senatorial chair, one dependent on the will of the voters, rather than the judgment of the legislature.

It was the Seventeenth Amendment to the Constitution of the United States, approved by the states in 1912 and proclaimed to be effective in 1913, that mandated the popular election of U.S. senators. Sentiment for this change had been building for several years as a part of the Progressive movement.

Adoption of the Seventeenth Amendment did nothing to interrupt the full terms of senators who had earlier been put in office by actions of the state legislatures. For such terms that were ending in 1915, election by the voters was first required in 1914. In Illinois, in 1914, the voters opted to return Lawrence Y. Sherman to a full term in the Senate. Previously, he had been chosen by the legislature to fill the vacancy left by the expulsion of William Lorimer.

Albert Jarvis Hopkins (1903–9)

The first new face to be sent to the Senate from Illinois after the turn of the century was Republican Albert J. Hopkins, a lawyer-politician from Aurora who had served for eighteen years in the U.S. House of Representatives. Earlier he had practiced law and spent four years as state's attorney for Kane County.

Hopkins was one of the few Illinois senators in his time and before who was completely native to the state. He was born in DeKalb County on August 15, 1846. After graduating from Hillsdale College in Michigan in 1870, he was admitted to the Illinois bar in the following year.

The selection of Hopkins by the legislature to replace Senator William Mason in 1903 was the result of an agreement between Republican Governor Richard Yates, son of the Civil War governor, and Congressman William M. Lorimer, the "blond boss" of Chicago, styled by Robert Howard as "the evil genius of Illinois Republicanism" (*Illinois* 420). Hopkins was also favored by President Theodore Roosevelt. His selection was "boss directed" and a surprise to many citizens.

Only the year before, in an advisory referendum on public policy, the electorate had voted overwhelmingly for the direct election of senators. Too often in the past, it seemed to the people, the choice of senators had reflected political manipulations that had little to do with merit and ability.

Hopkins chaired the Committee on Fisheries while serving in the Senate, not the most significant assignment. Other than that, his record was quite modest. Still, with his term running out in 1909, he was endorsed by the Republican state convention and given the nod, though not a majority, in an advisory primary election.

Then one of the most scandalous and corrupt episodes of Illinois political history took place. There were a number of aspirants to the position, including former Senator Mason as well as the incumbent Hopkins, and with a near-even balance of the major parties in the legislature, balloting went on during 126 days.

When deadlock seemed inevitable, Congressman Lorimer insinuated himself into the running and, on the ninety-fifth ballot, was given the nod with the vote of fifty-five Republicans and fifty-three Democrats. The explanation coming from the latter was that Lorimer was "less offensively Republican" than the other candidates of that party. In view of his past, that is improbable.

99

While Lorimer moved his things from one end of the Capitol to the other, Hopkins moved back to his law practice in Aurora and Chicago. He must have marveled at the strange disclosures of the first few years that followed his retirement from the Senate. He died on August 23, 1922.

William H. Lorimer (1909–11)

Congressman William H. Lorimer, who was serving his sixth term in the House at the time he was advanced to the Senate, had played a key role in the elevation of Richard Yates to the governor's mansion in 1901. Yates returned the favor by helping make Lorimer a senator.

According to Howard, writing of Lorimer:

> The blond boss had the appearance and habits of a Sunday school superintendent. The orphaned, English-born son of a minister, he had lived on Chicago's west side since his ninth year. He prospered in years of bargaining with friend and foe in a kaleidoscopic succession of deals. Lorimer gave Illinois government a bad name. To the civic minded, he epitomized Tammany at its worst. (*Illinois* 427)

Lorimer was born in Manchester, England, on April 27, 1861. He emigrated with his family to the United States in 1866. They moved to Chicago in 1870. Lorimer was apprenticed to a sign painter at the age of ten. Later he worked in the meatpacking plants and for an electric streetcar company. He became a Republican ward leader, by the time he was twenty-five, and a constable. He branched out into real estate, construction, and the manufacture of bricks.

In 1894, Lorimer was elected to Congress for the first of three terms, then defeated once, and elected again for four more terms beginning in 1902. In 1909, he was elected to the Senate by the legislature, in the process described above.

In spite of having little formal education, Lorimer managed to become the "boss" of the Republican Party in Chicago. He played a role in the making of governors—not only Yates but also Charles Deneen and Frank Lowden—and backed Chicago's mayor William Hale "Big Bill" Thompson.

Almost a year after Lorimer was sent to the Senate, a Democratic legislator stated that he had received a bribe of one thousand dollars to vote for Lorimer. Soon he was joined by others with the same assertion. President Theodore Roosevelt was scheduled at that time to attend a dinner in Freeport, Illinois. He sent word that he would not be present if Lorimer were. The senator's invitation was withdrawn.

A Senate investigating committee with a Republican majority looked into the matter and ruled that since Lorimer had had a fourteen-vote majority and it could not be proven that that many bribes had been given, he should remain in office. A remarkable finding—essentially, "guilty, but not guilty enough." A minority report was filed from the committee to the effect that Lorimer's election was not valid.

Even so, the whole Senate voted forty-six to forty to allow him to keep his seat. Senator Cullom was with the majority. Still the matter would not die. Soon a committee of the Illinois Senate uncovered new evidence. A major corporation making farm machinery had been asked to contribute ten thousand dollars toward a fund of one hundred thousand dollars to be used to elect Lorimer. The committee reported that his election had been corruptly obtained. The whole Illinois Senate concurred by a vote of thirty to ten.

The U.S. Senate reopened the case. Finally, on July 3, 1911, it voted fifty-five to twenty-eight in favor of a resolution that held Lorimer's election to have been invalid. Senator Cullom again was with the majority, but the result was quite different—Lorimer was expelled from office.

Illinois had lost a senator and gained a black eye in the world of politics. Senator Cullom was discredited by his earlier vote to retain Lorimer, and by reversing his position in the second vote. The movement for the direct election of senators had gained considerable momentum. Soon Illinois ratified the Seventeenth Amendment to the U.S. Constitution, which made such election mandatory.

Lorimer faded from view in the active world of politics, surfacing from time to time to wield some influence. He returned to his business pursuits in Chicago. From 1910 to 1915, he was president of the LaSalle Street Trust and Savings Bank. He got into the lumber business. He was reportedly a wealthy man.

Lorimer ran unsuccessfully for both the U.S. House and Senate following his expulsion from the Senate. In 1927, he was a quiet force in the election of Mayor Thompson to a third term.

A political bombing in 1928, however, turned the voters of Chicago against the tolerance that Thompson had shown toward gangster Al Capone, and Lorimer's group began to lose its grip on power. His Republican organization in Chicago was taken over by Fred Lundin, the self-styled "Poor Swede." Others called him "Foxy Fred."

William Lorimer died on September 13, 1934, at the age of seventy-three. Beyond doubt, he was the most unsavory character ever to represent the state of Illinois in the U.S. Senate. He was buried in Calvary Cemetery in Chicago.

James Hamilton Lewis (1913–19)

James H. "J. Ham" Lewis proved certain things about Illinois senatorial politics during the first four decades of the twentieth century: One did not have to spend a lifetime in Illinois to get elected to high office in the state; loyalty to the Democratic Party, and to Chicago, paid off; and flamboyance counted for more than a record in the making of public policy.

When Lewis landed in Chicago in 1903, he already had lived a life fuller than that enjoyed by most. Born in Virginia in 1866 and reared in Augusta, Georgia—his father had been a Confederate soldier—Lewis was well schooled. He attended the Houghton school in Augusta and the University of Virginia and studied law in Savannah. In 1883, he was admitted to the bar in Texas.

An adventurer at heart, Lewis headed for Washington Territory, where he immediately dived into politics. He was chosen as a member of the territorial legislature, and when Washington became a state in 1889, he was elected to an at-large congressional seat. He won on a coalition, or "Fusionist," ticket, bringing together a majority from among populists, Democrats, and "silver" Republicans. He failed to win reelection in 1891 and left the state.

Lewis went into military service in the Spanish-American War. He served as inspector general with the rank of colonel. After the war, he moved to Illinois and began the practice of law in Chicago.

He had a knack for politics at the local level, and knew how to use the art to promote himself. Longtime Chicago Mayor Carter Harrison, who benefited from Lewis's political organization skills, wrote that "Jim Ham always has been a freelance, something of an individual fighter, playing a lone hand principally for his own good" (Harrison 318). Lewis attached himself to the people he thought would help him get to the next rung of the political ladder.

He wasted no time in taking a political direction in Chicago. Lewis became an associate of Edward Fitzsimons Dunne, a likable

Democrat Progressive. Dunne served a term as mayor of Chicago from 1905 to 1907; his corporate counsel was J. Ham.

From the inside, Lewis rediscovered a thirst for public office. He sought the Democratic Party's nomination for governor in 1908 but ran fifty thousand votes behind the first Adlai E. Stevenson in the primary. We shall see that losing a political contest did not deter Lewis in the least.

As Dunne's most loyal and powerful ally, Lewis was at the Irishman's side when Dunne decided to run for governor in 1912. It was one of the oddest gubernatorial elections in the state's history. Dunne won but did so only after Republican votes were split between party regulars and Theodore Roosevelt Progressives. The legislature, reflecting the same split statewide, convened in 1913 with neither party having a majority.

With Dunne's help, Lewis won a statewide advisory primary for the Democratic nomination for one of the two Senate seats that were to be filled that year. Then Dunne became the principal promoter of Lewis in the legislature, where the contest would be decided.

Another anomaly in state politics in 1912 was the fact that it was the first time since the beginning of statehood in 1818 that the legislature filled two Senate seats at once. One full six-year term was open, the seat that Shelby M. Cullom had held for thirty years. A second seat was available because of William Lorimer's having been removed from office. When he was forced to step down, there were four years remaining in his term.

Filling the two positions proved to be a real ordeal for the legislature. Balloting began on February 1, 1913, but final decisions were not reached until May 26. From the beginning, the Democrats wanted both positions. But that was not to be the case. Lewis won the statewide preferential primary on the Democratic side, and Lawrence Y. Sherman won on the Republican side. The Democrats, though greater in number, did not have the necessary majority of votes. If that had been the case, no doubt they would have chosen two Democrats—Lewis and one other.

Seeing that the Democrats could win only one of the Senate seats, Governor Dunne offered a compromise. He suggested Lewis for the full term and Sherman for the other, shorter one. The Democrats howled in protest and would not accept the governor's proposal. Finally, they came to terms after the national figure William Jennings Bryan intervened and called the Dunne plan workable.

Even then, seventeen of them refused to accept the compromise and vote for Sherman.

Lewis, of small stature, dressed in striking fashion unlike anything Illinois citizens had seen among all its previous members of the Senate. One way adequately to describe Lewis's appearance is to quote from a published account of the time. Of the Senate swearing-in ceremony in Washington, the *Chicago Daily News* wrote: "Mr. Lewis was clad in a tight fitting dark grey cut-away suit, dark puffed tie, white vest, grey gloves and a silk hat and carried a silver-tipped cane, with a light lavender handkerchief peeping from the pocket of his coat" (Tingley 184).

To call him a "dandy" was an understatement. This was not a uniform for taking the oath of office alone; Lewis dressed in this manner each time he was on public display until the day he died. Historian Richard N. Smith described Lewis as "an Edwardian dandy with pink whiskers and a florid oratorical style that looked back to Daniel Webster and forward to Everett Dirksen" (210).

Dirksen, who had a long career in the Senate as party leader and confidant of presidents, studied the performances of other senators who were known to him so that he could hone his own legislative skills. Of Lewis, he once said, in a casual moment, "Jay Ham Lewis. He had a facility with words. He was a good student. When the time came, on a dramatic subject, Jay could charm the Senate and the galleries, but when it came to the mechanics [of parliamentary procedure], he was completely lost" (MacNeil 8).

As a member of the Senate, Lewis went to work in 1913 with a strong partisan purpose. Acknowledging his political organizational skills and history of public service, his Democratic colleagues chose him as whip, the man who counted and solicited votes for the party leaders. He served in that position for the full six years of his term. Lewis became one of President Woodrow Wilson's stalwarts in Congress, and a firm loyalist to the president's actions.

Lewis never shirked from supporting Wilson's policies before and during World War I. He showed his dedication to the war effort by spending much time visiting training camps for soldiers who later were sent to Europe. He especially spent time visiting companies of black soldiers. As a political technician, he was sensitive to the growing presence of blacks in Chicago.

Wilson liked Lewis so much that he put his full support behind the Illinois Democrat for reelection in 1918. The circumstances under which Lewis had won the seat in 1912 had changed, however. In 1918, it was a matter of popular election by the voters instead of choice by the legislature. Lewis's opponent was Joseph Medill McCormick, brother of Colonel Robert McCormick, publisher of the *Chicago Tribune*. Not surprisingly, the *Tribune* endorsed McCormick and called Lewis a "carpetbagger."

It was a slam-bang contest, and Lewis gave it his best. But this was a time of Republican dominance across the state of Illinois at all levels of government. Lewis carried Chicago by fifty-one thousand votes but lost statewide by sixty thousand.

True to form, however, Lewis barely wasted a moment before gearing up for another contest. This time he aimed for the 1920 gubernatorial race. His opponent was Len Small, a downstate Republican from Kankakee who had served as state treasurer.

Lewis ran a vigorous campaign on a platform that supported tax reform, home rule for Chicago, lowering the cost of living, protection of tenants from profiteering landlords, better roads, and improved waterways. He accused Small of corruption in the state treasurer's office, a charge that was later justified in the courts.

Unfortunately for Lewis, it was revealed during the campaign that he held decidedly racist views of African Americans. On one occasion in Chicago, he stated, "I want a just community here, but before God this is a white man's government. I want no white man's government that will misgovern Negro or any white man. I will have no criminal Negro misgovern any white man by crooked manipulation of the ballots" (Tingley 369). This comment obviously cost him dearly in Chicago, where the black press made much of it.

Even with the endorsement of the *Tribune*—Colonel McCormick did not favor the alliance between Small and Chicago Mayor William Hale Thompson—Lewis could not make a respectable showing. He lost to Small by half a million votes in a strong Republican year.

For the next decade, Lewis practiced international law and remained active in Democratic politics. When his party made a comeback in 1930, he was elected to another term in the U.S. Senate. (His next term is discussed in chapter 12.)

Lawrence Y. Sherman (1913–21)

Lawrence Y. Sherman of Macomb was a member of the Illinois House of Representatives in 1903. When a group of angry legislators literally drove the Speaker and a group of his followers from the chamber, Sherman became acting Speaker long enough for the rump session to reconsider the controversial matter at hand. It was part of a bill that would give a degree of home rule to the city of Chicago.

No doubt that episode helped to elevate Sherman in the ranks of his party and in public recognition, and to make possible in 1904 his election to the office of lieutenant governor, as a Republican. Sherman had served four terms in the House altogether, two of them as full-blown Speaker. Republican Charles S. Deneen of Chicago headed the ticket and was elected governor.

Like most Illinois statesmen who came to maturity during the nineteenth century, Lawrence Sherman was born in a more eastern state—Ohio. He graduated from McKendree College in Lebanon, Illinois, and set up a law practice in Macomb. A contemporary historian of his party evaluated him as "one of the keenest intellects in the public service in Illinois today. He is a commoner of the old school; he has kept in touch with the people and believes in them, in their sense of justice and the accuracy of their judgment" (Tingley 183). There is no doubt a good deal of puffery in that, but it probably also holds a grain of truth.

Since William Lorimer had been expelled from the Senate, and Cullom's sixth term was ending, it was necessary in 1913 for two senators to be chosen by Illinois. It was to be the last time that choice would be by the legislature. Senator Cullom had been weakened by his early support of Lorimer, and then his reversal of it, and time had taken its toll on his strength and vigor.

When Cullom and Lieutenant Governor Sherman contested for the senatorial seat in the preferential Republican primary—one not binding on the legislature—Sherman won. J. Hamilton Lewis won the Democratic preferential primary, setting the stage for a showdown in the legislature.

There no party had a majority. The Democrats were most numerous but did not have enough votes to dictate the choice of two senators. This story was told from one point of view above, but elements of it will be repeated here. That situation also held up the selection of a Speaker of the House and the inauguration of the new governor, Edward F. Dunne of Chicago, who had been its mayor. To this day, he remains the only mayor of Chicago to become governor. Most Chicagoans would regard such a movement from the seat of power in the city to the one in Springfield as a political demotion.

Balloting for the senatorial positions in the legislature began on February 11 and went on until May 26. This long delay illustrates one of the great defects of choosing senators by legislative action. An inordinate amount of time that should have been given to other matters was used up in endless balloting.

Finally compromise, in which Governor Dunne had a hand, paved the way to a solution. With a full term and a partial one on hand, the more numerous Democrats got to name Lewis to the former, while the Republicans had to be content with the two years remaining in the term initially begun by Lorimer, for Sherman. At last Cullom was retired.

Lewis and Sherman were sworn in on the same day. The difference in their appearances was noticeable. According to a reporter for the *Chicago Daily News:*

> [T]he contrast between the two senators was most striking. Senator Sherman not only was devoid of whiskers of any sort [Lewis wore pink whiskers], but his raiment consisted of a dark sack business suit, with a black string tie, and showed no form of outward adornment. (Tingley 184)

Lewis, of course, was dressed more ornately.

Before Sherman's brief term ended, the Seventeenth Amendment to the Constitution had been ratified, and it was the privilege of the voters in general to name a successor to him. He won a full term in 1914 by about twenty-five thousand votes.

Lawrence Y. Sherman spanned the distance between election of U.S. senators by the legislature and by the voters. He and J. Hamilton Lewis were the last to be chosen by the legislature. Of the two, only Sherman followed with immediate reelection by public vote. Lewis too won another term under the new system, but it came several years later. It is noteworthy that the last two to be chosen through the old system both managed to win another term by means of the new.

Lawrence Y. Sherman was sent to the Senate by the Illinois legislature in 1913 and again as the result of a vote of the people in 1914. He must have been doing a creditable job, for in 1916, the Illinois Republicans agreed to back him in their national convention as their candidate for nomination for president of the United States. Part of the same political bargaining gave the Republican nomination for governor to Frank O. Lowden, who ousted Governor Edward F. Dunne after he had served one term.

The Illinois delegation to the Republican national convention, in 1916, largely held together for Sherman for the presidential nomination through two ballots, but he had no other strength to speak of, and on the third vote, Justice Charles Evans Hughes of the U.S. Supreme Court was the winner. He lost to Woodrow Wilson that November in a close contest.

The United States was soon at war with Germany. Senator Sherman supported the declaration of war, unlike former Senator William E. Mason, who was then serving in the U.S. House. Sherman was critical of President Wilson, not surprising in view of the party difference between them, for what he felt was a lack of preparedness for war during Wilson's first term.

Senator Sherman was generally viewed as antilabor in his attitudes toward such things as the mandatory eight-hour day and the right of labor to strike during wartime. When the mailing privilege of the *American Socialist* was suspended because of an antiwar publication, he turned a deaf ear toward its appeal for assistance in the Congress.

When a piece from the "Goodyear blimp" fell through the roof of a commercial building in Chicago in 1919, killing thirteen persons, Sherman not surprisingly demanded federal regulation. He was not successful in that effort, and aviation went largely unregulated, so far as the Congress was concerned, until 1926.

When the East St. Louis race riot broke out in 1917, with eventually fifty persons killed and 250 buildings destroyed, Senator Sherman called for a committee of five representatives and five senators to be sent from Congress to the city to investigate. No such action was taken.

When the Eighteenth (Prohibition) Amendment to the Constitution was proposed in the Congress, the two Illinois senators split their vote. Senator Sherman voted in favor; Senator Lewis was opposed. In view of the habits of dress and demeanor of the two, and their general approaches to living, that result might have been predicted.

One of the issues that became central to the presidential campaign of 1920 was approval of the Treaty of Versailles, which ended World War I and with it the involvement of the United States in the League of Nations. President Wilson struggled earnestly to win acceptance for the League. Senator Sherman was hostile to it, as was Republican Senator McCormick, who had replaced Senator Lewis in 1919. Sherman was one of the Senate "Irreconcilables" who could not be persuaded to accept the concept of a League of Nations.

With the refusal of the Senate to approve the Treaty of Versailles and with it the League of Nations, the way was paved for the gathering storm clouds of aggression that were to bring on the second World War only twenty years after the first had ended. Bear in mind that for the Senate to approve any treaty, a vote of two-thirds of its membership was needed. Put another way, one-third plus one could stand in the way of any treaty the president might propose.

Lawrence Y. Sherman chose not to run again for the Senate in 1920.

11 ★ An Unraveling of the Republican Fabric

The most troublesome foes of Illinois Republicans from the Civil War to the Great Depression were not Democrats. They were Republicans. Just as Republicans after Abraham Lincoln could not fully capitalize on their post–Civil War strength, from 1912 to 1932, internal quarrels, combined with a topsy-turvy national economy, eventually ended Republican domination.

There were two main philosophical camps among Illinois Republicans during those twenty years. The first division surfaced with the elections of 1912, when Progressive Republicans, following the leadership of Theodore Roosevelt, split from traditional and more conservative Republicans in Illinois as well as nationally.

This disagreement cost Republicans the governor's chair, the statehouse, and a U.S. Senate seat, the cleanest Democratic sweep in decades. By 1916, when the Progressive movement had faded, a vicious internal party fight set in among moderates, leftover Progressives, conservatives, and Chicago interests. Earlier alliances changed, political organizations came and went. With it all, the Republicans returned to and continued in power until 1932, but only at great cost to many persons and the party.

The central figure in the second round of dissension was William Hale "Big Bill" Thompson, mayor of Chicago, who had pulled together an influential statewide G.O.P. organization with down-staters such as Len Small of Kankakee. Lingering Progressives, moderate Republicans who were embarrassed by Thompson's antics, and Chicago media—primarily the *Tribune*—formed the other wing of the party.

In the midst of this Republican strife, two contests for a Senate seat epitomized the internal wars. The first was in 1918, when the first term of Democrat J. Hamilton Lewis was coming to an end. Waiting in line to run against him were two of the biggest names in Republican circles, Joseph Medill McCormick and Big Bill Thompson. The second intraparty clash over a Senate seat occurred in 1924 between McCormick and Charles S. Deneen.

Joseph Medill McCormick (1919–25)

Medill McCormick, a scion of the newspaper family that dominated media in the Midwest for much of the first half of the twentieth century, was born in Chicago on May 16, 1877. He had a good education—Groton for preparatory school and an undergraduate degree from Yale. He went straight to the newspaper business from college, serving as a reporter, publisher, and member of the family that owned the *Tribune*. By all accounts, he was intellectually brilliant.

Medill McCormick also was a tormented man. He lived in the shadow of his mother, Kate McCormick, a domineering woman who pestered and prodded her children. He also suffered from a manic-depressive condition that ultimately was the cause of his suicide in 1925. In a time before medication was available to treat his illness, McCormick turned for relief to alcohol.

In 1903, McCormick married Ruth Hanna, the daughter of U.S. Senator Mark Hanna, who had advanced the career of William McKinley. She became a soul mate to her talented but troubled husband.

Forced to leave the newspaper business in 1912, for personal and business reasons, McCormick turned to politics. His departure from the *Tribune* allowed his brother Robert—the controversial Colonel McCormick—to become its publisher.

As a leader in the Roosevelt Progressive movement, Medill served as vice chairman of its national campaign committee from 1912 to 1914. In both of those years, he also was elected to the Illinois House of Representatives, where he earned a reputation as an effective legislator with a Progressive agenda. Continuing on the upswing, he was elected at-large from the state to Congress, where he served from 1917 to 1919.

During his Progressive Republican years, McCormick worked hand in hand with some of the state's best known political activists. Harold Ickes, later to become a member of Franklin Roosevelt's cabinet, was one. Loyalty to Theodore Roosevelt brought the two together, but otherwise an enmity between them was fully apparent. Ickes hated the *Tribune,* and naturally, then, McCormick.

As the Progressive movement weakened in the years after its high-water mark in 1912, the acid-tongued Ickes expressed his disdain for the other. "He was Medill-on-the-make," he said. "What he had done was to climb up over our shoulders and kick us in the face as he dived headlong into the party of his fathers' [traditional Republicanism]" (Tingley 186).

McCormick's string of political victories, which started in 1912, brought him face to face with what his family and the *Tribune* believed to be the evil empire of Republicanism—Big Bill Thompson and his followers. Thompson was elected mayor of Chicago in 1915 and almost immediately set his sights on becoming president of the United States. As one of his associates reminded him, however, no one had ever gone from being a mayor to being president. He then aimed at the U.S. Senate as his next step toward the White House.

Congressman George J. Foss of Chicago, Thompson, and Medill McCormick were on the ticket for the nomination for senator in the Republican primary in 1918. McCormick's previous statewide run just two years earlier gave him a leg up against his opponents. His support of U.S. entry into World War I, and Thompson's well-known opposition, played heavily in McCormick's favor in downstate voting.

Of course, the *Tribune* promoted McCormick relentlessly. Foss was not a major factor, but he pulled votes in Chicago from Thompson, and that may have been his major purpose in being in the race. McCormick won the primary even though he lost in Chicago by eight thousand votes.

Senator J. Hamilton Lewis, of the pink beard and spats, was no pushover for McCormick in the hard fought general election. The Republicans neutralized Lewis's advantage in Chicago, and McCormick won statewide by the narrow margin of fifty-three thousand votes.

In the Senate, McCormick espoused the *Tribune's* nationalistic agenda by opposing President Wilson and the League of Nations. He worked for a federal budget law and a constitutional amendment outlawing child labor. Unfortunately, his poor health and alcoholism prevented him from making a name for himself as a senator.

McCormick was favored to win reelection in 1924, although his Republican primary opponent was Charles S. Deneen, one of the best known names in Illinois politics. McCormick had the backing of remnants of the Progressive or reform wing of the party, while Deneen received strong support from the Thompson-Len Small faction, which was dedicated to thwarting the McCormick family and the *Tribune*.

The Deneen-McCormick battle, complete with Thompson as an activist, illustrated just how jumbled Republican politics had become. Deneen had built a good reputation during his two terms as governor, from 1905 to 1913, as a Progressive executive and party leader.

In 1912, when he sought a third term, he favored Theodore Roosevelt for the Republican presidential nomination at the party's national convention. Despite his progressive credentials, Deneen refused to run as a Progressive and lost in a three-way contest. Medill McCormick had wanted Deneen to have a third term, and the *Tribune* had endorsed him in that contest. By 1924, that alliance of a dozen years earlier had disintegrated.

When in 1924 all the primary returns were in, Deneen had upset McCormick by only five thousand votes out of seven hundred thousand cast. Big Bill Thompson had revenge for his 1918 primary loss to McCormick, and Deneen's career was revived.

The loss devastated McCormick. He sought in turn several federal appointments but failed each time. On February 25, 1925, with just one week left in his term, he was found dead in his hotel room. His death certificate listed "heart attack" as the cause of death. His wife, however, found empty vials of barbiturates in a trunk, after McCormick's death. For years the suspected suicide remained a closely guarded family secret.

McCormick was buried in Middlecreek Cemetery near Byron, Illinois.

William Brown McKinley (1921–27)

By 1920, both the public and persons interested in holding high office began to understand the opportunities and complexity inherent in the method of electing U.S. senators by popular vote. Repub-

lican William B. McKinley, who was not related to the president
of that name, won election to the Senate in 1920 by eight hundred
thousand votes, after a three-way primary contest in which victory
had not come so easily.

McKinley was a native of Illinois. He was born in Petersburg,
Menard County, on September 5, 1856, near the ruins of the tiny vil-
lage that since has come to be called, in its restored form, Lincoln's
New Salem.

He was educated in the public schools of Petersburg and attended the University of Illinois during its early years. He clerked
for a time in a drugstore in Springfield and then returned to Champaign. He became a banker.

In the years that followed, McKinley made a fortune in the
ownership and operation of interurban electric-powered rail lines
connecting a number of Illinois's larger cities. His system began in
Danville. It eventually grew to contain four hundred miles of track
and was one of the largest of its kind in the United States. It connected with St. Louis over the McKinley bridge, one that his company built. McKinley's empire owned its own electric company,
which eventually became Illinois Power.

McKinley also operated streetcar lines in a number of Illinois
cities, and several shorter interurban lines. As late as 1929, when the
automobile had made great inroads into its business, the main system still ran twelve trains a day from St. Louis to Peoria and Springfield. McKinley was no longer active in its management at that time.

Persons still living today can recall riding the electric-powered
cars of that system during World War II, in getting about between
St. Louis, Champaign, Springfield, and Peoria. With the limited
supply of tires and gasoline and a thirty-five-mile-an-hour speed
limit of those times, it was often the preferred way to go.

McKinley must have been a busy man, for he was elected to the
University of Illinois Board of Trustees in 1902 and to the Congress
in 1904. He served in the U.S. House of Representatives for four
terms but was beaten in the Republican split between Taft and
Roosevelt in 1912. With that rift healed two years later, he went
back to the House for three more terms.

In 1920, McKinley was elected to the U.S. Senate to take the
place of Lawrence Y. Sherman. He chaired the Committee on Manufactures during the Sixty-ninth Congress but was otherwise undistinguished in his service. Republican voters must have thought so,

too, for he was beaten by Frank L. Smith in the primary election in 1926 by one hundred thousand votes. Before McKinley's term ended, he died in Indiana, on December 12, 1926. He was buried in Mount Hope Cemetery in Champaign.

His name is honored by the presence of McKinley Presbyterian Church in Urbana, near the University of Illinois campus. It enrolls a number of students and faculty among its congregation.

Charles Samuel Deneen (1925–31)

By the time Charles S. Deneen was elected to the Senate in 1924, he already had one of the outstanding resumes in Illinois political history. The Senate experience, which should have been a splendid cap to his career, turned instead into a personal failure and a public disappointment.

With his primary victory over incumbent Medill McCormick in 1924, Deneen had run his election course to thirty-two years of public service. He accomplished that record as a native Illinoisan, born May 4, 1863, in Edwardsville. Unlike so many political achievers in Illinois, he never lived in another state for any lengthy period of time.

Deneen was reared in Lebanon and received a degree from its McKendree College. His father was a professor of Latin at McKendree, his grandfather a Methodist minister. McKendree, of course was, in its origin and much of its history, a Methodist institution. After teaching in downstate public schools, Deneen graduated from Union College of Law, later a part of Northwestern University.

From that time, Deneen was of Chicago. He began practicing law in the city and, in 1892, was elected to the state House of Representatives, where he served a single term. Cook County voters elected him county prosecutor in 1896 and again in 1900. His next step was toward the governor's chair

He won a first term in that office in 1904 with almost 60 percent of the popular vote and soon established for himself a record as a Progressive Republican. He promoted a direct primary law, municipal courts for Chicago, a state highway commission, and a deep waterway from Lake Michigan to the highest navigable point of the Illinois River. He championed sound welfare management, paved highways, and funds for dependent and neglected children. Historian Robert Howard evaluated Deneen as "one of the strong governors of Illinois" (*Illinois* 21).

Deneen had a more difficult time in the election of 1908, when he was pitted against Democratic icon Adlai E. Stevenson and won by only a percentage point. He probably could have been elected to a third term in 1912 if it had not been for the Roosevelt Progressive movement that shattered the Republican Party. Deneen refused the nomination of the Progressive Party and ran as a traditional Republican. He captured only 27.4 percent of the vote and finished second to Democrat Edward F. Dunne, the mayor of Chicago.

Thoroughly beaten, Deneen retreated to practice law in Chicago. Still, he was never far from the Republican political activity that was all around him. During the time of Big Bill Thompson as mayor, failure of the Progressive movement, and anger and retribution in his own party, Deneen kept out of the fray, until 1924.

Senator McCormick was in the battle sights of a faction of the party that disliked him, and thoroughly hated his brother Robert and his *Chicago Tribune*. At the head of that group was Mayor Thompson, who was beaten by McCormick in the 1918 Senate primary. Thompson wanted revenge. Deneen wanted to resurrect his political standing. They came together in 1924 and defeated McCormick by just five thousand votes in the primary.

Deneen ran up a huge plurality of 650,000 in the general election against little known Democrat Colonel A. A. Sprague. Thompson had defeated his mortal enemy, and Deneen had won a Senate seat. Given the Republican factionalism of the time, however, and the unpredictable nature of Thompson within his alliances, it was only a matter of time until another split occurred. Deneen proved to be too independent to suit Thompson's taste.

Deneen stood for election in 1924, won, and served in the Senate as a Coolidge conservative in economic matters. He strongly supported the League of Nations and the World Court, positions that would haunt him when he sought reelection in 1930.

He added to his reputation as an honest politician during his Senate term. Political turmoil within the Republican Party was almost the rule during that time. He and Thompson went their separate ways over the elections of 1926 and 1928, both in Chicago and across Illinois. Deneen's supporters won in direct clashes with the Thompson forces.

In 1928, Ruth Hanna McCormick, Medill's widow, decided to run statewide in the Republican primary for an at-large seat in the U.S. House of Representatives. She defeated six other primary candidates and became the first woman to win a statewide election in Illinois. Her political star soared as she entered the Congress.

Almost immediately, McCormick announced her candidacy for the Senate in 1930. In retrospect, it is understandable why no one took her seriously. A woman in politics was a rarity then. Not only had Illinois never elected a woman to the Senate, but there had never been a woman elected from any other state. She faced serious obstacles. As her biographer Kristie Miller wrote, "Although she already represented a statewide electorate, there was more opposition to her senatorial campaign. 'People won't vote for a skirt,' it was said" (195).

Appealing strongly to women, McCormick campaigned tirelessly across Illinois. She disavowed Thompson's support, leaving him without a candidate. She attacked Deneen for his support of the League and the World Court, saying the League was predicated on the use of force to validate the Treaty of Versailles. Deneen weakly defended his position and still did not take McCormick seriously.

In advance of the April 1930 primary, Deneen associated himself with Republican reformers but was largely idle politically and finally launched a weak campaign in March. It was too late. McCormick buried him 714,505 to 496,412, ending the senator's long career in public office and bringing public attention to her candidacy. It was Ruth Hanna McCormick's time for revenge.

Then she turned her attention toward the Democratic candidate, former Senator J. Hamilton Lewis. (That contest is discussed in chapter 12.)

Deneen, loser to Ruth Hanna McCormick in the primary election, again returned to Chicago, where he practiced law until his death on February 5, 1940, at age seventy-six. He was buried in Oak Woods Cemetery.

Frank Leslie Smith (elected in 1926)

The expulsion of William H. Lorimer from the Senate in 1911 on account of corrupt and fraudulent practices in his selection by the legislature reduced to a low degree the reputation of Illinois as a political entity. As if that were not enough, it had to suffer the embarrassment, during the 1920s, of having a senator-elect denied the right to take his seat on similar grounds.

This time it was one who had been chosen by the voters. It seemed that neither system of choice during the first third of the twentieth century was adequate to produce U.S. senators of the quality of Lyman Trumbull, Stephen A. Douglas, and John M. Palmer, who came earlier, or Scott Lucas, Paul Douglas, Everett Dirksen, and Paul Simon, of later date.

Frank L. Smith was born in Dwight, Livingston County, Illinois, on November 24, 1867. He was the son of a blacksmith and became an orphan while still in his boyhood. With only a basic public school education, he taught school briefly, then became a telegrapher. With the help of the Keeley family, famous for the "Keeley cure" of alcoholics, he went into the real estate and insurance business, and eventually into banking and the ownership of farmland.

Smith's first political office was that of village clerk in Dwight, in 1894. He played a considerable role in local politics. During the Spanish-American War, he was on Governor Tanner's staff and acquired the title of colonel. From that time forward, he used it faithfully in his political campaigning.

And campaign he did, over and over. He ran unsuccessfully for the Republican nomination for lieutenant governor in 1904 and 1908. During the intervening four years, he was a collector of internal revenue.

Apparently, broader ambitions seized him as time went on. In 1912, he managed President Taft's campaign in Illinois. He was a generous contributor to William Hale Thompson's first campaign for mayor of Chicago in 1915. He ran unsuccessfully for the Republican nomination for governor in 1916. The least one can say of him is that he was persistent.

Republican politics presented a complex picture in 1916. Frank O. Lowden was also interested in running for governor and had considerable support. Former Governor Charles F. Deneen was still dabbling in the mix, and the new mayor of Chicago, Big Bill Thompson, was now one of the players.

Lowden, Thompson, and Senator Sherman pooled their followings and worked out an agreement in which Sherman would be a favorite-son candidate for the presidency, Lowden would get the primary nod for governor, and Thompson would have the satisfaction of being a "king-maker." Smith was the odd man out.

As a consolation prize, he was nominated and elected to Congress in 1918. Two years later, while also serving as chairman of the state Republican committee, again he wanted to run for governor. Fred Lundin, who had inherited William Lorimer's role as the Republican boss of Chicago, favored Len Small, however, and Smith, rather grudgingly, sought the party's nomination for U.S. senator.

William McKinley also wanted to run for the Senate. Governor Lowden supported McKinley, while former Governor Deneen withheld support from Smith. Those alignments forced Smith to make common cause with Fred Lundin and Mayor Thompson, who was backing State Treasurer Len Small for governor. Small won the primary race against Lieutenant Governor John G. Oglesby, son of former Governor and Senator "Uncle Dick" Oglesby, by a slim eight thousand votes, but Smith was beaten by McKinley.

His disappointment in that loss was salved by an appointment from Governor Small in 1921 to the chair of the Illinois Commerce Commission. He bided his time there. Given the effect the commission had on public utilities, the opportunity its members had for yielding to bribery and other corruption was great.

In 1926, Smith entered the Republican Senate primary once more, against the incumbent McKinley. This time Smith won, by one hundred thousand votes. In the general election in the fall, he defeated the Democratic candidate. The Thompson-Small-Lundin forces campaigned principally against Woodrow Wilson and internationalism.

A few weeks after the general election, Senator McKinley died, leaving the seat vacant. Governor Small did the obvious thing in appointing Senator-elect Smith for the short time remaining in the term.

The Senate had heard rumors of unduly large campaign expenditures on Smith's part and had launched an investigation. It was learned that he had spent more than a quarter of a million dollars, a large sum for the time. Of that amount, $125,000 had been donated by Samuel Insull, the public utilities magnate of Chicago.

Since the Illinois Commerce Commission, which Smith had chaired, had a great deal to do with setting public utility rates and other conditions of service, Insull's contribution to Smith's campaign fund was clearly beyond the line of acceptability. While these facts were being uncovered, Senator McKinley had died and Governor Small had appointed Smith to fill the remaining portion of the term.

When he presented his credentials, however, the Senate refused to allow him to take the seat. The fact that he had been appointed by a governor who had been indicted and tried, while in office, on the charge of embezzlement of state funds while he was state treasurer added to the distaste that the Senate felt for Smith.

We should take note here that Governor Small had been found not guilty by a jury of his peers. The Small trial was held in Waukegan, on a change of venue, about as far from Springfield as one could get and still be in the state. Many believed Small to be guilty of the charge, and that belief was strengthened when subsequently four of the jurors who had voted for his acquittal were given state jobs in the Small administration—two as highway patrolmen, one as a game warden, and one as a foreman in one of the state's penitentiaries.

In a civil action after the criminal trial, Small agreed to pay $650,000 into the state treasury in recognition of interest he had withheld from deposits of state funds. One can't escape the question, If he was innocent of embezzlement, as the jury found, why did he agree to turn a sizable fortune in cash over to the state?

Beyond any doubt, corruption and nepotism flourished during Len Small's two terms as governor. In an era of paved highway building, the first in the state's history, he appointed his son Leslie to be head of the Department of Construction and his son-in-law, A. E. Inglesh, as internal auditor of the Department of Finance. In short, what one member of the family stole another one could cover up. Eventually, Leslie was put on trial for rigging road contracts.

All of this added to the feeling of the Senate that Senator-elect Smith should be turned away when he presented his credentials for a second time, having been rejected previously following his appointment to the balance of McKinley's term. The seat remained vacant. Smith finally resigned on February 9, 1928. It was not until the general election in November of that year that a successor was chosen.

Thus, Illinois was represented by only one senator, rather than the usual two, from the time of the death of Senator McKinley, late in 1926, until the election of Otis F. Glenn in 1928 and his acceptance by the Senate. Governor Small had been beaten in the 1928 Republican primary by Louis Emmerson. A sorry chapter in Illinois politics was coming to an end.

According to Donald Tingley:

> The Springfield, Massachusetts, *Republican*, described Chicago as the "rottenest city in the rottenest state in the Union." William Allen White, writing in his *Emporia Gazette*, commented that "under primary, under convention, under a despotism or under a pure democracy Illinois would be corrupt and crooked. . . . it has been that way for two generations. It is in the blood of the people." (382)

Frank L. Smith would not be easily discouraged. He attempted to win the Senate nomination in 1928, predictably without success, and ran without avail for Congress two years later. He did manage to become a member of the Republican National Committee in 1932. He had a long record of political struggle with very little by way of office holding to show for it.

Out of fairness to him, it should be pointed out that he never really wanted to be in the Senate; his real goal was to be governor. For that prize, he could not gain the blessing of those who pulled the strings of his party's nominations. With the coming to power of the Democratic Party in 1932 in Illinois, he retired to a life of business in Dwight, where he died on August 30, 1950. He was buried in the Oak Lawn Cemetery there.

Otis Ferguson Glenn (1928–33)

Otis F. Glenn was born in Mattoon, Coles County, Illinois, on August 27, 1879. At twenty-one, he completed work on a law degree at the University of Illinois, was admitted to the bar, and began a practice in Murphysboro. Twice he served as state's attorney for Jackson County, from 1906 to 1908 and from 1916 to 1920. He was elected to the Illinois Senate as a Republican in 1920 for a four-year term.

One historian reports that at that time Glenn had "an unblemished reputation." Perhaps it was his distance in space from Big Bill Thompson, Fred Lundin, and Len Small that permitted him to be an honest Republican, of the stripe of Deneen and Lowden.

No doubt it was that reputation for honesty, in addition to his experience as a prosecutor, that caused him to be selected as one of the principal attorneys for the state in the trial of six men from Williamson County, for murders committed in the so-called "Herrin mine massacre" of 1922.

The Herrin massacre was the killing of a group of mine guards and strikebreaking miners who had been brought in from outside the region. One trial had ended in a jury finding of "not guilty" for five defendants. A second trial on a different set of indictments was initiated for two of the defendants in the first trial, plus four others. It was in this second trial that Glenn was one of the prosecutorial team.

In a lengthy address, that consumed most of one morning, he made the closing argument for the state. Speaking to the jurors, he concluded fervently:

You have an opportunity to strike at murder and lawlessness. If this crime is endorsed murder will grow upon the community and assassination will increase. Life, home and family will not be safe. You have the opportunity of stamping this out and I believe you will do it. (Angle 61)

The defense chose not to make a closing argument. The jury was out for seven hours, and the verdict, as in the earlier trial, was "not guilty" for all defendants on all counts. Public opinion in Williamson County simply would not allow a conviction.

No doubt the widespread attention Otis Glenn received in the course of that trial strengthened his hand when he ran for the U.S. Senate in 1928. He was opposed in the primary by Frank L. Smith, who was seeking vindication from the voters after being rejected twice by the Senate itself. Governor Small, with his ties to Mayor Thompson, was running for nomination for a third term.

The primary contest turned violent in a way that benefited Glenn and Secretary of State Louis Emmerson, who was opposing Small. A Republican operative in Chicago, "Diamond Joe" Esposito, was machine-gunned to death. The coroner counted fifty-eight bullet holes in his body.

Many believed that gangsters who favored the Small-Smith-Thompson faction had done the shooting. Former Governor Charles S. Deneen, now a U.S. senator, was present at Esposito's funeral. His house was bombed that night, as was the home of a candidate for Cook County state's attorney.

There was widespread public revulsion against such goings-on, which was to the benefit of Glenn and Emmerson. After the fact that hand grenades were often called "pineapples," this election became known as the "pineapple primary."

A final act of violence took place on the day of the primary itself. A black candidate for ward committeeman on the Republican ticket was machine-gunned and died.

Otis Glenn defeated Frank Smith in the primary by almost a quarter of a million votes. Lou Emmerson won by almost two to one in ending Governor Small's hopes for a third term. The public seemed to be reacting strongly against the kind of public officialdom they felt the two losers represented.

Otis Glenn served without particular distinction during the four years that remained of the term to which he had been elected, although he did chair the Committee on Privileges and Elections. The political tide was running strongly against the Republican Party when he ran for reelection in 1932. He was beaten by William H. Dieterich, a minor political figure from Beardstown. Not one to give up, he tried again in 1936 but lost to the incumbent, J. Hamilton Lewis.

Glenn resumed his law practice, but in Chicago rather than Murphysboro. That may explain why so little is known of him now, in southern Illinois, while another senator from that region, John A. Logan, has been immortalized in the naming of a community college and is made much of in Murphysboro, where he was born and lived during his boyhood days.

12 ★ Democrats Come to Power

The intraparty wars that engaged Republican leaders and office seekers during the third decade of the twentieth century were merely a prelude to the economic and social upheavals that came with the Great Depression of the 1930s. One of its results was a reversal of the traditional dominance in Illinois politics that had been in effect, with little exception, since the Civil War.

Following the stock market crash of October 1929, one of the first indications of that coming to power was the election to the Senate once more of the perennial Democratic candidate J. Hamilton Lewis. This time for Lewis it was by a different method of choice—by vote of the people rather than by the legislature.

The resurgence of the Democratic Party in 1932 and 1934, both nationally and in Illinois, represented a revitalization of both Jeffersonian Republicanism and Jacksonian Democracy. The coalition that swept its representatives into power in Springfield and Washington consisted of blue-collar labor, the poorly educated, organized labor, the economic underprivileged, and marginal and subsistence agrarians. It found its philosophers in the academy and many of its leaders in affluent families long Democratic on ideological grounds.

The Republicans in defeat were the "Yankee" element that had placed its trust in efficiency, education, capitalism, and good government. In Jensen's words, the "traditionalists" rode a wave of economic depression to victory over the "modernists" (121).

Following the Civil War, the Senate was in retreat from its Golden Age, which had lasted from 1819 to 1859. The South may have lost on the battlefield, but as time went on, it prevailed in the Senate. Robert Caro speaks of the Senate as the South's "revenge for Gettysburg" (xxiii). Through the workings of the seniority system in determining committee chairmanships, the "solid South," consistently Democratic, returning its senators to office over and over, became more and more a Senate force.

As the clouds of worldwide depression darkened the economic sky during the 1920s, the Senate remained an agent of reaction as far as economic remedies were concerned. Under the guise of reforming the protective tariff, it made its rates only higher. It provided no creative spark in the relief of human suffering and no action at all in the field of civil rights. Few blacks voted in the South during the 1920s.

By 1930, desperate times had come to the farms, mines, factories, and centers of capitalism of the United States, and through the ballot, change was in the wind.

James Hamilton Lewis (1931–39)

Among the forty-six men and one woman who have been elected to serve in the U.S. Senate from Illinois, J. Hamilton Lewis is a rarity in more ways than one. He is one of only three persons who served two or more nonconsecutive terms. Of the three, John A. Logan and he are the only ones to be selected for a third term. What is more, Lewis is the only senator to be chosen for a first term by the state legislature and two later terms by public vote.

Lewis owes his length of Senate service—fourteen years—spread over just slightly less than four decades, as much to the peculiarities of party politics as to his popularity. As reported in an earlier chapter, Lewis was chosen for a six-year term in 1913 by a legislature that took almost three months to make up its mind. This occurred primarily because of a split in the Republican ranks brought about by the formation of the Theodore Roosevelt Progressive Party. Lewis might not have won the seat without help from the Progressives in the legislature. He failed in the popular vote in a reelection bid in 1918, with the Progressives effectively out of the picture, as the Republicans regained control in Illinois of almost every elective state office. His bid for governor in 1920 fell before a Republican avalanche.

Lewis reentered the picture in 1930, when Democrats again were on the rise due to a worsening economic situation, blamed on the Republicans, plus internal strife among G.O.P. leaders. He then rode the crest of Democratic victories during the 1930s, due in large part to the coattails of Franklin D. Roosevelt.

The flamboyant Lewis—pink whiskered and outrageously tailored—had by 1930 proved himself a capable Democratic infighter and a strong campaigner. He demonstrated both talents again as that year's elections approached.

Lewis owed his political resurrection in 1930 to Anton Cermak, a Democratic leader in Cook County. Cermak believed in paying his debts—one of his secrets in holding political power—and he owed big ones to former Governor Edward F. Dunne, and former Chicago Mayor Carter Harrison, who had given Cermak his start in politics. It was in discharging those debts that Cermak and his allies chose Lewis to run for the Senate. They thought they knew what they were getting. Lewis, however, although a Democratic loyalist, held his strongest allegiance to himself.

Lewis was thrown into the general election contest against Congresswoman Ruth Hanna McCormick, the widow of Medill McCormick, who had buried with votes her primary opponent, incumbent Senator Charles S. Deneen. McCormick was a strong favorite to be the first woman in the U.S. Senate. But several things got in her way.

First, she spent, for the time, a huge amount of money in winning the primary election over Deneen. She admitted to spending more than $250,000. In 1930, that was big money for a campaign. This led to discrediting congressional hearings and dogged her throughout the general election campaign. That issue, combined with her gender, made for an uphill run against Lewis.

Lewis, referring in the early part of his campaign to his opponent as "the lady," avoided open warfare based on gender. But as election day neared, he became more demonstrative on the subject. On the primary campaign expenditure issue, Lewis said, "When a woman dishonors the state of Illinois far beyond the corruption even attempted by any man, no appeal of sex will save her from the just judgment of the voters." In predicting victory, Lewis said Cook County would "cast a big vote against a woman whose inherited riches were wrung from the poor."

Lewis and Democratic candidates all across the state won what some then called the biggest party victory since the Civil War. His plurality over McCormick exceeded 685,000. Lewis carried 88 of the 101 "downstate" counties. In Chicago, he won forty-seven of the fifty wards. When asked about the cause of her defeat, McCormick said, "Somebody else got more votes."

Feuding within the Republican ranks for two decades plus public concern over what was becoming in many counties a desperate economic condition due to worldwide depression was beginning to cause the political tide in Illinois to flow in the Democratic direction. Good fortune continued for candidates of that party in Illinois and nationally in 1932. It began with the election of Cermak as mayor of Chicago in 1931, climaxing a struggle for power that began twenty years earlier. This was followed by the election of FDR as president and Henry Horner as governor in 1932. Before the 1932 elections, however, the first signs of trouble between Lewis and Cermak surfaced.

Mayor Cermak was not convinced early in 1932 that the Democrats would nominate Franklin Roosevelt. He wanted FDR to come courting him and his influence. Therefore, he announced before the Democratic national convention in midsummer that the votes he controlled would be cast for Lewis as a "favorite son."

Lewis went along with that ploy, although there is evidence that he secretly plotted his own course with Roosevelt partisans. Just before the convention, with Cermak holding fast for Lewis, the latter cut a deal with Roosevelt and announced support for him. Cermak, furious with Lewis, found another stalking-horse to be his favorite son and continued his boycott of Roosevelt at the convention.

Convention votes under Cermak's control finally were cast for Roosevelt but only after other states' votes had clinched the nomination for him. Cermak had missed the Roosevelt "train." Lewis became the Illinois "darling" with Roosevelt. When federal patronage began to flow after the election, in Illinois it came through the hands and office of Lewis, not Cermak.

This situation made such a strained relationship that Cermak sought a personal conversation with Roosevelt to straighten out their differences. The mayor went to Florida for such a meeting, but before it could be accomplished, he was shot while with the president at a public appearance. He died a few days later.

It was generally thought that the assassin's bullet was intended for Roosevelt, but there has been a persistent view that Cermak himself was the true target, that enemies of his in Chicago had masterminded the shooting, making it appear to be an attempt on Roosevelt's life, to divert suspicion from them. The assassin was tried, found guilty, and silenced by execution in a matter of only a few weeks. His real intent probably will never be known.

During the turmoil that followed among the Democrats of Cook County and throughout the state, Lewis went to work as a loyalist for Roosevelt and the New Deal. He was a predictable vote for Roosevelt's policies until his service in the Senate ended with his death in 1939.

The Democratic leaders in Chicago after Cermak, Edward J. Kelly and Patrick Nash—whose organization was known as the Kelly-Nash machine—moved in. They quickly fell out with Governor Horner and, in 1936, supported his opponent in the Democratic primary. They slated the seventy-three-year-old Lewis for reelection against former Senator Otis F. Glenn, who had been in office from 1928 to 1933. Embarrassed and inconvenienced by the machine's split with Horner, Lewis remained on the sidelines in the primary, providing silent support for the governor, who prevailed.

Riding the crest of Roosevelt's landslide victory in 1936, Lewis was easily reelected to his third term in the Senate. He served as chair of the Committee on Expenditures in Executive Departments. He died while in office in Washington, D.C., on April 1, 1939. There is no doubt that he qualifies as one of Illinois's most durable and colorful political figures.

After funeral services in the chamber of the Senate, he was buried in the Abbey Mausoleum, adjoining Arlington National Cemetery, at Fort Myer, Virginia. It was an appropriate resting place for one who had traveled from state to state looking for a political home and whose final years of public service had been in the U.S. Senate.

James M. Slattery (1939–41)

In no more time than it took Governor Henry Horner to take the train from Florida to Illinois, James M. Slattery was appointed to succeed J. Hamilton Lewis in the U.S. Senate.

The governor, ill and fading, had been recuperating in Florida, and his archenemy, Lieutenant Governor John Stelle, who was allied with the Kelly-Nash machine, was acting as governor in his absence. Horner was just an hour inside the borders of the state when Lewis died, having crossed on the railroad bridge at Shawneetown. Informed of Lewis's probable demise, he had made all haste to return to Illinois. Had he still been out of the state, it is probable that Stelle would have named Patrick Nash to serve in the Senate for the brief balance of Lewis's term.

This anecdote illustrates Slattery's situation in the Illinois political picture. He was a Horner partisan and as such an enemy of Kelly and Nash. The Chicago machine vowed to thwart the governor at every opportunity after Horner's primary victory and reelection in 1936, and that made Slattery less than welcome at city hall in Chicago.

Slattery, who had never been elected to public office, had run Horner's campaign in 1936 in Cook County. The governor then appointed Slattery chairman of the Illinois Commerce Commission. He was serving in that position when Lewis died.

Born in Chicago on July 23, 1878, Slattery served in a series of academic positions after graduating from the Illinois College of Law in 1908. Until 1936, he also held appointive positions in Chicago, such as legal counsel for the Lincoln Park Commission and the Chicago Park District.

Before Horner's death in 1940, Slattery won the Democratic primary nomination for the Senate seat he was temporarily occupying. His opponent in the general election was Republican Charles Wayland Brooks, who was strongly supported by the *Chicago Tribune* and Colonel Robert McCormick. Brooks won by just 20,827 votes.

The spirit of isolationism was running strong in Illinois in 1940, and that tended to aid Republican candidates for office. Paul H. Douglas, then a member of the Chicago City Council and later a U.S. senator, suspected that deals were made between McCormick and Mayor Kelly that influenced late returns from Chicago precincts and turned the tide for Brooks.

His brief tenure as a senator ended, Slattery turned to the private practice of law. He died at his summer home at Lake Geneva, Wisconsin, on August 28, 1948. He was buried in Calvary Cemetery in Evanston.

William Henry Dieterich (1933–39)

The hard times that accompanied the Great Depression of the 1930s marked an end to Republican dominance in Illinois politics. After the election of Lewis in 1930, Otis Glenn was beaten in 1932 by the Democratic candidate William H. Dieterich.

Dieterich was born near Cooperstown, in Brown County, Illinois, on March 31, 1876. After service as a corporal in the Spanish-American War, he received a law degree from Northern Indiana University in 1901 and began practice in Rushville, Illinois.

He was city attorney in Rushville from 1903 to 1907, and city judge from 1906 to 1910. After a move to Chicago, he was settled in Beardstown by 1912. From 1917 to 1921, he was a member of the state House of Representatives and was elected to Congress in 1930.

In 1932, Dieterich was elected to the U.S. Senate with the backing of the Kelly-Nash organization in Chicago. That fact proved to be his undoing after one term. Governor Henry Horner had fallen out with the Kelly-Nash group during his first term (1933–37) and won the nomination in the 1936 primary without its support and against its opposition. In 1938, he backed Scott W. Lucas of Havana, Illinois, in the Democratic primary against Dieterich, and Lucas won.

Thus, Dieterich was retired from the Senate after one undistinguished term. He resumed his law practice and died in 1944. He was buried at Rushville.

With Dieterich's tenure in the Senate, a time ended in which popular election seemed to produce a succession of relatively obscure and not very able men. Possible exceptions to that rule would be Medill McCormick and Charles S. Deneen, and neither of the two was a great success in the Senate. Perhaps it simply took a decade or two for the political system to absorb the fact that a new tool of democracy, the popular election of senators in place of their selection by the legislature, was ready at hand.

Senator Jesse Burgess
Thomas, 1818–1829.
Courtesy of the Illinois State
Historical Library.

Senator Ninian Edwards,
1818–1824.
Courtesy of the Illinois State
Historical Library.

Senator Elias Kent
Kane, 1825–1835.
Courtesy of the Illinois
State Historical Library.

Senator Stephen A.
Douglas, 1847–1861.
Chicago Historical Society,
ICHi-10090. Photo by Taft.

Senator James Shields,
1849–1855.
Library of Congress.

Senator Lyman
Trumbull, 1855–1873.
U.S. Senate Historical Office.

General John A. Logan and other Corps commanders with Major General
George G. Meade in June 1865. *Left to right:* Horatio G. Wright, Logan,
Meade, John G. Parke, and Andrew A. Humphreys.
Library of Congress.

Senator John
Alexander Logan,
1871–1877,
1879–1886.
U.S. Senate Historical Office.

Senator Richard James
Oglesby, 1873–1879.
U.S. Senate Historical Office.

Senator David Davis, 1877–1883.
U.S. Senate Historical Office.

Senator Shelby Morris Cullom, 1883–1913.
U.S. Senate Historical Office.

Senator John McAuley Palmer, 1891–1897.
U.S. Senate Historical Office.

John A. Palmer campaigning for the Senate in 1884.
Courtesy of the Illinois State Historical Library.

Senator James
Hamilton Lewis,
1913–1919,
1931–1939.
U.S. Senate Historical Office.

Senator Charles
Samuel Deneen,
1925–1931.
U.S. Senate Historical Office.

Senator Scott Wike
Lucas, 1939–1951.
U.S. Senate Historical Office.

Senator Charles
Wayland Brooks,
1941–1949.
U.S. Senate Historical Office.

Right, Professor Paul H. Douglas filing petitions for candidacy in a Chicago municipal election.

Chicago Historical Society, ICHi-35715.

Senator Paul Howard Douglas, 1949–1967, receiving a pen from President Lyndon Johnson during the signing of H.R.7984, the Housing for Low and Moderate Income Families Act of 1965.

Chicago Historical Society, ICHi-35716.

"Illinois Republican chiefs." *Left to right:* U.S. Representative Bob Michel; unidentified; U.S. Representative Les Arends; Governor Richard Ogilvie; Senator Everett McKinley Dirksen, 1951–1969; Senator Charles Harting Percy, 1967–1985.

The Dirksen Congressional Center.

Senator Everett McKinley Dirksen, 1951–1969.
The Dirksen Congressional Center.

Senator Charles Harting Percy, 1967–1985, aboard Air Force One in
June 1973, explaining to President Richard M. Nixon the Senate-
approved resolution calling for a special Watergate prosecutor.
White House photo.

"Making peace." Adlai Ewing Stevenson III, shaking hands with Chicago mayor Richard J. Daley.

Courtesy of the Illinois State Historical Library.

Senator Alan John
Dixon, 1980–1983.
U.S. Senate Historical Office.

Senator Paul Martin
Simon, 1985–1997.
SIU Media and
Communication Resources.

Senator Carol Moseley-Braun, 1993–1999, with Senator Richard J. Durbin, 1997–.
Photo by Heather Moore. U.S. Senate Historical Office.

Senator Richard J.
Durbin, 1997–.
Office of Senator
Richard J. Durbin.

Senator Peter Gosselin
Fitzgerald, 1999–.
Office of Senator Peter
Gosselin Fitzgerald.

13 ★ Popular Election Comes of Age

The decade of the 1940s was one in which Illinois was represented by two senators whose selection by the voters represented a maturing of the system of popular election. It was initiated by the Seventeenth Amendment to the Constitution thirty years earlier. Thereafter such decisions were to be made by vote of the people, rather than by the legislature.

So long as U.S. senators were chosen by the legislature, the voting public had at best an indirect voice and influence in that process. True, persons wishing to be sent to the Senate could attempt to influence the election of legislators who would look on them with favor, but at the same time, other factors might prove to be of greater weight.

When the procedure was changed by the Seventeenth Amendment to require the popular election of senators, it seemed for at least twenty-five more years that the voters were willing to allow party leaders, legislators, the governor, and the news media to continue to play leading roles in determining who would become members of the Senate from Illinois.

The old ways died hard, and it was not until 1938 that the voters of Illinois seemed fully to understand the power that was theirs in this essential process. With that realization came the elections of Scott W. Lucas in 1938 and C. Wayland "Curly" Brooks in 1940.

Lucas ran and won as a Democrat in spite of the efforts of the Democratic organization in Cook County in behalf of another. As a Republican, Brooks was swept into office in 1940 in a popular wave of feeling for isolationism and pacifism. If the choice had still been in the hands of the legislature, then under Democratic control, he would not have prevailed.

The fact that Lucas eventually became the majority leader in the Senate, the most prominent Senate post that an Illinoisan had achieved, suggests that popular election was capable of worthy choices. The record since supports that belief.

Scott Wike Lucas (1939–51)

Scott W. Lucas entered the Democratic primary in 1932 seeking to be nominated for the U.S. Senate. He did not have the support of the Democratic organization in Chicago, however, and did not succeed. He allied himself with incoming Governor Henry Horner and was appointed head of the State Tax Commission.

Governor Horner urged Lucas to run for Congress in 1934, when the incumbent in his district did not; he did and won. He became a solid supporter of the New Deal program and was re-elected in 1936.

Lucas was capable of charting an independent course, however, as in 1937, when he asked the House, in regard to President Roosevelt's plan to enlarge the Supreme Court, "Is there a single Democrat in this historic hall who believes that continuation of this fight will accomplish a single constructive thing?" (D.A.B. VI, 391). Roosevelt's proposal broke on the rock of the Senate. In that action, it did as much to preserve the separation of powers in the structure of national government as the Senate's refusal to remove President Johnson had seventy years earlier. It is noteworthy, too, that never again was the Senate to approve any significant social measure that Roosevelt proposed.

In 1938, Lucas again took on the Kelly-Nash organization of Cook County, with the backing of Governor Horner, who had broken with the machine two years earlier, and this time won the Senate nomination over the incumbent William H. Dieterich. It was a triumph of the power of the people over machine politics, as was Horner's primary victory in 1936.

Scott W. Lucas was born on February 19, 1892, in Cass County, Illinois, the youngest of six children. His father was a tenant farmer of little means. The fact that his father's middle name was Douglas suggests a family attachment to the Democratic Party. That suggestion is strengthened by the fact that Lucas was named after Scott Wike, who had been a Democratic state legislator in Illinois and was a member of the U.S. House of Representatives at the time the future senator was born.

Lucas grew up in and near the small towns along the stretch of the Illinois River lying below Peoria. During that time, he acquired a lifelong interest in hunting and fishing. He attended public school in Bath and graduated from Virginia High School in Illinois. Pretty much on his own as far as education beyond grade school was concerned, he did some public school teaching before and after he left high school.

He fired furnaces and waited tables to make his way in college at Illinois Wesleyan in Bloomington, and one legend is that at times he would warm his supper on top of one of the furnaces. At six feet two inches and heavy boned, he played center in basketball and end on the football team and was a star at both positions. As a freshman third baseman he hit over .400 for the baseball team before signing to play with the Bloomington "Bloomers" of the Three-I league.

His older brother Allen, who was an attorney, had encouraged Lucas to study law. In 1914, he graduated from Illinois Wesleyan with an L.L.B. degree. He read law for a year in an established office, and after a second try at the bar examination proved successful, he set up a practice in Havana, Illinois.

During World War I, Lucas entered the army as a private and came out as a lieutenant. Like so many of his generation, participation in veterans' organizations accompanied political success. He served as state commander of the American Legion and from 1928 to 1932 as its national judge advocate. His first public office came in 1920 as state's attorney for Mason County.

After he had bested the Kelley-Nash organization in winning nomination and election to the U.S. Senate in 1938, Lucas made up his differences with that machine and thereafter had its full support, notably in 1944 for the vice presidential nomination. If that effort had been successful, Lucas, not Harry Truman, would have become president of the United States in 1945.

In the Senate, Lucas sided with President Roosevelt in his efforts at building up the national forces for defense. After World War II began, he served on the Joint Committee of the Congress on Pearl Harbor, concurring with the majority findings as to the location of responsibility for that disaster. Chicago Democrats supported him for vice president in 1940, 1944, and 1948, and in 1944, he was one of those whose names was formally put in contention and who was voted on for nomination.

Clearly, Scott Lucas was much more than a run of the mill U.S. senator. He became majority whip in 1946, and in 1948, when Alben Barkley was elected vice president, Lucas became the majority leader of the Democratic Party. It was at the time the most prestigious position in the Senate that an Illinoisan had gained.

Harry Truman, of course, had just stunned the political world with his defeat in 1948 of Republican Thomas E. Dewey, who was governor of New York. Given Truman's background, one might assume that it would be a good time to be in the Senate, and to be its majority leader. Not so in Lucas's case, however, for he could never depend on the votes of more than forty of the fifty-four Democratic senators.

Southern opposition in the Senate prevented the passage of legislation that would have strengthened civil rights, federal aid to education and housing, and national health insurance. The issue of communists in government was raised by Republican Senator Joseph McCarthy, of Wisconsin. Lucas set up a McCarthy-oversight committee chaired by the respected Senator Millard Tydings of Maryland, but it was not successful in curbing "Tail Gunner Joe's" conduct during the time that Lucas continued to be majority leader.

In Lucas's time, real power in the Senate lay in the hands of the committee chairmen. Most were southern Democrats. The majority leader was virtually powerless—with "nothing to promise, nothing to threaten." Lucas said later that his two years as majority leader were the worst two of his life. He developed a bleeding ulcer. He even took to composing little poems in an effort to control his temper—"Senators who preside / Shouldn't rhyme, shouldn't chide" (Caro 162).

When the election of 1950 approached, Lucas was one of the incumbent senators up for reelection who had earned McCarthy's dislike. That was a telling factor. In addition, the growing lack of popularity on the part of President Truman, with the conflict in

Korea under way, reflected badly on the Democratic Senate's majority leader. His opponent stated that "all the piety of the administration will not put any life into the bodies of the young men coming back in wooden boxes" (McCullough 814).

Lucas had neglected the electoral home front in Illinois in the face of his duties in the Senate as military action in Korea commenced in the summer of 1950. When he returned to begin his campaign in September, he found himself up against a formidable opponent. China's coming into the fighting in October added to the Truman administration's woes, and to Lucas's problems in Illinois. When election day came and went, he found that he had been beaten by Republican Everett Dirksen.

It may be that defeat coming at that time lengthened Lucas's life, for unknown to the public he had had two severe heart attacks. After he left office in 1952, he practiced law in Havana and Springfield, Illinois, and Washington, D.C., and became a lobbyist, a pattern others had shaped before him. He wished to be nominated for the Senate seat in 1956 but could not gain the blessing of the Chicago Democrats. That was his last attempt at public office.

In personal terms, Scott Lucas possessed considerable charm and magnetism. He dressed well, favoring double-breasted suits and a homburg hat. His greying hair, worn long but neatly, lay in soft waves across his head. On one occasion, a group of Capitol Hill female secretaries voted him the congressman they would most like to see in a leopard skin costume.

At home in Illinois, in waterfowl season, he enjoyed duck hunting along the backwaters of the Illinois River. Athletic from youth onward, he was a persistent golfer and served as president at one time of the prestigious Burning Tree Golf Club, a favorite of President Eisenhower and many other political figures.

Although he was not an insignificant figure as majority leader in the Senate, Lucas's stature pales in comparison to Alben Barkley, who preceded him in that office, and to Lyndon Johnson and Everett Dirksen, who came later. He appeared to be not so liberal as Johnson nor as conservative as Dirksen and so has been lost sight of to a degree in the judgment of history (Deason 274).

Scott Lucas suffered the loss of a leg due to diabetes near the end of his life. En route by train from Washington to Florida in February 1968, he suffered a stroke and died in Rocky Mount, North Carolina.

Charles Wayland "Curly" Brooks (1941–49)

The Senate career of C. Wayland Brooks, who was known to many simply as "Curly," suggests a truth of World War II politics. Not all elected officials in Congress fell in behind the leadership of Franklin D. Roosevelt or applauded the concepts of mutual security and foreign aid after the conflict.

With hindsight, much of what Brooks said and did in his eight years in the Senate looks narrow-minded, shortsighted, and wrongheaded today. But there were elected officials in those years who honorably and consistently supported the idea of "America for Americans" and battled against everything Roosevelt and Truman proposed. That characterizes Brooks's eight years in the Senate.

An Illinois native, Brooks was born on March 8, 1897, in West Bureau, Bureau County. His father was a Methodist minister who moved frequently; consequently, young Brooks went to school in several small Illinois communities. He acquired the nickname "Curly" because of his hair, which also drew snide remarks from political opponents. *Nation* magazine once described Brooks as "round, heavy, with pinker [than his hair] face capped with tight curls, which look as though they are wet down with a patent hair concoction."

After spending 1916 at the University of Illinois, Brooks enlisted in the U.S. Army and went to war. He earned a battlefield commission and was wounded seven times. Among many decorations, he received the Distinguished Service Cross and the Croix de Guerre. Throughout his political career, he capitalized on his heroic war record.

Brooks finished college at the University of Chicago after the war and received a law degree from Northwestern University in 1926. He served seven years as an assistant state's attorney in Cook County, where he helped prosecute members of organized criminal associations. It was during this period that he earned the undying gratitude and loyalty of Colonel Robert R. McCormick, editor and publisher of the *Chicago Tribune*.

In 1931, a *Tribune* reporter—actually a "legman" who gathered information but rarely wrote a news report or article—named Jake Lingle was murdered in Chicago. McCormick promptly called for justice and spoke glowingly of Lingle.

To McCormick's embarrassment and that of the *Tribune,* Lingle was shown to be something less than an ethical and honest reporter. He had hung out with Al Capone and his associates and lesser lights in the underworld. In that way, he was able to gather "inside" information for his newspaper work. After his death, it became known that Lingle had taken money for providing information about the police to the mob. It is not surprising that he met a violent end.

Brooks came to McCormick's rescue in this matter by leading the prosecution and conviction of one Leo Brothers for Lingle's murder and putting the case to rest. He made it possible for McCormick and the *Tribune* to claim victory in the end.

McCormick sent Brooks into the political arena in 1934 against Democrat Mike Igoe for an at-large seat in Congress. Brooks lost narrowly. Wasting no time, McCormick groomed him for a more ambitious office.

Backed by McCormick and the state Republican Party, Brooks ran for governor in 1936 against incumbent Henry Horner. In a landslide for Franklin D. Roosevelt and other Democratic candidates, Brooks lost by 385,000 votes. He had been a stalking-horse for both Republicans and Democrats who wanted Horner out of office.

The confrontation between Horner and Brooks had been put together by McCormick and Chicago's Mayor Kelly, a Democrat, with the long-shot hope of embarrassing and defeating the popular Horner. Although their ruse failed, the Kelly-McCormick combination was to surface again in the political life of Curly Brooks.

After the death of J. Hamilton Lewis in 1939, the appointment of James Slattery to the Senate set up the next contest for Brooks and his mentor McCormick. In 1940, Slattery and Brooks contested for the remaining two years of what had begun as Lewis's term. It also was a gubernatorial election year, and McCormick's man in that race was Dwight H. Green.

While Green won easily over a nondescript opponent, Brooks struggled and finally pulled out a twenty-thousand-vote triumph, but only after alleged voter shenanigans in Chicago. While Slattery built a lead over Brooks on election night, Mayor Kelly held back the returns from four hundred precincts in Chicago until it could become known what sort of lead Brooks had to overcome.

Organization Democrats were not enthusiastic over the man—Slattery—whom their enemy Governor Horner had appointed when Lewis died. When the tardy returns finally came in, Brooks had won.

With Brook's election to the Senate, at last McCormick had his man in Washington. Brooks voted the *Tribune* line in opposition to President Roosevelt and all his policies, including the Lend-Lease policy of providing ships to Great Britain, and the military draft of Americans. Brooks and McCormick together gave unlimited support to the isolationist organization America First.

Richard M. Smith provides this unflattering description of Senator Brooks in his biography of McCormick: "a World War I hero with a clutch of medals and a spread-eagle platform style [who] rarely expressed a thought that didn't come from McCormick" (442).

Throughout the 1930s, in the face of rising aggression on the part of the fascist dictatorships in Germany and Italy and the Japanese expansion into China and Korea, the Congress of the United States had steadfastly refused to strengthen the nation's armed forces. If anything, the opposite was true. The feeling that the two great oceans were all the defense that was needed was in command.

Shortly after taking his seat in the Senate, Brooks made a political gaffe that has trailed him throughout history. On December 6, 1941, he sent Illinois voters franked copies of his speech entitled "This Is Not Our War." The mailing arrived in Illinois homes a few days after the Japanese attack on Pearl Harbor and the declaration of war by the Congress. In the face of overwhelming support for armed action after Pearl Harbor, Brooks was embarrassed by the mailing.

Brooks was no sooner safely in Washington in 1941 than he and Colonel McCormick had begun planning for the election in 1942, which would fill the position for a full six-year term. Although Mayor Kelly was urged by associates to make the run himself on the Democratic side, and he would have been a formidable opponent, he decided against it. The understanding between him and McCormick seemed still to be in effect.

Kelly passed over several better-known Democrats before choosing an undistinguished Chicago congressman and Kelly loyalist, Raymond S. McKeough, as the opposition for Brooks. It seemed again that Kelly wanted Brooks to win. Labeled immediately by the *Tribune* as "Small Potatoes," McKeough had no chance of winning against a resurgent Republican Party. Brooks prevailed by 407,000 votes.

Comfortably in the Senate for six more years, Brooks added to his anti-Roosevelt record at every turn until the president's death in 1945 and continued in that posture with Harry Truman. McCormick disliked Truman only slightly less than he did Roosevelt.

Brooks and the *Tribune* fought determinedly against formation of the United Nations and the concept of mutual security.

As the 1948 elections approached, Republicans were encouraged. Truman, battling uphill against a Republican-led Congress, did not show well in the polls. In Illinois, Republicans had every reason to believe they would triumph again with Brooks running for reelection and Green seeking a third term as governor. They looked especially good against two Democratic newcomers: Adlai E. Stevenson II, who had not previously sought public office, and Paul Douglas, a University of Chicago economics professor who had served on the Chicago City Council.

Democratic Party officials liked Douglas's chances. He had volunteered for the Marine Corps at far above the usual age, had been severely wounded, and was a certified war hero. It was felt that with that record, he could neutralize Brooks's heroics in World War I.

Campaigning tirelessly across the state on a financial shoestring, Douglas challenged Brooks to a series of debates, and when Brooks declined, Douglas debated an empty chair. He stood on street corners and public squares and spoke with a bullhorn to often small audiences.

Douglas and the Democratic sweep of 1948 from top to bottom in Illinois ended Brooks's Senate career. In spite of the *Tribune's* headlines proclaiming Dewey the winner, Truman was returned to office as president. Green lost the race for governor to Stevenson. McCormick, however, was one of the biggest losers. The top voices he had in Springfield and Washington for his policy agendas went down in defeat.

Brooks was just fifty-two, though in many ways, he seemed older. He returned to Chicago to practice law and remained active in Republican politics. He served as a member of the Republican national committee from Illinois.

C. Wayland Brooks died in Chicago on January 14, 1957. He was buried in the Pleasant View Cemetery in Kewanee, in the rural portion of the state where he had grown up. While his record in the Senate was one of opposition to most of the progressive movements of his time, there is no doubt that he truly represented the feelings of many thousands of his constituents. There is equally no doubt that he and Colonel McCormick of the *Chicago Tribune* made up a team.

14 ★ A Professor in Politics

When Paul Douglas took his seat in the Senate in 1949, he joined fellow Democrat Scott Lucas to make up a team of two from Illinois. Lucas was majority leader in the Senate, and the newly inaugurated president was one-time Senator Harry S Truman, who now had a term of his own in the nation's highest office. As vice president, he had succeeded Franklin D. Roosevelt in 1945.

It must have seemed to Douglas to be quite a good time to begin Senate service, yet his naturally suspicious nature made him see conspiracies against himself on all sides. The good times were not to last, perhaps to confirm his fears, as Lucas fell before Everett Dirksen in 1950 and the war in Korea brought increasing unpopularity to President Truman.

Paul Howard Douglas (1949–67)

Paul H. Douglas, scholar and wounded war hero, entered the U.S. Senate from Illinois in the company of men destined to become national political stars. The class of 1948 (senators newly elected in that year) included Lyndon Baines Johnson of Texas, Estes Kefauver of Tennessee, Russell Long of Louisiana, and Robert Kerr of Oklahoma. Johnson brought a new force to the Senate, and before his first six-year term ended, he had become the minority party leader.

Following Johnson's landslide reelection in 1954 (in contrast to his first hair-breadth win six years earlier, which had earned him the name "Landslide Lyndon"), and his party coming to majority status in 1955, he became majority leader, the youngest in the history of the Senate, as he had been the youngest minority leader.

Each of these newcomers, in his own way, became a pillar of the Senate, judged at the end of his senatorial career as a mover and shaker of the institution and a major influence on public policy. Douglas chose a different path from the beginning of his three full terms. He spoke loud and often but did not carry a big stick when it came to determining the outcome of legislation.

As a result, Douglas has been placed by historians in the category of long on principle, short on votes. Edward L. Schapsmeier evaluated Douglas's work in the Senate in this way: "Douglas . . . was more prone to view rigid consistency of principle, even in defeat, as more important than flexibility. Therefore, he was less effective as a legislative leader and more often found himself standing alone" (83). From his earliest days in the Senate, Douglas was defiant toward authority. He wrote in his memoir, titled *In the Fullness of Time:*

> I began my senatorial career by becoming involved in no fewer than five struggles. . . . This did not make me popular with the elders of the Senate, who demanded decorous silence from newcomers during first year of service and allowed only muted murmurs during the second. But these struggles, largely forced on me, helped to set the pattern for my later activities in the Senate. (269)

The five issues that Douglas became embroiled in combat over were civil rights, equal housing opportunities, repeal or modification of the Taft-Hartley Act, preservation of legitimate economic competition, and pork barrel legislation.

Douglas was relentless in his lack of respect for colleagues with whom he disagreed. In a speech early in his Senate career, he denounced southern Democrats for their racist approach to civil rights legislation. He never let up in his criticism of fellow party members who did not share his view of the need for equal rights, and it cost him dearly.

The southern senators, many of whom held leadership positions coming to them through the working of seniority, never allowed Douglas a place of honor or strength. In this characteristic of differing sharply with others on matters of principle, Douglas was very different from Everett Dirksen, who served during nearly the same period of time as Douglas. (Their differences are discussed in the next chapter.)

Even though Douglas in 1955 was eminently qualified for a seat on the Finance Committee, the Senate's principal arm for writing tax legislation, Majority Leader Johnson did not place him there. The committee had to do with the oil-depletion allowance against the income tax, and it was stacked with senators favorable to the oil and gas industry. Douglas might have been a thorn in their sides.

Instead, economist Douglas was put on the Joint Economic Committee, one with little power except to issue reports. "'I'm gonna name him chairman,' Johnson told Bobby Baker. 'It can't do a damn thing. It's as useless as tits on a bull. But it'll give Professor Douglas some paper to shuffle'" (Caro 565). Nor did Johnson give Douglas any explanation. It is no wonder that the relationship between the two was a distant one.

A review of Douglas's life prior to his election to the Senate provides us with a glimpse of the influences that brought him to the points of principle that seemed to motivate him. Born on March 26, 1892, in Salem, Massachusetts, he was reared by his stepmother in the backwoods near Newport, Maine. He claimed a distant blood relationship to Stephen A. Douglas, who also was a native New Englander.

Poor but full of ambition, the young Paul Douglas worked his way through Bowdoin College, graduating Phi Beta Kappa in 1913 with a degree in economics. He studied political science and economics at the Columbia Graduate School of Economics for two years and received a master's degree there. Then he attended Harvard University for a year and finished work for the Ph.D. degree in economics at Columbia in 1921.

Douglas aimed directly for a career in the college classroom. Starting in 1916, he taught for a year at the University of Illinois, another at Reed College in Portland, Oregon, a year at the University of Washington in Seattle, and then joined the economics faculty at the University of Chicago in 1920. There he had his academic base until he retired in 1969 after leaving the Senate.

For many of the intellectually curious in the United States, the 1920s were filled with the exploration of new ideas. Douglas was no exception. In 1918 and 1919, he underwent a spiritual conversion to pacifism, then became a follower of the Quaker faith in

1920. Apparently, family responsibilities or a physical defect kept him out of military service during World War I. He gained further inspiration for his beliefs from friendship in Chicago with social worker Jane Addams, the founder of Hull House, who also was a Quaker.

This was the early period of Marxist control of the Soviet Union, and scholars throughout the world visited Moscow to see how the communist experiment was going. Douglas joined a trade union visit to the Soviet Union in 1927 to inspect the social experiments under way. He quickly became skeptical of communism and the authoritarian nature of the Soviet system, although he urged the U.S. government to recognize the Marxist regime. Douglas never joined any organization with communist affiliations or leanings.

Instead of communism, Douglas turned to socialism as a means of bringing reforms to society in the United States. In the 1932 presidential election campaign, he supported socialist candidate Norman Thomas, in part because he did not believe Franklin D. Roosevelt advocated the basic reforms needed for economic recovery. At that time he had not.

The 1930s became a period of intense activism for Douglas, both in Chicago and at the national level. On the city front, he worked with activist Harold Ickes to form the Illinois Utility Consumers and Investors League, which was opposed to the policies of Chicago utility magnate Samuel Insull. Through friendships with Ickes, who joined the Roosevelt administration as secretary of interior, and Frances Perkins, who was secretary of labor, Douglas abandoned the socialists and became a staunch supporter of the president's New Deal program.

As an academic activist, Douglas wrote books on wage theory, social security, unemployment insurance, and the control of economic depressions. He worked for passage of the Social Security, Wagner Labor Relations, and Fair Labor Standards Acts. During this period, he became a stalwart friend of organized labor, a position he never abandoned during many years of public service.

Douglas's activism in Chicago led him to run for mayor in 1935 on a fusion ticket. Without organization support, he was soundly defeated. His next attempt at public office came in 1938, when he ran as a candidate for alderman in the Fifth Ward and won. He served three years in that position on the city council.

While a man of principle on issues, Douglas took a decidedly practical view of Chicago-style politics. He sought and gained Mayor Kelly's endorsement in 1938, saying in explanation:

> During the last year Mayor Kelly has shown signs of improvement. He fought hard for adequate relief and has allowed complete civil liberties to the unemployed in their demonstrations. He has also begun to recognize the Negroes and his police were absolutely neutral and nonprovocative in the recent stockyards strike. (Schapsmeier 79n)

In the 1930s, Douglas also altered his views of pacifism in light of aggressive military actions by fascists Benito Mussolini in Italy and Adolph Hitler in Germany. "No more Munichs," became Douglas's motto after the appeasement efforts of British Prime Minister Neville Chamberlain with Hitler. He was one of the early members of the Committee to Defend America by Aid to the Allies—the William Allen White Committee.

Those were the symbols and actions of a fiercely patriotic internationalist. He said of his change in philosophy, "To turn the other cheek was interpreted by them [Hitler and Mussolini] as a sure sign of weakness, and yielding brought danger ever closer. One must resist with the weapons of the flesh" (Schapsmeier and Schapsmeier, "Douglas" 314).

Douglas took his political ambitions a step further in 1942 when he sought the Democratic Party nomination for the U.S. Senate. He wanted to run in the general election against Senator C. Wayland Brooks, the isolationist and anti-Roosevelt Republican who had been elected in 1940 to a portion of a term and was seeking reelection.

Douglas conducted a courageous primary campaign on a shoestring, without the support of Mayor Kelly, who was backing Congressman Raymond S. McKeough of Chicago. Douglas won in 99 of the state's 102 counties, but still lost by almost three hundred thousand votes. His opponent carried Cook County by a huge majority, and that made the difference.

Douglas had learned once more that "you can't beat city hall!" McKeough lost to Brooks in the general election, as Douglas perhaps would not have. If so, his impact on the politics of the war years would have been considerable. The experience of losing once more convinced Douglas that he had to embrace the Chicago political machine if he wanted to serve in high state or federal office.

At the age of fifty in 1942, Douglas was above the age limit for enlisting in the armed services. With the help of Adlai Stevenson II, who was then working in the Roosevelt administration, Douglas, the former pacifist, prevailed on Navy Secretary Frank Knox, a former Chicago newspaper publisher, to waive the age limit for him. He then enlisted in the Marine Corps as a private and went off to basic training with men thirty years younger.

Douglas survived the rigors of boot camp and went into combat in the South Pacific. He was wounded at Peleliu and Okinawa, honored with the Purple Heart and Bronze Star, and promoted to the rank of major. He spent the last fourteen months of his time in the service in hospitals for five operations in an effort to regain partial use of his left arm. Functional use of the arm was never restored. He was discharged as a lieutenant-colonel in November 1946 and returned to Chicago.

When Douglas was seen campaigning on the public square in Urbana, Illinois, in 1948, speaking to a group of a half dozen, he used that withered arm effectively, holding it stiffly across his body and chopping the air with it for emphasis. No voter could miss seeing it and knowing Douglas was a wounded hero of World War II.

While Douglas was in service, his wife, Emily Taft Douglas, the daughter of the famed sculptor Lorado Taft, was elected as an at-large congresswoman from Illinois in 1944. She ran for reelection in 1946 against Republican William G. Stratton, who had held that position from 1941 to 1943, and who later became state treasurer for the second time in 1951 and governor in 1953.

Douglas and his wife never forgave Stratton for the campaign he waged against Emily, which he won by 367,000 votes. Her opponents had insinuated that she was too friendly toward communism. Douglas wrote in his memoir, "My gallant wife was attacked by both left and right and went down to defeat" (127). Douglas had a long memory for those he felt had wronged him or Emily. She later became a successful writer of children's books.

Douglas returned to teaching at the University of Chicago and became a vocal supporter of the new United Nations, the Truman administration's postwar policies, and the concept of mutual security with European allies. As the 1948 primary election neared, he was the first choice of Chicago Democratic king-maker Jacob Arvey to take the party's nomination and run against incumbent Senator Brooks.

Arvey described the moment he knew Douglas was the party's man for 1948:

> In 1946, Douglas came to a mass meeting in uniform. He did not make a speech but he waved a greeting to the crowd. I saw his withered hand. Brooks never made a speech without saying "I got shrapnel in my back at Chateau-Thierry and I learned what it means to serve our country." I knew the shattered hand would dispose of that. (Martin 274)

Adlai Stevenson and his supporters did not see the race that way. He wished to run for the Senate. In the end, he had to settle for his second choice, the nomination for governor. He and his supporters never forgot it. Douglas would have preferred to run for governor. Some felt that the Chicago Democratic machine wanted him out of the city council and out of the state. In the end, each man ran for the office that the other most wanted.

Democrats swept all the top positions on the ballot in 1948, led by President Truman at the national level. Douglas attacked Brooks for being an isolationist and opponent of every social and international policy of the Roosevelt and Truman administrations. He defended Truman's foreign policy and supported a social agenda that included civil rights, federal aid to education, social welfare, and economic reforms.

In this contest, Douglas developed a style of campaigning that he carried forward through two future victorious efforts at reelection and one that ended in defeat in 1966. He went to the people, shook hands at the factory gates, spoke with a bullhorn on street corners in small towns, and made countless speeches to small groups.

In the 1948 campaign, Douglas's finances reached such a low point that he borrowed all the money he could and took out a mortgage on his vacation cottage to pay for staff, literature, and radio time. Fortunately for him, television was not yet in use in campaigns. One friend warned him, "Paul you are about to lose your life, your fortune and your sacred honor" (Douglas 36). Instead, he won by 407,000 votes.

While Douglas focused largely on issues of high personal interest, his relationships with colleagues and presidents form some of the lasting impressions that others have of his three terms in the Senate. He had been in the Senate just two years when Everett Dirksen, a longtime member of the U.S. House, defeated Senator Scott Lucas, the Democratic Party's majority leader. This set in motion a key relationship in the lives of both Illinois senators that lasted for fifteen years, until Douglas was defeated in 1966.

The two could hardly have been less similar in personality, background, and style. Historian Edward L. Schapsmeier drew the contrast with these words:

> Dirksen's smiling, cherubic countenance seemed to invite colleagues to become his close friends. His shock of unruly hair and the honeyed tones of his sonorous voice attracted the immediate attention of his audience. Douglas, in sharp contrast, was endowed with a gaunt visage and staid and serious demeanor. His cropped white hair made him appear stern. His speeches—highly articulate, factual and logical—were uttered in a raspy voice. (88)

Dirksen was a pragmatist who eventually endorsed most of the modern Republican agenda. Douglas was an idealist who followed no one and led only a few liberals. Dirksen became the epitome of compromise at a time when Democrats controlled the Senate and Lyndon Johnson rose to leadership. Historians like to point out that while Douglas was one of the most vocal and courageous advocates of civil rights, it was Dirksen who broke the southern filibusters that could have doomed the Civil Rights Acts of 1964 and 1965.

Douglas shed little light on his personal relationship with Dirksen or his feelings about his Republican counterpart. In his memoir, the kindest comment Douglas made was in a discussion of Dirksen's 1962 Senate contest, when he said Dirksen "had won a national reputation and was well-liked by the voters" (572).

For all their differences on policy, the two followed virtually the same position on the Vietnam war. Both were strong supporters of President Johnson's policies and of pressing the full force of the military. Douglas shared the experience of Senate service under four presidents, three of them Democrats. He defended Harry Truman and his goals, including the war in Korea. He was often at political odds with John F. Kennedy, and he never had a particularly close relationship with Lyndon B. Johnson, whether in the Senate or the White House. The only Republican president during Douglas's time was Dwight D. Eisenhower, whom Douglas viewed as lethargic toward issues of importance.

Perhaps Douglas's difficulties with presidents of his own party reflected the fact that he had higher expectations of Democrats. When Kennedy became president, Douglas was critical of what he saw as inaction from the president on civil rights. After the fact, Douglas said of Kennedy, "[A]s much as I admired John Kennedy, I regretted his delay in proposing effective civil rights legislation." Recognizing the shortness of Kennedy's tenure, Douglas added, "[I]f Kennedy had lived I believe he would have come out more strongly for civil rights" (295).

Kennedy was president long enough for him and his aides to have a full-scale public brawl with Douglas over the election of a senator from Illinois in 1962. Douglas was not himself a candidate. Dirksen was seeking a third term, and the Chicago Democrats chose Representative Sidney Yates of the U.S. House, a respected member of Congress and a Daley loyalist, as his opponent.

The disagreement over Kennedy's treatment of Yates and support of Dirksen began when the president nominated a Republican from Illinois to be a federal judge. He had not informed either Douglas or Yates of what he was doing. Douglas considered that to be an affront to him and to Yates.

"I was dispirited that the administration should treat so shabbily a good candidate who supported the forward-looking practices of our Democratic party," Douglas wrote in his memoir (144). Historians agree that Kennedy wanted Dirksen to win not because he did not wish to have another Democratic senator from Illinois but because of the senator who would have taken Dirksen's place as minority leader if Dirksen had been defeated. Bourke Hickenlooper would have succeeded him in that position, and his conservatism would have made it more difficult for the president's legislative agenda to have been approved.

Douglas vented his anger in a letter to Kennedy denouncing the judicial appointment and criticizing the Democratic leadership for supporting Dirksen. He was especially irked at Senate majority leader Mike Mansfield and Senator Hubert Humphrey for offering "glowing praise" of Dirksen on the Senate floor. In final insults, in Douglas's opinion, President Kennedy and Vice President Johnson made lukewarm endorsements of Yates and only brief appearances in Illinois. Dirksen won reelection over Yates handily.

The long, turbulent struggle over civil rights legislation consumed much of Douglas's time. The issue also set up confrontation and frustration in the relationship between the senator and Lyndon Johnson, when the Texan was minority then majority leader and again when he was president. Douglas wanted Johnson to reject the counsel of southern Democrats in the Senate and press ahead with legislation proposed by Senate liberals. That was not Johnson's way, and Douglas knew it.

Douglas simply did not like the way Johnson engaged in politics. He once told an aide:

> Under Johnson, the Senate functions like a Greek tragedy; all the action takes place offstage, before the play begins. Nothing is left to open and spontaneous debate, nothing is left for the participants but the enactment of their prescribed roles. (Caro 578)

When Johnson tried and failed to win the nomination for president in the Democratic national convention in 1956, he realized that if he were to have any chance four years later, he would have to have a more liberal stance toward civil rights legislation. "He knew now that the only way to realize his great ambition was to fight—*really* fight; fight aggressively and effectively—for civil rights." Yet to achieve such legislation would mean for him to lose the support of the South. The dilemma that he faced seemed cruel and unredeemable (Caro 832).

Finally, in 1957, Johnson reached the conclusion that he could seek civil rights legislation *and* retain southern support by convincing southern senators that it was his only road to the presidency. As a result, the Senate approved the first civil rights bill enacted by that body in eighty-seven years.

Southern senators again and again had effectively blocked civil rights legislation through effective filibustering. To vote closure and end a filibuster took a two-thirds vote. That was difficult to accomplish. The civil rights measure in 1957 was majority leader Lyndon Johnson's bill, and he was responsible for getting it passed. The media cheered, and Johnson took the bows. Douglas thought it was too weak and gave Johnson no credit. He had been repeatedly humiliated by Johnson in the civil rights struggle.

Historian Doris Kearns Goodwin, a Johnson biographer, described the majority leader's approach to getting the necessary votes:

> Johnson moved from one side of the cloakroom to the other, assuring one side, then the other. He'd tell Senator Douglas to ready his troops and arguments so "we can make sure this long-overdue bill for the benefit of the Negro-Americans, will pass." Later, in another

corner, he would whisper a warning to Senator Sam Ervin that the worst part of "the nigger bill" was coming up. (150)

When Johnson became president in 1963, one of his first orders of business was to resurrect Kennedy's civil rights plan and move it through Congress. It became the Civil Rights Act of 1964, a true breakthrough. It and the Voting Rights Act of 1965 were the legislative initiatives Douglas had worked for since 1948. The irony was that they passed mainly because Lyndon Johnson and Everett Dirksen—not Douglas—did the legislative work. Only after passage of both acts did Douglas acknowledge that he had buried the hatchet with Johnson.

Other hot-button issues for Douglas included civil liberties and Supreme Court rulings upon them. Douglas had been a member of the American Civil Liberties Union since its beginning in 1920 and was vigilant toward issues of equality. He also became a strong supporter of the Court led by Chief Justice Earl Warren. After a series of controversial decisions that angered members of Congress, Douglas helped fight off a number of actions designed to reverse the Court's decisions. Douglas was especially protective of the Court's 1954 school desegregation ruling.

After his election victory against Brooks in 1948, Douglas received the blessing of the Democratic organization in Chicago when needed, and he faced relatively weaker opponents. His winning percentages in 1954 and 1960 were 53.6 and 54.6—not exactly runaways but still comfortable margins.

Douglas made an accommodation with Richard J. Daley during the mayoral campaign in Chicago in 1955, Daley's first. "I greatly prefer Dick Daley," he announced (Biles, *Crusading* 62). Daley won, of course, and backed Douglas thereafter. The senator maintained that Daley never attempted to influence his voting or made an improper request. Still, an awareness of the importance of the Chicago vote must have always been in Douglas's mind.

His opponent in 1954 was Republican Joe Meek, a conservative and an ineffectual campaigner. Douglas won by 241,000 votes. In 1960, when Kennedy eked out a win over Nixon in the presidential contest in Illinois, in an election that had some Republicans crying "fraud!," the senator bested respected Republican Samuel Witwer by 437,000 votes. His stock with the voters must have been rising and strong.

It was a different story when Douglas attempted to win election to a fourth term in 1966. With eighteen years of Senate service behind him, he had served longer than any Illinois senator since Shelby Cullom's five terms ended in 1913. Douglas was seventy-three years old, and generally in good health, though naturally not as vigorous and durable as he had been six years earlier. Like old ballplayers and many old politicians, he believed he still was good for another inning or two. Work remained to be done on issues to which he was devoted.

The Republicans chose Charles H. Percy as Douglas's opponent. A corporate executive with Bell and Howell in Chicago and a millionaire, Percy had been active in party affairs since the 1950s, inspired by Dwight Eisenhower, and had run unsuccessfully against incumbent Otto Kerner for governor in 1964.

While not a particular favorite among conservatives in Illinois or those who valued candidates who had worked their way up through the ranks doing party chores—"carrying water for the elephant," as some put it—Percy presented a new, moderate look that appealed to independent voters. In short, he was "an Eisenhower Republican," of the stripe of Nelson Rockefeller in New York.

The war in Vietnam became a major issue between the two candidates. Douglas was an unapologetic supporter of the U.S. military position. It was a matter of patriotism for the senator, and he could not accept its interpretation as an immoral war. Douglas defended his position with these words: "If the history of the last third of a century teaches us anything it is that resistance to aggression is both constructive and necessary and that courage is contagious" (Schapsmeier and Schapsmeier, "Douglas" 322).

Percy took a more dovish position on the war, criticizing the Johnson administration and calling for a negotiated solution. He supported an all-Asian peace conference, an idea that drew approval from Republican Party leader Richard Nixon. Douglas called the idea "half-baked." So went the campaign rhetoric until the morning of September 18, 1966. At that time, the race appeared to be about an even one.

That is when the world learned that Percy's daughter Valerie Jeanne was murdered in her bed in the Percy's Kenilworth, Illinois, home, during the night. The tragedy brought the campaign to a halt. Douglas suspended his activity and asked Chicago Democrats not to take advantage of the situation by starting rumors and innuendo.

Even so, suspicions were circulated about the possible involvement of Percy himself, and Mrs. Percy, who was Valerie's stepmother. These rumors were completely without foundation.

Douglas believed that news of the crime would subside soon and that the campaign would resume. Instead, Valerie's death dominated headlines through the final weeks, and sympathy for the Percys became a major factor in the general election.

One Democrat was quoted later as saying, "To vote for Percy seemed the least one could do." Douglas was beaten by 420,000 votes, receiving about 45 percent of the total. He won in only 8 of the 102 counties. In his concession speech on election night, he said, "Let us remember that ours is one country and one state. Let us purge ourselves of any trace of bitterness or divisiveness. Let us start with ourselves for no one of us is perfect or free from fault" (Douglas 593).

After this defeat, Douglas continued an active interest in public affairs, although his health deteriorated and he sought no other public office. He had retired from academic life and spent his remaining years in the Washington, D.C., vicinity. He died on September 24, 1976, at the age of eighty-four.

15 ★ "The Wizard of Ooze"

As a young veteran of military service in World War I, Scott W. Lucas had recruited one of his friends from a nearby river town to join the American Legion. Both had political ambitions, and both understood the added strength at the ballot box that active legion membership might give. They shared that understanding and that advantage with other Illinois politicians such as Senator C. Wayland Brooks, Governor Dwight Green, and Lieutenant Governor and eventually Acting Governor John Stelle.

It is quite possible that Lucas in later years looked back with some regret on his suggestion to his friend Everett Dirksen that he join the legion. In 1950, Lucas, the majority leader in the Senate, in his effort to win a third term, was beaten at the polls by Dirksen. It is an irony that Senator Dirksen, who also became the floor leader of his party in the Senate, seldom had the strength of majority status yet on the whole wielded more power than Lucas, who had headed the majority party.

Everett McKinley Dirksen (1951–69)

Everett M. Dirksen was born in Pekin, Illinois, on January 4, 1896. His parents were emigrants from Germany. The family name, however, was Danish. Like so many who had come to the United States from Germany in midcentury, his parents, Johann and Antje, were solidly Republican in their politics. Everett's middle name was given to him in honor of President McKinley. He had a twin brother who was named Thomas Reed after the Speaker of the House in Washington, and their older brother Ben had been named for President Benjamin Harrison.

Everett and his brothers grew up in a home where hard work was the accepted way of life. The family lived in a large, old house on a sizable plot of ground at the edge of town. Part of Everett's chores was tending the garden, and he continued to enjoy growing vegetables and flowers for the rest of his life. His father suffered a stroke when Everett and his brother were five and was totally incapacitated. He died four years later, leaving his sons more chores and family responsibilities.

Everett attended high school and gained a diploma. Neither of his brothers finished the eighth grade. He was an honors student—first among the males in his class—played football, and ran the distances on the track team. Indicating talents to be employed in the Congress in later years, he was a finalist in a national oratorical contest.

He thought of attending the University of Illinois but felt it was beyond his means. Instead he went to work for a corn refining company in Pekin. After a year, he took an unpaid vacation and visited a half brother in Minneapolis. There he discovered that jobs were plentiful and that he could afford to attend the University of Minnesota.

That he did, with his mother's encouragement, beginning in 1914. The course of study he favored was directed toward the law. He became active in campus and presidential politics, campaigning and speaking in behalf of the Republican candidate, Chief Justice Charles Evans Hughes, in 1916.

When the United States entered World War I in the spring of 1917, Dirksen enlisted. One of his objectives was to demonstrate the patriotism of his family, in spite of its German background. Eventually, he was commissioned a second lieutenant and survived several weeks of hazardous duty as an artillery spotter in a hot air balloon, thirty-five hundred feet above the ground, vulnerable to enemy aircraft attack and with only a rudimentary parachute as an escape device.

Dirksen traveled widely in Europe before returning to the United States. He became enamored of a German woman and thought of marrying her. His mother opposed the match, fearing it would damage his political opportunities later in life. Apparently, she was already thinking of him as one who would enter politics. Dirksen yielded to her judgment and returned to the United States alone.

When he did, it was not to go back to college but to begin a life of work in Pekin. He was employed in a grocery run by his two brothers and then in the family bakery. In the life of the community, he was active in amateur theatricals and wrote a number of plays, poems, and short stories, and five novels. Almost nothing that he wrote was published.

Dirksen lived with his mother in the family home and cared for her in her declining years, until her death in 1923. Perhaps it was out of concern for her that he had not gone back to college after his military service. As a death bed promise to her, he forswore any effort at a professional career in the theatre. Amateur theatricals, however, helped him become acquainted with Louella Carver, whom he married in 1927.

His activity and office holding in the American Legion helped him substantially in entering and succeeding in electoral politics. He was elected to the city commission, Pekin's principal legislative and administrative body, in 1926, and, as the most successful vote-getter, became commissioner of finance. His chief interest in politics was the national level, however, and in 1930, he entered the primary election of the Republican Party against the incumbent congressman. In an uphill struggle, he came out second best.

Almost at once, Dirksen went to work campaigning for the next primary period, then less than eighteen months away. This time he was successful in winning the nomination, and in November 1932, he was elected to the U.S. House of Representatives. He was one of only four Republicans to go to the House from Illinois that year, out of twenty-seven. He managed to win in a year of Democratic landslides, by low-profiling his partisanship and appealing to "citizenship" in the face of depression.

Always conscientious, Dirksen went to Washington, D.C., early in order to find his away around. Arriving there, he had to ask directions to the Capitol. Already an astute politician, Dirksen took pains not to offend Democratic sensibilities. On many New Deal measures, his vote was "aye." In foreign policy matters, however, his views were consistently antiadministration and isolationist.

By attention to hard work, of the sort he had learned while growing up in Pekin, and adherence to ideals of "good government," Dirksen made steady progress upward in the House hierarchy. In 1937, he became a member of the powerful Appropriations Committee, a post that conferred considerable status.

His attention to duty was simplified by the fact that he had left his wife Louella at home in Pekin. He lived alone in the Mayflower Hotel until 1938, usually walking to his desk in the Capitol. He had few social distractions. His usual schedule was to retire at midnight, after an evening of work, and to rise at 5:30 A.M. to begin the next day's round of duties.

He read and studied law in the office of a practicing attorney and, in 1936, with the college work he had already done, became qualified to practice law in the courts of Washington and Illinois. In 1938, he apparently felt that he could enjoy a greater degree of domesticity, and he and Louella rented a small apartment on Rhode Island Avenue, where they and their daughter Joy lived for a number of years.

Leadership qualities were already apparent in Dirksen, and in 1938, he became chairman of the Republican National Congressional Committee, an organization devoted to the election and reelection of members of that party to the House. He held that position for almost a decade and, in that time, caused many of his colleagues to feel that they owed their positions at least in part to him.

Dirksen could see what was coming on the international scene and, in September 1941, abruptly reversed his position to become an internationalist. His timing was good, for it was just three months later that the Japanese attack on Pearl Harbor brought about the entry of the United States into war against both Japan and Germany and their allies.

That move alienated him from much of his power base in Illinois, in the persons of Governor Green, Senator Brooks, and Colonel McCormick of the *Chicago Tribune.* Although he was aware of the influence that McCormick wielded through the pages of the *Tribune,* Dirksen was never his puppet. Dirksen had broader ambitions and made an unsuccessful gesture at seeking first the presidential and then the vice presidential nomination of his party in 1944.

By the time the war ended, he was one of the leading internationalists in the Congress. During the winter of 1945, he utilized unspent campaign funds for a prolonged tour of Europe, to survey the damage that war had done and to appraise the state of politics there. When he returned, President Truman asked for and received a detailed report on what he had seen. He favored large-scale economic aid to European countries as early as 1946, of the sort that the Marshall Plan brought about two years later. He backed much of Truman's program but consistently opposed deficit spending.

Late in the spring of 1946, Dirksen began to experience trouble with blurred vision. His difficulty continued, and by 1948, he was almost blind. He was reduced to memorizing speeches by having them read back to him after he had dictated them to his secretary. He reached the difficult decision early that year not to enter the primary election to seek another term in the House. Both the Republican Speaker of the House, Joseph Martin, and the Democratic minority whip, John McCormack, later to be Speaker, urged him to reconsider.

Many tests resulted in the diagnosis of cancer of the retina. Dirksen was advised to have his right eye removed. While he delayed that decision, he and Louella rented an isolated cottage in Maryland near Chesapeake Bay. There he rested, prayed, meditated, and consumed massive amounts of vitamins. Which of those procedures worked best we will never know. Improving, he decided against removal of the eye.

When he informed the specialist who had advised him to have the eye removed of his decision, he said that he had gotten another opinion. "From what doctor?" he was asked. "Oh . . . a very big Doctor. He lives upstairs," Dirksen answered (Schapsmeier and Schapsmeier, *Dirksen* 47).

By midsummer, he had recovered sufficiently to make another try for the vice presidential nomination of his party, and again he was not successful. He was dismayed when in November his friends and fellow Republicans Governor Dwight Green and Senator C. Wayland Brooks were beaten in Illinois, and Democrat President Harry Truman won another term.

Dirksen went home to Pekin, by one account to spend a good deal of time recuperating on the front-porch swing of his mother-in-law's home, where he and his family also were living. He decided to practice law for a livelihood and joined a Pekin law firm. But politics ran very near the surface of his mind.

It was not long until Dirksen was planning, with the encouragement of his wife and daughter, to run for the Senate seat held by Scott Lucas, his friend and neighbor from Havana, Illinois, whose second term would end in 1951. Free of legislative duties himself, Dirksen could devote all of his time to campaigning. In doing so, he traveled a quarter of a million miles up and down the state, wore out two automobiles, and made two thousand speeches!

Dirksen and Lucas were much alike in some ways and very different in others. Both were big, heavy-boned men, athletic in appearance. Lucas dressed handsomely, almost elegantly, in double-breasted suits; Dirksen offered a rumpled appearance as if he had slept in his clothes. Lucas's hair was always neatly arranged and worn long; Dirksen's was usually rumpled as if it were deliberately done. Dirksen liked to mingle with crowds and "press the flesh"; Lucas was more reserved and less given to humorous stories of the sort that his rival liked to spin out one after another.

Dirksen knew in 1949 that his separation from the *Tribune* group had cost him dearly in his national ticket ambitions in 1944 and 1948. He also knew that his chances of beating Lucas in 1950 would be better if he could win *Tribune* endorsement again. He courted Colonel McCormick by veering sharply to the conservative side, in both domestic and foreign policy issues.

He called on the colonel in his *Tribune* Tower office the week before he announced for the Senate. When McCormick suggested that Dirksen could have the newspaper's support in exchange for "certain things" he might do in Washington, Dirksen later reported, "[T]here was no deal." He refused to sell himself to the *Tribune*. Colonel McCormick, he said, ended the interview at that point with a curt "Good day" (Schapsmeier and Schapsmeier, *Dirksen* 56).

Even so, the newspaper came over strongly to Dirksen's side. Although he claimed there had been "no deal," many of those who had shared internationalist sentiments with him were dismayed by the changes that Dirksen displayed.

Lucas was confined to Washington with his duties in the Senate in 1950. He had little time to campaign. President Truman was denounced by Republicans for much of his foreign policy, including the "police action" in Korea, and as majority leader in the Senate, Lucas took the heat for matters that were beyond his control. When the vote was taken in November, Dirksen was the winner, 951,984 to 657,630.

The Everett Dirksen who took his seat in the Senate early in 1951 proved to be a man quite different from the one who had been a leading internationalist from 1941 to 1948. The dignity of his new position appeared to change his general demeanor. Observers of him late in 1951 found him to be something of a "dandy." His suit was pressed, his hair was neatly combed, and he was wearing a homburg!

Senator Dirksen opposed most of President Truman's domestic and foreign policies. He supported General MacArthur when the general was removed from command in Korea by the president. He allied himself with Senator Robert Taft and backed him for the presidential nomination in 1952. Like Taft, he supported Senator Joe McCarthy in the early years of McCarthy's anticommunist tirades. In the 1952 Republican national nominating convention, he played a prominent part.

Unhappy over the strength that the Eisenhower forces brought to the convention, Dirksen committed a blunder from the convention speaker's stand that probably cost him any chance of being nominated for vice president, then or in the years that followed.

Senator Taft had chosen Dirksen to make a critical address in the matter of seating rival delegations. He began well, but his tone became bitter. Gradually, his venom focused on Thomas E. Dewey, the Republican presidential candidate in 1944 and 1948, who was seated on the convention floor. He had campaigned for Dewey, he said, in eighteen states in 1944 and in twenty-three states in 1948. "From the podium he looked down at Governor Dewey. He shook his finger dramatically in Dewey's face. 'We followed you before,' Dirksen cried out, 'and you took us down the path to defeat!'" (MacNeil 104).

The whole convention, and the galleries as well, broke into an uproar. Some were venting their dislike of Dewey, others anger at what Dirksen had so bluntly said. On the whole, the performance earned him more dislike than any previous action he had ever taken. It marked the end of Taft's hopes, as the convention then moved to seat the Eisenhower delegates and nominate the general on the first ballot. That action ended Dirksen's hope of second place on the ticket.

There was one final grim note for Dirksen at this convention:

The chief supporters of Eisenhower caucused in a hotel room to choose a . . . running mate. . . . Taft [telephoned to say he] wanted Dirksen considered. . . . The proposal took the Eisenhower chiefs aback. Finally Governor . . . Beardsley of Iowa spoke up. "Mr. Chairman," he said, "all I have to say is after what Dirksen said the other night, the people of Iowa would not use him to wipe their feet on."

"That," wrote Governor Sherman Adams of New Hampshire, who was there, "was the end of Dirksen." (MacNeil 105)

The years that followed were the blackest that Dirksen was to know as a member of Congress. He was an ally of Robert Taft, and after Taft's death, he lacked a leader. He was ridiculed by the media for his appearance and mannerisms and for the changes in policy direction that he had exhibited. He supported Senator McCarthy for a time and opposed his censure by the Senate. By 1954, he was reduced to the depths of what had become for him a "wilderness" time.

Facing reelection in 1956 and without Taft as his leader, Dirksen came over to Eisenhower's side so that he might benefit from the president's popularity in Illinois. Fairness to Dirksen requires that it be noted that he was never at any time antiadministration during the Eisenhower presidency.

By 1957, after the voters had returned Dirksen to the Senate for a second term, he had become Eisenhower's foremost supporter in that body. That was not just a boast on his part; by an actual counting of votes, no senator had been on the president's side more often than Dirksen. His support level in that year was 95 percent, up twenty points in two years. In explaining such change in his opinions, he liked to say:

> I'm just an old-fashioned garden variety of Republican, who believes in the Constitution, the Declaration of Independence, in Abraham Lincoln, who accepts the challenges as they arise and who is not unappreciative of the fact that this is a dynamic economy in which we live, and sometimes you have to change your position. (MacNeil 151)

Dirksen campaigned hard for reelection for ten weeks in 1956, leaving nothing to chance. His opponent was the little known Richard Stengel, a state legislator from Rockford and a second cousin to the legendary baseball manager Casey Stengel. Dirksen won in November by slightly more than a third of a million votes. At the same time, President Eisenhower was favored in Illinois for a second term by a margin of 847,845.

Clearly, it was Ike at the head of the ticket who helped Dirksen's cause, and not the other way around. Even though the president won in a landslide, many Republican candidates for Congress were defeated, and the Democrats took over control of both House and Senate.

After his reelection in 1956, Dirksen was becoming a different man. He was beginning to regard service in the Senate as an end in itself. He became the minority whip, generally recognized as next in line to be the minority leader. No longer did he yearn for executive office. Perhaps he had come to realize that his time to think of being nominated for higher office had come and gone.

Following the model that Lyndon Johnson had established as floor leader on the Democratic side of the Senate, Dirksen reached out to the liberal wing of his own party in order to gain and consolidate his leadership position. Neil MacNeil has summed up Dirksen's style in this way:

> Dirksen made it a point to be, in his phrase, "one of the boys" with his fellow senators. "I try to be cooperative," he said, explaining as leader how he dealt with his colleagues, "not to be selfish—to try to help." He was a pragmatic, flexible, politician, not inclined to judge his colleagues in moralistic terms. "I am a man of principle," he once said, smiling, "and one of my basic principles is flexibility." He wanted power, influence, and the prestige that comes with them, and he wanted to shape and temper the course of American political affairs. "I am not a moralist," he had said. "I am a legislator." (167)

Dirksen entrenched himself as party leader in the Senate through offering social activities to his colleagues, cultivating good relations with the news media, and being helpful in such things as election campaigns and committee assignments. He followed Lyndon Johnson's example of pleading and cajolery in persuading his party members to vote as he wished them to. In fact, he seemed to model himself so closely after Johnson that some felt he was his complete clone.

One story that circulated widely has to do with Dirksen's great desire to have a telephone in his limousine, just like Johnson. Bear in mind that that was long before the day of the cell phone, and such a luxury in an automobile was unusual.

Dirksen finally got his telephone and could hardly wait for the moment when both party leaders were limousine borne. He rang Johnson at once. "'Hello, Lyndon,' Dirksen supposedly said. 'This is Everett Dirksen. I'm calling you from my limousine on my new phone.' 'Wait a minute, Everett,' replied Johnson in his limousine. 'The other phone is ringing'" (MacNeil 172).

Unlike Johnson, Dirksen never threatened, never preached. His "tools of the trade as a leader were his mastery of details, open candidness, cordiality, concern for the principles espoused by his colleagues, and the ability to persuade without being obnoxious"

(Schapsmeier and Schapsmeier, *Dirksen* 113). He did his work with a sense of humor, often saying, "[T]he oil can is mightier than the sword."

In 1959, Dirksen worked skillfully at consolidating his position with both wings of his party and his relationship with President Eisenhower so that he would be chosen to replace William Knowland as minority leader. In the Republican caucus, he won, over the more liberal John Sherman Cooper of Kentucky, twenty to fourteen.

In the same year, Dirksen and his wife Louella left the modest apartment they had rented for eight years for the home that they had built on the bank of the Potomac River near Leesburg, Virginia. About an hour's drive from the Capitol, its three and a half acres allowed space for the gardening that the senator still liked to busy himself with in his infrequent hours of relaxation.

By 1960, Dirksen was President Eisenhower's acknowledged champion in the Senate. Eight years earlier, you will recall, he had backed Taft for president and opposed Eisenhower's policies. There was some talk of him for the vice presidential nomination in 1960, but that went nowhere. The presidential nominee Richard Nixon chose Henry Cabot Lodge as his running mate and might have done better with Dirksen. And "better" by only a few thousand votes could have meant victory.

When John F. Kennedy became president in 1961, Dirksen was the spokesman for his party in the Congress so far as Kennedy was concerned. He represented both wings of the Republican organization, and the president valued his help. Often Republican votes were needed to help pass Kennedy administration measures.

When Dirksen ran for a third term in 1962, he was almost certainly "the best known member of the Senate" (MacNeil 208). At home in Illinois, however, he was weak among the party's conservatives. Some liberals, at the same time, thought him too far to the right. He feared being beaten at the polls and even composed a farewell message in case his worst fears were realized.

He campaigned briefly but won without difficulty. It is generally an accepted fact that President Kennedy preferred that Dirksen win, rather than his opponent, Democrat Sidney Yates (Schapsmeier and Schapsmeier, *Dirksen* 45). Paul Douglas, the other senator from Illinois, was angry that Yates had been treated this way by the White House. He wrote the president a long letter of protest that was never answered.

After election day in 1962 had come and gone, Dirksen was exhausted. He had used his body hard for many years. He smoked three packs of cigarettes a day. When his doctor told him to cut back on his smoking, he made the concession of no longer carrying cigarettes. He "mooched" smokes from others, however, at such a rate that his total use of tobacco was not reduced.

His daily schedule called for him to be up at 5:30 A.M. and at work in the Capitol long before others were on hand. Often it was mid-evening before he returned to his home, and he took heavy loads of work with him. He went often to Illinois, taking his briefcase, which held thirty-five pounds of work papers. When Dirksen could weekend at his home near Leesburg, he often gardened, raising both vegetables and flowers. He had gardened at home in Pekin from boyhood on, at first of necessity and then, as an adult, for relaxation. After his marriage, while he lived in Pekin, his gardening was at the home of his wife's mother, where the Dirksens also made their home.

He became a champion of the marigold and annually would rhapsodize to the Senate about its merits, usually nominating it to be named the national flower. This sampling of his oratory is a fair example of the ornateness of his speech:

"It is as spritely as the daffodil," he said of the marigold . . . , "as colorful as the rose, as resolute as the zinnia, as delicate as the chrysanthemum, as aggressive as the petunia, as ubiquitous as the violet, and as stately as the snapdragon. It beguiles the senses and enobles the spirit of man. . . . Since it is native to America, and nowhere else in the world, and common to every state in the Union, I present the American marigold for designation as the national floral emblem of our country." (MacNeil 216)

When Dirksen's wife, Louella, wrote a memoir of her husband, following his death, she titled it *The Honorable Mr. Marigold*. According to her, his ten-year effort to have the marigold made the national flower was an earnest one. She continued that campaign but met no more success than had her husband. The Burpee Seed Company developed a marigold with a five-inch blossom and named it the Senator Dirksen, and the city of Pekin annually in the fall holds a marigold festival.

When President Eisenhower was succeeded by Democrat John F. Kennedy in 1961, Dirksen made the adjustment with relative ease.

He opposed most of Kennedy's domestic program but finally came over to his side on the nuclear test ban treaty, in 1962. Kennedy valued Dirksen's assistance in providing Republican votes on critical matters of legislation.

The Democratic floor leader, Mike Mansfield, was so low key and retiring that to many, Dirksen, actually the minority leader, at this time came to seem to be the leader of the whole Senate. That appearance was intensified when Lyndon Johnson became president following Kennedy's assassination. Dirksen and Johnson had been close friends for many years, and that relationship deepened.

One afternoon, Lady Bird Johnson left the two visiting in the west hall of the White House. When she returned some time later, she found them still there, heads close together, chatting away as if time meant nothing. She overheard Dirksen say, "[Y]ou don't mind if we denounce you once in a while, do you, Lyndon?" (Schapsmeier and Schapsmeier, *Dirksen* 150). The two old professionals would often engage in trading favors, as, for example, an appointment by the president for a Republican for Dirksen's support of a piece of legislation. They understood one another.

Friends since their days in the House together, both understood the importance of negotiation and compromise in the making of legislation. That did not rule out substantial disagreement and even the raising of harsh voices from time to time. Johnson, in his memoir, remarked on Dirksen's ability to "take the long view without regard to party" when the national interest was at stake (Schapsmeier and Schapsmeier, *Dirksen* 151).

In 1964, Dirksen became one of the dominating figures in the passage of the civil rights bill. President Johnson courted him on the issue personally and through Senator Hubert Humphrey. On this bill, Humphrey said later, he "was ready to kiss 'Dirksen's ass on the Capitol steps'" (Dallek 119).

Once convinced, Dirksen drove the Senate hard on this most important of domestic issues. It took a tremendous toll on him physically. He maintained the same dawn-'til-long-after-dark schedule as always. He had long before given up any exercise or relaxation, except for the occasional hour spent in his garden.

When the crucial vote came on the civil rights bill, it was not on the substance of the bill itself but on "closure," the ending of debate that was the only weapon against endless filibustering.

Dirksen brought twenty-seven Republican votes to the table in favor of closure, and it carried. He felt it to be a great victory, one that would help candidates of his party at the polls.

His pleasure at the voting of closure and enactment of the civil rights bill was tempered by the fact that his friend and fellow senator Barry Goldwater, who seemed assured of getting the Republican presidential nomination that year, was not among the twenty-seven Republicans who were on Dirksen's side in the closure vote. Goldwater was one of only six Republicans who voted "no" on both closure and final passage of the bill, which was decided by a vote of seventy-three to twenty-one.

Dirksen feared that that would hurt Goldwater and his party among black voters in the North in the November election. Probably he was right and it did.

In spite of his misgivings, Dirksen was loyal to Goldwater during the Republican nominating convention. He gave the speech that presented Goldwater's name to the convention. The two remained close. Goldwater's massive defeat left the Republican Party in chaos, with its liberal and conservative wings hostile to one another, and rendered Dirksen's task of party leader in the Senate more difficult.

Even so, he continued to hone his leadership skills and gained a level of power that no other senator in the history of the institution could match. He was working as hard as ever, attending to every detail, employing his highly cultivated persuasive powers, both from the platform and in more private settings, and flexing his arm in political "hardball" when necessary.

His long-standing personal relationship with President Johnson was helpful to him. While the president generally could rely on Democrats for support, when he needed Republican votes in the Senate, Dirksen became of great importance to him.

That combination was effective in the passage of another civil rights bill in 1965. Dirksen opposed most of Johnson's domestic program, but he felt that support of the civil rights measures was critical to the electoral success of many Republicans. That support was lacking for the civil rights "open housing" bill of 1966, and the bill failed. Dirksen sensed that it ran far ahead of public opinion on the matter. Its failure was in part a "white backlash" in Cook County against the 1964 and 1965 civil rights bills, which caused the veteran three-term Senator Paul Douglas to be defeated in 1966 by Republican Charles Percy, even though Douglas had taken a low-profile stance on the measure for fear of what a more aggressive posture might do.

Foreign policy was another matter. Dirksen expected to be briefed by the White House on foreign policy issues, but once that had been done, he accepted the judgments of the president without question. It was true that he had opposed Truman on Korea at the time he was first elected to the Senate. He explained that it was necessary for him to take that position if he expected to win.

His acquiescence with presidential decision making in foreign policy led him to support Johnson on Vietnam. Earlier he had given the same approval to the decisions of Presidents Eisenhower and Kennedy on Vietnam matters. A younger generation of Republicans were coming on in the Senate, however, and Dirksen's stance on Vietnam began to erode his position of leadership with them.

Signs of that erosion began to appear. In 1966, Dirksen offered a proposed amendment to the constitution, on public school prayer—he wished it to be allowed, as the Supreme Court did not—and the proposal was defeated in the Senate. Of that effort, Dirksen declared, "I'm not going to let nine men say to 190 million people, including children, when and where they can utter their prayers. I can see no evil in children who want to say that God is good and to thank him for their blessings" (Schapsmeier and Schapsmeier, *Dirksen* 180).

Senator Howard Baker of Tennessee, who was Dirksen's son-in-law, married to his only child, Joy, had, in 1965, led a successful opposition to another amendment Dirksen offered. It would have left the matter of reapportioning the state legislatures to the states themselves, in place of a Court required standard of "one person, one vote." The Dirksen amendment read in part: "The people of a state may apportion one house of a bicameral legislature using population, geography, or political subdivisions as factors, giving each factor such weight as they deem appropriate" (Schapsmeier and Schapsmeier, *Dirksen* 178). That was obviously a reactionary response to the Supreme Court decision in *Baker v. Carr* (1962), which directed use of the "one person, one vote" principle.

Dirksen was also beaten in the Senate when he moved to curtail the busing of school children in integration efforts. This time the opposition was led by a freshman senator, Robert Griffin of Michigan. Older Republican senators resented their party leader's close relationship with President Johnson. And gradually in 1967 and 1968, the whole Senate was moving away from Dirksen's position on Vietnam.

The result of such an erosion of power was that by 1968, many Republicans in the Senate wished to topple Dirksen from his leadership post. But the question of who would take his place puzzled them. Thurston Morton of Kentucky was a logical choice, but he did not want the hard work that went with it. He said,

> "It's a drudgery job. He works like hell at it." Morton believed that there was not a senator in the party who really wanted Dirksen's job. . . . "I don't want it," Morton said. "I'm too lazy to do the work he does. I've told him that if he has a contest for the leadership, I'll be his campaign chairman. . . . There's no [other] choice." (MacNeil 304)

As his hold on power loosened, Dirksen still retained an array of political tools that had served him well in the past. He was still a cunning strategist and a master of parliamentary procedure, and he had many favors owed to him.

Not the least of his problems was the condition of his health. In 1967, he experienced a series of physical illnesses. Even though he suffered from emphysema, he still smoked cigarettes. His heart was enlarged, and it had a leaky valve. Twenty years later, surgical repairs would probably have been made.

He experienced congestive heart failure and had to have the excess fluid taken out of his body on a number of occasions. He had a persistent bleeding ulcer. For years, he wore a heavy, uncomfortable steel back brace. For a time, he "lived" at Walter Reed Hospital, checking in there each evening and going to the Capitol in his limousine each morning. He refused to take a vacation. It almost seemed that he was exercising a death wish.

Dirksen continued his weekly hour-long news conferences. He was quite open with news gatherers, so far as public policies and his own political views were concerned. By 1968, the media had come to regard him as the leader of the whole Senate, not just its Republican portion. News people knew that he was closer to President Johnson than was Senator Mansfield, the majority leader. He was the unchallenged leader of his party in the Congress, a condition that spanned the time between the retirement of William Knowland from the Senate and the election of Richard Nixon as president in 1968.

Consistently, however, Dirksen refused to reveal or discuss his own financial affairs. That silence aroused suspicion on the part of some, that he might be accepting money from affected interests, or from the law firm in Pekin that he was associated with, for influence he might wield in Washington.

He seemed largely indifferent to money. He and his wife had never owned a home until he was in his sixties, when they built the house in Leesburg. Their home was roomy and comfortable, and pleasing in appearance, but not a mansion by any means. They also had acquired a modest place in Florida that was little used.

They lived simply. Dirksen paid little attention to food, saying he "ate to live." He liked a good drink of bourbon whiskey every day. He dressed carelessly and, after losing forty pounds at one time, went for months before buying new clothes. He usually looked like he had slept in his suit. In 1959, he was named "one of the 10 worst dressed men in the United States!"

When he died in 1969, his estate was valued at between $150,000 and $200,000—not very much for thirty-five years of service in the Congress!

His popularity among the public generally in 1967 and 1968 was greater than ever. Invitations for him to speak came in at the rate of 250 to 300 a month—this in spite of his declining influence in the Senate. In 1968, he was the grand marshall of the Tournament of Roses in Pasadena, California. He appeared on television with the comedian Red Skelton and was given the "High Order of the Open Mouth" by the National Press Club.

In 1968, Dirksen reversed himself on an open housing civil rights bill, of the sort, with modifications, that he had opposed and defeated two years before. He felt that public opinion had advanced sufficiently to allow him to do so. He could not carry the usual number of Republican votes with him, however, and closure was only barely voted so that the bill could move forward.

In the same year, he agreed to support President Johnson's choice of Associate Justice Abe Fortis of the Supreme Court for the position of chief justice. A number of younger senators, led by Robert Griffin, objected, on the ground that the incoming president in 1969 should have that opportunity. Johnson had already made it known that he would not run for reelection in 1968. Dirksen finally reversed his position, and the appointment did not go through. That hurt him badly, politically.

When President Johnson was nearing the end of his time in office, he wrote to Dirksen, saying:

> I leave with a sense of pride in the quality of friends I have made over the years. I am indeed proud to call you "my friend—a good friend, a steadfast friend, a loyal friend. You have helped lighten the load that I have carried as President and you have enriched my life. Thank you, from the bottom of my heart." (Schapsmeier and Schapsmeier, *Dirksen* 220)

Dirksen ran for a fourth term in 1968. The Democrats passed up several likely candidates and put forward one much less well known, leading to the suspicion that neither Mayor Daley of Chicago nor President Johnson wanted to see Dirksen beaten. Neither would accept a candidate who was critical of the U.S. role in Vietnam.

Dirksen's opponent, William G. Clark, became a critic of that role following his nomination, and Mayor Daley and the Chicago Democrats abandoned him. They took the A.F.L.-C.I.O. with them. Even so, Clark did much better at the polls than expected, and Dirksen, who did not return to Illinois to campaign until mid-October, received only 53 percent of the vote.

In 1968, Richard Nixon won the presidency over Hubert Humphrey, and Dirksen's role as minority leader in the Senate changed radically. No longer was he in a position to deliver much needed Republican votes to a Democratic president. Rather than President Johnson socializing with Dirksen, it was President Nixon courting Democrat Wilbur Mills, chairman of the House Committee on Ways and Means. Republican Senator Hugh Scott challenged Dirksen's choice for assistant minority leader and won. That was a substantial blow.

The younger, more liberal Republican senators were restive under Dirksen's leadership. On several occasions, Dirksen differed with Nixon and his administration over appointments, and that harmed his stature as leader. His stance on Vietnam was increasingly outdated. Time was passing him by, and he became more and more frustrated in his leadership role. He played the game as best he could, however, though threatened from several directions.

In August 1969, a chest X ray revealed a spot on Dirksen's lung that had not been present earlier in the summer. On the ground that they needed to know if it was a malignancy, his physicians scheduled exploratory surgery for September 2. His final words on the floor of the Senate were prophetic: "My time has run out."

Only days before the surgery, he completed writing his memoir. That may have been an omen. The operation showed that the tumor was cancerous, and major surgery followed immediately, with the removal of one lobe of Dirksen's right lung. He seemed to rally satisfactorily, but his greatly enlarged and weakened heart failed suddenly, and he died on September 7.

Dirksen's body lay in state in the rotunda of the Capitol. That was an honor that had been accorded only four other senators—Henry Clay, Charles Summer, John A. Logan, and Robert A. Taft. President Nixon eulogized him as a great political leader, and he was taken home to Pekin for burial. Senator Margaret Chase Smith of Maine placed a single marigold blossom on his desk in the Senate.

A greatly enlarged Pekin public library had become the Dirksen Library. In 1968, it was decided to enlarge the Dirksen portion of the library and rename it the Dirksen Congressional Leadership Research Center. Dedicated in 1975 by President Gerald Ford, it has become a significant research resource.

There can be no doubt that Everett McKinley Dirksen was one of this nation's political leaders for at least fifteen years. He came to power under Republican President Dwight D. Eisenhower and saw that power grow when Democrats John F. Kennedy and Lyndon B. Johnson followed Eisenhower to that office. His delivery of Senate minority votes to a president of the other party was of greater significance than similar action when one of his own party was in the White House.

Dirksen was a cunning strategist and a master politician. He understood how the game was played. Infinitely capable of changing direction when events dictated, he took pride in having flexibility of purpose as one of his ruling principles of action.

Some found him too responsive to the need for change. Others found his behavior offensive, a parody of a "Senator Claghorn" in many ways. More and more he was viewed by his younger colleagues as too conservative in his views, too much an agent of the corporate world, and too unresponsive to human needs. His support of President Johnson and U.S. policy in Vietnam harmed his reputation substantially during the last few years of his life.

Dirksen was driven to seek power. Perhaps the fact that his father was invalided when he was five and died four years later, leaving him to grow up in poverty, implanted in him an overwhelming compulsion to seek security through gaining political success in high office. It is clear that his work habits harmed his health and shortened his life. He was a true "workaholic" long before the word came into our vocabulary.

A gradual relinquishing of the reins of power and a graceful retirement in 1969 after three full terms in the Senate might have meant a happier end to Dirksen's political career and might have lengthened his life. But that would have been out of character, would it not? He lived the final years of his life in the only way he knew.

Paul Douglas and Everett Dirksen were almost complete contemporaries in Senate service. The former's years there were 1949 to 1967, the latter's 1951 to 1969. Edward L. Schapsmeier refers to them as "two stellar senators, each a dedicated public servant" (76).

At the same time, there were sharp contrasts between them in personality, political strategy, and background. They tended to agree on the war in Vietnam and on civil rights. They differed greatly on the war in Korea in the early 1950s, but that difference was largely due to the fact that Douglas was in the Senate when the war broke out, and Dirksen was not and was seeking to go there.

The two were vastly different in appearance. Douglas was gaunt, grim visaged, with short white hair. He spoke in a rather raspy voice and often came off as pedantic in style. Dirksen was tousled, smiling, affable, and a noted orator with honeyed tones.

In political discourse within the Senate, Douglas alienated southern Democrats with his views; Dirksen was compromising, pleasant, agreeable. The former was rigid in principle; the latter was pragmatic and conciliatory. It has been said that Douglas "despised" Dirksen; if Dirksen had felt the same way about Douglas, he would never have revealed it. The difference in style that fact represents is significant.

Douglas voted as a thorough-going Democrat but was never a leader within his party in the Senate. He was an idealist, a loner. Dirksen was a party and Senate leader, an adviser to presidents, an Eisenhower "modern Republican," a social moderate, and an economic conservative. Both were strong in support of the civil rights bills and acts of the 1960s.

In a poll taken in 1985 among historians, Dirksen ranked seventh among twenty-five leading senators of all time, and all the states judged according to historical significance. Douglas was not included.

While "each left a legacy of patriotism and public service," each today would be an anachronism in his own party (Schapsmeier 84).

Illinois was fortunate to have had two such senators serving at the same time for the equivalent of two and a half Senate terms.

Ralph Tyler Smith (1969–70)

Ralph T. Smith, as he was generally known until he entered the Senate, was serving as Speaker of the Illinois House of Representatives when he was favored by appointment to the U.S. Senate in 1969, following Dirksen's death in September. He had managed Governor Ogilvie's downstate campaign the previous year. No doubt the governor felt indebted to him.

Smith was a career legislative politician. Born in Granite City, Illinois, on October 6, 1915, he was educated at Illinois College, where he earned a degree in 1937. Three years later, he was granted a law degree by Washington University in St. Louis. He began a law practice in Granite City but soon entered the navy, where he served until 1946.

He resumed the practice of law, in Alton. In 1954, he was elected as a Republican to the first of eight terms in the Illinois House. He became majority whip in 1963 and was elected Speaker in both 1967 and 1969. He enjoyed a good reputation as a hard-working legislator.

Following his appointment to the Senate, Smith worked hard at taking on the mantle of a legislator at that level. He became Ralph Tyler Smith and claimed a distant relationship to President Tyler, for what that was worth. Nothing quite seemed to work well for him in his campaign for confirmation by the voters at the next general election, and he was soundly defeated by State Treasurer Adlai E. Stevenson III in November 1970. Smith received 42.2 percent of the vote.

Since he was to fill an unexpired term, Stevenson took office immediately after the election, and Smith returned to his law practice in Alton. He died there two years later at the age of fifty-seven and was buried in the Sunset Hill Cemetery Mausoleum in Edwardsville.

16 ★ A Modern Republican

In 1970, Illinois, as we have just seen, made the exchange of a Republican senator for one from Democratic ranks. Four years earlier, the tide ran in the opposite direction when Charles H. Percy beat Paul Douglas. Both events seem to be in accord with the image we have of Illinois being politically a "swing" state.

As a result of the latter one of those alternations, again Illinois was represented in the U.S. Senate by both a Republican and a Democrat. In the decade of the 1970s, it was Percy and Stevenson, as during most of the 1950s and into the 1960s it had been Dirksen and Douglas. During all of those years, on balance, it is probable that no state in the Union had better Senate spokesmen, even though there were often great differences between the two who represented Illinois.

Charles Harting Percy (1967–85)

During eighteen years in the U.S. Senate, Charles H. Percy fought for acceptance, understanding, and even sympathy. He wanted to be remembered as a political leader at the highest levels of the federal government. Colleagues, enemies, friends, and helpful critics have denied him the full measure of his wishes and instead have pronounced his period of Senate service as disappointing.

Notwithstanding this judgment, Percy labored to serve. In his own ways, he was mindful of the Illinois constituency and paid attention to its demands and needs. At the same time, he voted an independent line in the Senate, reflecting his long-held belief that senators must consider the national as well as the local interest.

This middle-ground approach to his senatorial duties is a framework for evaluating his outlook on politics. From earliest involvements in Republican Party affairs in the 1950s, Percy steered a middle course in support of state and national leadership. He chose the Dwight Eisenhower model rather than that of Richard Nixon. He backed Nelson Rockefeller rather than Barry Goldwater, Gerald Ford instead of Ronald Reagan. He spoke out for moderation on issues and avoided the extremes. One who follows such a course may not arouse great enmity, but at the same time, he or she does not stir great enthusiasms.

Critics looked at Percy's choices of committee assignments and concluded that he had a self-serving agenda that did not include the interests he represented in Illinois. He never got past an early decision to leave the Appropriations Committee, one of the most powerful in the Senate, for membership on the Foreign Relations Committee, one of the "show horse" committees with little Senate clout.

Political operatives observed those choices and declared Percy to be naive and ineffective. He made no excuses for his allies or positions on issues. Unrepentant, his approach made it difficult for him to build coalitions and a deal-making base among his fellow senators.

Percy charted a course designed to avoid being a captive of narrow interests. He proved that this independent route could win elections as he cobbled together a successful electoral majority from middle-of-the-road voters of both major parties, in 1966, 1972, and 1978. Prior to his tenure, only four Illinoisans in the states's history had served three full terms without interruption.

Finally, timing contributed to the judgment of those who observed Percy as senator. He had the unfortunate circumstance of being a moderate Republican in an increasingly conservative party. Leadership of the G.O.P. from 1967 to 1985 did not appreciate his only nominal support of the party's right wing. Additionally, Percy served all but four of eighteen Senate years in the minority party, where his power would have been limited even if he had played ball with its leadership. Republicans exulted in winning a majority of the Senate in 1980, and Percy soon found himself surrounded by Reaganites.

Charles H. Percy was born on September 27, 1919, in Pensacola, Florida. His family soon moved to the Rogers Park area of Chicago. As a teenager, he worked at a variety of part-time jobs and contributed to the family's meager finances during the Great Depression. During his student years at the University of Chicago, where he received a degree in economics, he earned much of his way by means of his own business ventures. Serving in the navy from 1943 to 1945, he enlisted as a seaman and finished as a lieutenant.

Percy's rapid ascendance to the top of the corporate world is legendary. As a teenager, he had made the acquaintance of Joseph McNabb, a Sunday school teacher in the Wilmette, Illinois, First Church of Christ Scientist. McNabb, president of Bell and Howell, a firm that manufactured movie camera equipment, projectors, and the like, took a liking to the young Percy and hired him for part-time jobs during his college years. After graduation, and again after naval service, Percy worked in full-time capacities at Bell and Howell, eventually in close proximity to McNabb.

McNabb chose Percy as his successor, and shortly after McNabb's death in 1949, Percy became president and chief executive officer of the company. He was twenty-nine years old. The media quickly labeled him the "Whiz Kid of U.S. Business."

Percy held the top position at Bell and Howell until 1963. During that time, the company entered the consumer products camera business. Under his guidance, the firm became highly profitable, and Percy benefited personally. When he left the corporation in 1966 to run for the Senate, he was a millionaire several times over.

In 1943, Percy had married Jeanne Dickerson. In the four years of their marriage—she died in 1947—they became the parents of three children. The oldest were twins, Valerie Jeanne and Sharon, and the third a son, Roger. Percy reared the children on his own for three years before marrying Loraine Guyer in 1950. Together they had three children, Jay, who lived only a week, and Gail and Mark. All five of his children were active in Percy's later political adventures.

On the personal side, Percy believed in a disciplined and orderly life, with an emphasis on physical fitness and a high energy level. He skied and swam and took pride in his good looks and trim body. One friend said in admiration, "He's got a body like a moose" (Hartley, *Percy* 30). To some, that would be a dubious compliment. Percy also took seriously his beliefs in the Church of Christ Scientist.

175

Percy was initiated into Republican Party politics at the national level during the 1950s. He worshipped Dwight Eisenhower from a distance, then up close when the two forged a personal relationship during the president's second term. Eisenhower had a reputation for befriending corporate leaders.

Through the Eisenhower connection, Percy met people who formed the moderate wing of the Republican Party. He gave Eisenhower credit for turning him toward politics. "General Eisenhower was the controlling influence that caused me to come into public life. He was the only man who could have caused me to seek elective office" (Hartley, *Percy* 38).

The other significant relationship for Percy that came out of those years was with Vice President Richard Nixon. They were thrown together as the party prepared for the end of the Eisenhower years and the 1960 Nixon campaign for the presidency. The two had a testy relationship from the beginning, one that was renewed in 1969, when Nixon became president.

Percy made his first run for public elective office in 1964 against incumbent Illinois Governor Otto Kerner, a product of the Chicago Democratic organization. It was a bad time for his debut, for no Republican was going to do well with Barry Goldwater at the head of the national ticket.

Democrats held most of the state offices in Illinois, and it was a landslide year for the party at the national level, with Lyndon Johnson thrashing Goldwater for the presidency. It might have been a minor piece of the Percy picture except for the bitterness of the Republican campaign and the animosities that arose between Percy and the traditional party conservatives in Illinois.

Before running against Kerner, Percy had to defeat an aggressive conservative Republican primary opponent, William J. Scott. Later Scott served as Illinois attorney general and became a political ally of Percy. In 1964, Scott made an issue of party loyalty and ideology, casting Percy as a beginner in politics and a moderate to boot. Percy survived the challenge, but afterward, Scott partisans who remained active in state affairs rarely gave him the benefit of the doubt.

On the national level, however, the media took a look at candidate Percy and liked what they saw. *Time* magazine gushed in 1964:

Chuck Percy really looks and acts the part of the Algeresque hero. . . . He has frank brown eyes, a frank, open face, a trim exercise-toned body. He is hard-working, fun loving, self-disciplined and perfectly organized. He reads deep think books, takes religion, politics and self-improvement seriously. . . . He neither smokes nor drinks.

Percy may have basked in that glow, but party workers at the precinct and county level in Illinois did not think much of such praise. They called him "Mr. Prissy."

Kerner prevailed against Percy, but the challenger took 49 percent of the vote and lost by only 179,000. Percy had shown doubters and detractors that he could get votes across the prairies of Illinois. As soon as the gubernatorial contest was over, Percy began running for the Senate against incumbent Paul Douglas, whose third term would end in 1967.

Percy first met Douglas at the University of Chicago, when he was a student there and the other was a professor of economics. By 1966, Douglas had begun to show his age, although he was an energetic and healthy seventy-four year old. Percy, exuding youth and a beaming smile, with a wrinkle-free face and melodic voice, was forty-six. As the campaign went on, Douglas seemed to tire more easily than he had in the past, and the contrast between the two was more apparent.

Initially cordial, the campaign became a bruising battle. Public opinion polls showed the two contestants nearly equal by mid-September. Feeling was that it would go on that way until election day. But fate intervened on September 18 to make a difference.

During the early morning of that day, an intruder entered the Percy home in Kenilworth and murdered the candidate's daughter, twenty-one-year-old Valerie Jeanne, in her bed. The crime and its aftermath seriously altered the political landscape. Douglas immediately halted his campaign and urged his Chicago operatives to refrain from criticizing Percy. When the campaign resumed, the story remained in the headlines, generating sympathy for Percy, and he won 56 percent of the vote. After three terms in the Senate, Douglas's political career was ended.

The shadow of Valerie's murder hung over the Percy family for years while investigations meandered on without resolution. The family finally asked officials to halt inquiries and put the matter to rest. Although no individual was charged or tried, the Percys believed the culprit had died in prison, there on conviction for another crime.

Percy's first term in the Senate focused in large part on relationships with two major national political figures, Richard M. Nixon and Everett M. Dirksen. Percy's standing with Nixon had reached a low point when he announced his support for Nelson Rockefeller for the Republican nomination for president of the United States. After Nixon became president and until his resignation in 1974, he and Percy clashed over military expenditures, party loyalty, Supreme Court appointments, the Vietnam war, and other issues.

Meanwhile, Percy and Dirksen performed a delicate dance until the senior senator's death in 1969. Outwardly supportive of his younger colleague, Dirksen and his aides did not trust Percy and did not go out of their way to make the new senator's first years in the Senate easy ones. They disagreed on issues, choice of judges, and behavior in the Senate. Still, at Dirksen's memorial service, Percy said, in eulogizing his colleague:

> His secret perhaps was that, while a master of the reasonable compromise, he would never compromise a principle—and he would never ask another man to do so. . . . Before I came to Washington, he said that, whenever conscience dictated, we should simply agree to disagree, and he always honored that principle between us. (Hartley, *Percy* 173)

Percy's first term was not especially productive, in the Nixon environment, but the senator showed his strength at the polls when he ran for reelection in 1972. Against Roman Pucinski, a former Chicago alderman, member of Congress, and strong supporter of Mayor Daley, he racked up a huge plurality with 62 percent of the vote.

On two occasions in his early Senate years, Percy allowed his dream of being president to be apparent. One occurred shortly after he was first elected and generated little more than conversation. The second was more serious, at least from Percy's point of view. After his reelection in 1972, and at the first rumors of Watergate, Percy formed an exploratory committee and talked of seeking the Republican presidential nomination in 1976.

Before long, events at the White House changed the picture and ended Percy's effort. With the appointment of Gerald Ford as vice president, and then Nixon's resignation in 1974 and Ford's becoming president, it became obvious that the next nominee would be a gentleman from Michigan, not Illinois.

Percy found a soul mate in President Ford. Although Ford had a record of conservatism in the House of Representatives, he turned out to be a moderate president. Percy backed him on many issues, spoke glowingly of his importance to the nation, and worked diligently in 1976 to make sure the Illinois delegation cast most of its votes in the party's national convention for Ford rather than for Ronald Reagan.

Percy continued his interest in international affairs and foreign policy, becoming a supporter of and believer in the policies and initiatives of Henry Kissinger. He traveled regularly and, in 1975, visited the Mideast. That visit created a rift between Percy and American Jews and supporters of Israel that dogged him to the end of his days in the Senate.

After visiting with Palestinian leader Arafat, Percy had declared that an independent Palestinian homeland was necessary for Mideast peace. Further, he was quoted as labeling Arafat as a moderate. Forever after he denied saying that, but he was unable to correct that impression. He claimed that he said Arafat was "relatively moderate as compared with George Habash," the Marxist who was Arafat's major rival at that time. Jewish people in the Chicago area were incensed by Percy's positions and punished him at the polls in 1978 and 1984.

The next serious electoral challenge to Percy came in 1978 as he sought a third term. With Democrats again in power in Washington, and an off-year Senate race, the negatives for Percy loomed larger than they had in previous elections. Literally out of nowhere, a millionaire attorney from Chicago, Democrat Alex Seith, took full advantage of Percy's weaknesses and nearly defeated him.

Seith attacked Percy for not paying enough attention to Illinois concerns, taking committee assignments that did not benefit the state, and focusing on international rather than domestic issues. Critics in Washington said Percy was weak on day-to-day and behind-the-scenes work and that cutting deals was boring for him. After the election, Congressman Paul Simon of Illinois, a Democrat, said, "Percy wasn't touching bases back home as frequently as he should" (Isikoff 8).

During the campaign in 1978, Percy could not shake Seith and leave him behind in the public opinion polls. A month before election day, the race was a dead heat, and shortly thereafter, Seith was seen to have a lead over the incumbent. In an eleventh-hour desperation move, Percy went on statewide television to beg for his political life. He said, "I got the message," and he promised to be more attentive to the needs of Illinois citizens. It was a rare view of a U.S. senator groveling for his job. It worked. Percy's plea brought him a plurality of about 250,000 votes, with 53.3 percent of the total number cast.

Afterward, observers wondered aloud what Percy would do with a Democrat in the White House and his party still in the minority in the Senate. He held a ranking minority position on the Senate Operations Committee, but it had almost nothing to do with Illinois concerns. It looked as if Percy might serve out a third term with no better opportunity for leadership than before.

The victory of Ronald Reagan over President Jimmy Carter in 1980 changed all that. Suddenly Republicans controlled the Senate as well, and Percy had his pick of committee chairmanships. With the defeat of liberal Republican Jacob Javits, Percy was next in line to chair the Foreign Relations Committee. He also had top seniority on the Operations Committee. For Percy, the internationalist, it was not a hard decision. He became chairman of Foreign Relations early in the presidency of a man who had taken dead aim at communism and the Soviet Union.

Percy worked hard at being a team player with Reagan and his aides. They did not like having him in the foreign relations chair, but they could do little about it. Percy tried to accommodate Reagan's policies abroad, but in the end, he went off on his own with trips to Russia and other nations.

Percy's public statements often appeared to be in conflict with Reagan's goals, and he explained that he did not speak for the administration. Clearly, however, he enjoyed his position. He had the authority of a committee chair that pertained to the subject of his greatest interest.

The year 1984 came quickly, and Percy again was in the thick of a campaign for election to his fourth term. Reporters remembered that he had ended Paul Douglas's hopes of a similar gain in seniority in 1966. The person standing in Percy's way was a widely known and respected five-term veteran of the U.S. House of Representatives, Paul Simon. The congressman earned his right to run against Percy by surviving a Democratic primary election.

Simon picked up where Seith had stopped six years earlier. He did it with the backing of a supportive Chicago Democratic organization and a record of thirty years duration in Illinois electoral politics. He challenged Percy's constituency by pursuing black and Jewish votes in Chicago, as well as courting labor. It helped Simon's cause for Percy to have had a conservative primary challenge from Congressman Tom Corcoran, which drained the senator's resources and put his weak standing with conservatives on the front burner.

Percy defended President Reagan in his campaigning, calling him "my president," and pointed to Simon's liberal voting as out of touch with reality. They slugged it out until election day, when Simon upset Percy by about ninety thousand votes, taking 50.1 percent of the total.

In defeat, as in victory, Charles Percy confounded many among both his supporters and his opponents. Public comments by two Percy loyalists, in the *Washington Post Magazine* in 1981, provide some insight for assessing the senator's approach to public office.

Calvin Fentress, a Percy family favorite and an aide to the senator, said:

> He has the decency and the essential instincts, and when he's committed to something he'll say, "Hey, wait a minute!" He'll go along but only up to a point, and then he'll drive the administration crazy, he'll drive his colleagues crazy, but he'll be a lot more fun that way than when he's the team player. (McPherson 23)

Percy's daughter Sharon, the wife of U.S. Senator John D. Rockefeller IV, of West Virginia, added:

> As soon as you've described his qualities, his good points and his less good points, they don't seem to add up. All those parts are true and even consistent—they're not as mutually exclusive as they appear to be—yet they don't add up to a whole that is easy to understand. No one is simple, certainly not my father. (McPherson 23)

Percy spent his years following the eighteen he had given to the Senate in consulting work with foreign governments and leaders on the international scene. He lives in the Georgetown section of Washington, D.C., and maintains an active social life in the nation's capital.

17 ★ Ending an Illinois Tradition?

Perhaps the nearest thing Illinois has had to a "royal family" in politics has been the participation, for more than a century, of the Stevenson family in the public life of the state. The tradition began with the first Adlai Ewing Stevenson, who was state's attorney of Woodford County during the Civil War. By 1874, he had moved back to Bloomington and was elected to Congress as a candidate of the Greenback Party. Its single plank was an expansion of the currency by means of printing paper dollars. He was elected to Congress again in 1878, as a Democrat as well as a Greenbacker. Along the way, he lost at the polls three times.

When Democrat Grover Cleveland was elected president in 1884, he appointed former Congressman Stevenson first assistant postmaster general, with the specific assignment of firing forty thousand Republican post office employees. His performance in that task earned him the label "the Headsman!"

He must have carried out that duty effectively, for when Cleveland ran again in 1892, Stevenson was his running mate. In his role as the "headsman," he had acted pleasantly, giving a minimum of offense to those who lost their jobs. The Democratic ticket carried the day, and Stevenson brought the same affable personality to the office of vice president. As was often the case with vice presidents, his four years in that office were an exercise in obscurity.

Stevenson ran again for vice president in 1900, this time with William Jennings Bryan at the head of the ticket. The two were defeated by William McKinley, elected president for a second term, and Theodore Roosevelt, soon to become president following McKinley's assassination.

Stevenson was his party's candidate for governor in 1908 and lost by only 23,164 votes to the Republican incumbent, Charles S. Deneen. That was his "last hurrah" in seeking public office. He died in 1914.

Stevenson's son Lewis married into the family that owned Bloomington's principal newspaper, the *Pantagraph*. A friend of William Randolph Hearst, he worked for one of the Hearst papers in California and managed Hearst-owned copper mines in Arizona. Returning to Illinois, he followed his father into politics. He had been his father's secretary during the time he was vice president.

According to John Bartlow Martin, a Stevenson biographer, Lewis "never really amounted to much" (32). He attended Phillips Exeter Academy in New Hampshire but did not go to college. He resented Bloomington, and there is evidence that Bloomington resented him. After his time in the West, he managed farms in the area, most of them owned by members of his family.

Lewis Stevenson was appointed state pardons board chairman by Governor Dunne and, in 1913, was appointed secretary of state to fill a vacancy due to the death of the elected incumbent. He ran for that office on the Democratic ticket in 1916, unsuccessfully. That was the end of his career in elective politics. He hung on at the fringes of politics for a time. He died in 1929 and was buried in Bloomington beside his father.

Before he died, Lewis Stevenson advised his son, Adlai Ewing, "never to go into politics—it was an ungrateful business" (Martin 93). That advice went unheeded, for the second Adlai E. Stevenson was to become governor of Illinois in 1949 and twice the candidate of the Democratic Party for president of the United States.

Born in Los Angeles in 1900, the future governor spent most of his boyhood in Bloomington and attended the university high school there for three years. Then he was sent to Choate Preparatory School in Connecticut and from Choate, after two years, to Princeton. The atmosphere at Princeton can be suggested by the fact that F. Scott Fitzgerald and Richard Halliburton were students at about the same time. In many ways, it was a carefree, country club sort of life. Adlai's greatest distinction was becoming managing editor of the university's daily newspaper in his senior year.

An oddity of his college years was that his mother and sister Buffie came to live in the village of Princeton. That fact reminds one that such famous persons as Winston Churchill, Franklin D. Roosevelt, and Douglas MacArthur also suffered much attention from their mothers during their higher educations.

Adlai graduated near the middle of his class. At his father's insistence, he then enrolled in the Harvard Law School. He found the work there difficult, often complained of it, and ended by flunking out after two years. He went back to Bloomington to work for the *Pantagraph,* the newspaper owned by the Stevenson and Merwin families. Control of the paper was for years a matter of legal struggle between them.

In 1925, he enrolled in the Northwestern University Law School. There he did much better than at Harvard and graduated the following spring. He then traveled in Europe, as he had during and after Princeton, and returned near the end of 1926 to practice law in Chicago with the firm later called Sidley and Austin, one of the most respected in the city.

In 1928, Stevenson married Ellen Borden. Soon he became interested in the work of the Chicago Council on Foreign Relations and gave it considerable attention. Bored with the law in Chicago, he went to Washington, D.C., in 1933 to work in the Department of Agriculture. Later he was employed in the Navy Department and then in the State Department during the time the United Nations organization was being formed. Between Washington assignments, he returned from time to time to his family, his law office in Chicago, and his interest in the Council on Foreign Relations.

When World War II had ended and Stevenson's assignment with the United Nations was finished, he found the law office tame for his taste and aspired to run as a Democratic candidate for the U.S. Senate in 1948. Paul Douglas, an independent-minded professor of economics at the University of Chicago, had his sights set on the gubernatorial contest. He had been a thorn in the flesh of Chicago Democrats while serving a term on the city council.

The regular Democrats wanted Douglas out of Chicago and out of Illinois. Their king-maker at the time, Jacob Arvey, brokered an arrangement in which Douglas would run for the Senate, the position Stevenson wanted, and Stevenson would run for governor, the position Douglas wanted.

Both agreed to the switch, and in November 1948, with a faltering Republican presence, both were elected. While Harry Truman carried Illinois by only 33,612 votes, Douglas was prevailing over Curley Brooks by 407,728, and Stevenson was winning over Dwight Green by more than a half million votes, a record at the time. It is apparent that Illinois was ripe for political change.

Stevenson as governor was a novice in both state politics and state affairs. Much of his first two years was spent in learning his way around the bureaucracy and the legislature. Robert Howard states that he was "fairly successful with a legislative program. . . . He practiced fiscal . . . economy. . . . His . . . supporters could claim that the moral climate of state government had improved" (*Mostly* 275).

Stevenson claimed to want a second term as governor, but fate intervened; instead, he was nominated by the Democratic national convention in 1952 for the office of president of the United States. He appeared to shrink from that duty, but the record shows that he wanted and actively sought it. In the November election, he lost to General Eisenhower, 55.1 percent to 44.4 percent in the popular vote, a difference of over six and a half million, and 442 to 89 in the electoral college. His term as governor ended soon after.

While Governor Stevenson was the titular head of the Democratic Party in the United States during the years that followed, he never achieved real command either in Illinois or nationally. That is not surprising. He did provide leadership to a considerable segment of the voters, by means of his speeches and other public pronouncements.

In 1956, Stevenson actively sought and won the Democratic presidential nomination for a second time. In the opinion of his biographer John Bartlow Martin, who wrote speeches for him, the 1956 campaign against President Eisenhower was a better, more issue-oriented one than four years earlier.

Still, Stevenson lost in 1956 by a greater margin than in 1952, even though he was much better known. The second time around, his percentage of the vote fell, with Eisenhower taking 57.7 percent of the popular vote and 457 votes in the electoral college to Stevenson's 73. The latter did not carry a single northern state. The president's plurality—over nine and a half million votes—was historically second only to Franklin Roosevelt's in 1936. It is now

generally known that the Chicago Democratic organization abandoned Stevenson in a political sense before the election. Eisenhower
crushed him in Illinois.

Stevenson continued his speaking and writing as an expert in
foreign affairs. Even though he wanted the nomination again in
1960, he would not actively seek it. Time had passed him by, and
a newer generation had come forward. John Fitzgerald Kennedy
carried the Democratic banner to an exceedingly narrow margin of
victory, one that many believe was corruptly obtained, over Vice
President Richard Nixon.

Stevenson hoped and expected to be appointed secretary of
state. Kennedy, however, had other plans. Instead, Stevenson was
named ambassador to the United Nations. There, the necessity of
defending such actions as the "Bay of Pigs" attempted invasion of
Cuba tarnished Stevenson's reputation. U.S. policy in Vietnam became an increasing burden to him.

Adlai E. Stevenson II died in 1965 of a heart attack on a Lon-
don street. His funeral service was held in the National Cathedral
in Washington. Then his body was taken to Springfield, where it
lay in state in the rotunda of the Capitol. There he was further
eulogized, with Governor Otto Kerner saying, "Adlai Stevenson of
Illinois has returned."

He was buried in the Bloomington Cemetery near his forebears.

Adlai Ewing Stevenson III (1970–80)

Adlai E. Stevenson III, a numerical designation he did not favor
during his political lifetime, was born on October 10, 1930, in Chicago. He was the oldest of three sons of Adlai E. and Ellen Borden
Stevenson. Like his father and grandfather, Adlai attended preparatory school in the East. His was the Milton Academy in Massachusetts. There his marks were below the level that his perceived ability suggested, and despite his father's earnest efforts, he did not gain
admission to Princeton. Instead, he went to Harvard, where he
graduated on schedule in June 1952.

Adlai went into the U.S. Marine Corps and served during 1953
and 1954 in Korea and Japan. A commissioned officer, he commanded a tank platoon. From there he enrolled in the Harvard Law
School and received a law degree in 1957. In the year that followed,
he served as a law clerk to Judge Walter V. Schaefer of the Illinois
Supreme Court.

Judge Schaefer had been a close associate of Adlai's father and assisted him in his campaigns. During Adlai II's term as governor, Schaefer had headed for him a "little Hoover" commission, which studied the administrative organization of Illinois government. A number of its recommendations—but none of its most important ones—were made into law. Eventually, Judge Schaefer served as chief justice and was for many years a highly respected member of the Illinois Supreme Court.

Following his year with Judge Schaefer, Adlai III joined a law firm in Chicago and eventually became a partner in it. Thus far, his career was proceeding predictably, much after the pattern his father had set. There was speculation about the state and nation as to what his plans on entering politics might be.

That question was answered in 1964. It was a political year unique in all of Illinois history. A failure of the legislature to redraw district lines for the state House of Representatives, as the state constitution required it to do after each decennial census, led to the election of every member of the House *at large,* by the voters of the whole state.

That was accomplished by allowing each of the two major political parties to draw up, in convention, a list of 118 nominees for the 177 House seats. Voters then could mark as many as 177 individual candidate names from the two party lists, or any lesser number of them, or could mark a party circle to cast a vote for each candidate of that party, making a total of 118, and let it go at that, or could mark a party circle and then up to 59 names from the other party list, up to a total of 177. If all that sounds confusing, it was then and is now.

But one thing it did was allow each major party to pick and choose its 118 candidates without holding a primary election. It was a throwback to the old nineteenth-century practice of nomination by party caucus. And it permitted young Adlai Stevenson to make a running start in politics without going through the grimy business of working his way up from the bottom of the political hierarchy. His father had been able to do the same in 1948 in being anointed for governor by Chicago Democrats in need of a "reform" candidate.

After all, the first Adlai had been vice president, his son Illinois secretary of state, and *his* son, also Adlai, governor. The name could not fail to garner a great many votes for Adlai III, no matter how well or little known to the voters he may have been. No doubt many who voted for him in 1964 did so thinking they were voting for his father, and some with good long-term memories but less recollection of yesterday's headlines—a "senior moment"—may even have confused him with his great-grandfather.

In the same way, an unknown William G. Stratton had been elected congressman-at-large from Illinois in 1940, with many thinking they were voting for his father, William J. Stratton, who had been Illinois secretary of state from 1929 to 1933—no matter that the elder Stratton had been dead for two years. Nor did it matter that Adlai II in 1966, the year his son ran for the office of state treasurer, had been dead for one. The name in each case meant thousands of votes, even though its current bearer may have been completely unknown. That is proven by the fact that in 1964, in his first campaign, young Adlai was the leading vote getter of both party's at-large legislative tickets.

With that beginning, Stevenson's political career was launched. Two years later he ran for state treasurer and won. In 1968, he

> hankered after nomination to higher office . . . but found the state [Democratic] organization of another mind. When Mr. Stevenson couldn't endorse President Johnson's Vietnam policies to the satisfaction of Mayor Daley [of Chicago], the party found in turn that it couldn't endorse Mr. Stevenson for either governor or [U.S.] senator. One columnist reported that he didn't pass the "saliva" test. So he bided his time and went on building his own political base. (Kenney, *Basic* [1st ed.] 187)

Two years later his circumstances had changed. Everett Dirksen was dead, and Ralph T. Smith had been appointed by Republican Governor Richard Ogilvie to fill Dirksen's shoes in the Senate until the next general election. That came in 1970.

By 1970, "Stevenson had assumed leadership of a liberal revolt against what he had called the Democratic party's 'feudal' system in Cook county" (Howard, *Illinois* 187). He planned to announce his candidacy for the Senate at a picnic at the Stevenson "farm" near Libertyville, in Lake County. The Chicago Democrats had been weakened by the disorders accompanying the national convention of their party in their city in 1968.

Mayor Daley appeared unexpectedly at the Stevenson political rally and gave his blessing to Stevenson's candidacy for the Senate. Ever the pragmatic politician, he may have seen Stevenson as too great a threat to be slighted again. In return, in his campaign, Stevenson moved toward the political center and called for an end to violence on the part of his student supporters.

In an often repeated story, Stevenson sat down with one of his father's more reliable advisers and asked, "[I]f you could give me just one piece of advice, what would it be?" After a long silence, his friend replied, "Adlai, don't change your name!"

The name no doubt helped. Stevenson was elected in a Democratic landslide. The new income tax initiated during Republican Governor Ogilvie's administration hurt that party at the polls. Ralph Smith had no statewide presence to match that called up by the name "Adlai Stevenson." The new senator assumed office on the day after the general election because he was filling an unexpired term.

Senator Stevenson went to Washington, D.C., with the credentials of a liberal, largely on the basis of his father's reputation, although much of the latter's program as governor tended toward middle or conservative ground. The senator himself was seeking middle ground as early as the 1968 Democratic national convention, when he sought to bring together dovish followers of Eugene McCarthy and hawklike supporters of President Johnson.

He displayed similar tastes when in 1972 he backed Edmund Muskie for the presidential nomination as long as it was practical to do so and went to George McGovern only at the last moment. In the Senate, he tended to be a pragmatist and, at the same time, spoke of "reforming" government, whatever that might mean.

His pragmatism caused him to remain on a professionally cooperative basis with Mayor Daley and the Chicago organization he had once called a "feudal system." That relationship in turn tended to turn away some would-be Stevenson supporters who could not abide the mayor. It caused a certain coolness between the senator and Democrat Dan Walker, who became governor in 1973. He and Daley were at odds with one another, an alienation that grew deeper and wider as time went on.

Thus, reform and pragmatism tended to define the Stevenson style during his first term in the Senate (Hartley, "Middle" 28). It was abbreviated because he had been elected to complete the term that Dirksen began in 1969.

Stevenson's opponent in 1974 was a little-known Republican named George Burditt. By that time, Watergate was beginning to hamper Republican campaign efforts all over the nation, and Stevenson was one of the beneficiaries. He won easily with 62.2 percent of the vote.

Secure in the Senate for a full second term, Stevenson began in 1975 to edge over into the realm of international affairs, perhaps a signal that he was thinking of the presidency. Notable in that year was an attack on Secretary of State Henry Kissinger. In a speech at Jersey City College in February, Stevenson said:

> History has overtaken the personal diplomacy of Henry Kissinger. Impressionable members of the Congress and the press have awakened to the truth: his personal diplomacy . . . is threatening to make of the U.S. the apparition Mr. Nixon most feared—a pitiful, helpless giant. (News Release, 2/11/75)

Late in 1975, however, he announced that he "would not seek" the nomination of his party for president or vice president in 1976. Apparently, there had been some expressions of support from various quarters in Illinois. He shrank from subjecting himself and his family to yet another broad campaign effort. He did not wish to reduce the attention he could give to matters in the Senate. And he was critical of the process by which nominations were determined and campaigns carried out (News Release, 11/24/75).

That action seemed to remove him from any consideration yet did not rule out a groundswell of opinion such as the one that had claimed his father's participation in 1952. In fact, the reluctance of the son reminds one of the reluctance of the father.

That he might be "drafted" in 1976 remained a possibility. "If Adlai had as much charisma as the catsup bottle, he'd be a shoo-in for the presidency," Democrat Mike Howlett, Illinois secretary of state, had remarked earlier in the year. Still, Stevenson lacked the image in the public mind that a candidate for the presidency needed in order to be successful, and he probably knew it. Four more years in the Senate to develop his public persona might make it a different matter in 1980 (Hartley, "Adlai").

Still, after Jimmy Carter had been nominated by the Democratic national convention in 1976, and Stevenson's name was floated among those being considered as a running mate, he took the matter seriously and spoke to the media about his qualifications. He seemed to wish to be considered.

He was not chosen, of course. Walter Mondale was. Stevenson came away from the experience with a bitter taste in his mouth not because he had not been chosen by Carter but because of the way he had been treated by Carter's staff. The columnist Mike Royko reported one incident as follows:

> I happened to be in the lobby of Carter's hotel when Jerry Rafshoon, Carter's propaganda specialist, stopped and chatted with a few of us.
>
> We asked him about Adlai's chances. Rafshoon sneered . . . and said something to the effect that Adlai wasn't bright enough to find the men's room.
>
> Similar comments drifted out of other Carter sources. Some of them found their way into print. Sneering, arrogant, and patronizing remarks. ("Adlai")

What especially hurt Stevenson, Royko believed, was that the Carter staff was basically a band of political amateurs, fresh out of a Georgia political setting and with far less sophistication than the senator possessed. They had taken advantage of his eagerness to be chosen as Carter's running mate to demean him. All of that was to be remembered as time went on and especially four years later ("Adlai").

Following the death of Mayor Daley late in 1976, Stevenson became more assertive. He seemed to be freed from a certain restraint. During the Democratic national convention, he had remarked to a reporter that "some people say I am my grandfather's grandson. Some people say I am my father's son. And some people say I am Mayor Daley's pet rock" (Kelly 12).

Stevenson had formed a necessary alliance with Mayor Daley in order to be elected in 1970 and again in 1974, and with the latter's death in 1976, that connection was severed. Some of his friends who disliked Daley the politician were relieved.

Stevenson was becoming part of the Senate leadership structure by 1977. He was chairman of the Senate Ethics Committee and led an effort to restructure the Senate committee system. He was on the Select Committee on Intelligence, which provided oversight of the Central Intelligence Agency. He was becoming more of a party loyalist yet retained the role of critic of policies with which he found fault. He seemed to be maturing as a senator, and to be gaining a certain presence in the public mind.

And he was becoming less liberal. In the annual rating that Americans for Democratic Action made of all members of Congress, in 1974, he scored 100 percent. Two years later that mark had fallen to 60 percent. He was backing more conservative figures in intra-Senate politics.

As the Carter administration went about the nation's business, Stevenson became increasingly restive in the face of its mistakes. In one speech, he declared the president to be in "over his head" and surrounded by "bush leaguers."

Don Rose, a "widely known political strategist," described Stevenson in 1979 as "a generally retiring, slightly intellectual man, stodgy for his years" (8). He came from a liberal tradition, Rose believed, but was increasingly on the side of the monetarists and free-market economists. He appeared to be increasingly frustrated in the Senate and toying with the idea of making a run for the presidency in 1980.

Rose suggested that "Adlai's offenses are procedural, not substantive. He is not a good politician among politicians." "He has a tendency to be abrupt, impatient and 'moralistic'" (11), according to an aid to another senator. He seems often to seek "to offend." These qualities had reduced his chances to become a real leader in Senate affairs.

At five o'clock on a Friday afternoon, March 30, 1979, a time of the week least likely to attract media attention, Stevenson issued a 140-word news bulletin stating that he would not seek another term in the Senate. His reasons for giving up such a coveted and often prized office were not clearly stated. He seemed to friends to feel that little could be accomplished in the Senate, that it was not at center stage in the affairs of the nation.

Presumably, Stevenson yearned after higher office. Yet it appeared that he had no intention of seeking the presidency in any conventional way. William Furlong pointed out in 1979 that Stevenson was leaving the Senate not because it wasn't fun but because it wasn't significant. He, Furlong wrote, "is, by nature, a drudge. . . . Fun is not a word that comes [easily] to his mind. He spends most of his waking hours . . . going around with the expectant look of a man who has just been invited to be the guest of honor at a public execution" (174).

Furlong recalled that Mike Royko had done perhaps the best job of summarizing the Stevenson persona in a column written about the time Stevenson won election to a second term. It went like this:

The most dangerous element in our politics is charisma. It makes people get glassy-eyed and scream and clap without a thought in their heads. Adlai never does that.

He makes people drowsy. His hair is thinning. He has all the oratorical fire of an algebra teacher.

His clothes look like something he bought from the coroner's office. When he feels good he looks like he has a virus.

We need more politicians who make our blood run tepid. (176)

Would he run for governor in 1982? He had no intention of doing so, was the implication. On the other hand, he did not seem to be entirely ruling anything out. He had the one-thousand-acre farm in Jo Daviess County with its 250 head of cattle to retire to if he chose (Furlong 176).

I (Kenney) was in Governor James Thompson's inner office, talking with the governor, during a late spring afternoon in 1981, when the governor took a telephone call, something he seldom did while he was talking with a cabinet officer. From the conversation, it was apparent that he was speaking to Adlai Stevenson. Of course, I listened closely, all the while trying to appear disinterested.

Near the end of the telephone conversation, which was mostly small talk, the governor brightened perceptibly. When he put the telephone down, he turned to me and said happily, "That was Adlai Stevenson telling me he was not going to run for governor next year!"

Before 1981 ended, however, Governor Thompson learned differently. Stevenson filed in December for the Democratic primary for governor. Needless to say, he won the nomination, and he and Thompson squared off for the campaign.

Stevenson's efforts were inept. His opponent had set a record margin of victory in his first election to the office and, in his second, had set another for a reelection plurality. By 1982, Thompson was a thoroughly seasoned campaigner. As late as mid-October, it appeared to some that Stevenson would be badly embarrassed when the votes were counted early in November.

It did not turn out that way at all. A massive turnout of black voters, as they looked forward to the mayoral election the following spring, helped Stevenson take 74 percent of the vote in Chicago. Concern over the economy and support for the perceived underdog probably also helped him. The outcome was in doubt for several days while the count was being completed.

It was not until the state supreme court decided against order-
ing a recount that Thompson was declared the winner by a margin
statewide of 5,074 votes. The day its decision came down, Thompson ended a luncheon talk with "God bless the Supreme Court!"
The magic of the Stevenson name had almost done it again.

But that is to get ahead of our story. In 1980, while Stevenson
was serving his last year in the Senate, his party was to nominate
its candidate for president and try to win the election in the fall.
He had made it clear at the time he announced his decision to leave
the Senate that he was unhappy with the Carter presidency. "The
entire world," he had said then, is "trembling," but America is led
by an "embarrassingly weak" president who is "surrounded in the
White House by bush leaguers" (Kaiser).

It almost seemed that Stevenson was readying himself to announce his candidacy. Still he stopped short of doing so. At a break-
fast meeting for reporters and news makers hosted by Godfrey Sperling of the *Christian Science Monitor,* after Stevenson had spoken,
Sperling observed that "'it seems to me that you have dealt too much
with nuances.' That was a polite expression of bafflement" (Kaiser).

Nothing came of it. Stevenson did not mount a candidacy in 1980
for the Democratic nomination and eventually ruled out a third party
effort. He appeared to be a "wannabe" candidate in search of an
invitation to run. None was forthcoming. His term in the Senate
ended early in 1981, and he came back to Illinois to brood over his
future and eventually to launch his effort to become governor.

The fact was that Stevenson did not like the rough and tumble
of politics. The following anecdote is an example of that dislike:
When I (Kenney) was serving in the Thompson cabinet in 1977, I
was invited to attend the Sunday afternoon dedication of a nature
preserve in southern Cook County. I accepted gladly, especially so
because I had been told that Senator Stevenson would be present.

When I arrived at the site, there was a sizable group already assembled. I asked to be taken to the senator so that I could pay my
respects. To my surprise I was led not to a cluster of eager citizens
but to an automobile, where Stevenson sat alone in the backseat.

And there he remained until near the time he was to speak. He
spoke in a monotone not likely to arouse any enthusiasm. I was
perplexed. I could not fully understand the senator's reluctance to
mingle joyfully with his constituents, pressing the flesh and cement-
ing friendships that might prove useful. Reflection on the record of

Stevenson's father brought the understanding that the two were quite similar in their views of the political system and how it ought to work. In this case, truly "the apple did not fall far from the tree."

Following his near victory over Governor Thompson in 1982, Stevenson made his "residence" on his farm at Hanover and practiced law in Chicago. He took part in the necessary associations that would preserve his claim to a later gubernatorial nomination. He exercised that claim in 1986. Surely, many felt, this time he would be elected governor.

He did win the Democratic nomination, but in a primary election that contained a discrepancy that hinged upon a flaw in the state constitution. It was "one of the strangest episodes of Illinois political history" (Kenney, *Basic* [3rd ed.] 93). In the Democratic primary, for lieutenant governor, the voters preferred an unknown rather than the "slated" candidate. Perhaps it was because of his boy-next-door name, Mark Fairchild. Many voters might have believed that someone with a name like that must be a virtuous and deserving candidate.

The fact was that *this* Mark Fairchild happened to be an avowed follower of the political extremist Lyndon H. LaRouche Jr. His views simply were not acceptable to mainstream Democrats. The Illinois constitution, however, stated that the candidates of each party for governor and lieutenant governor had to run as a unit, with each voter casting one vote for the unit of his or her choice.

This meant that if Stevenson were to accept the nomination of the Democratic Party for governor, his running mate, Fairchild, would be a "disciple of a man who professed to believe that Queen Elizabeth was a drug pusher, that Henry Kissinger was a Russian agent, and that the International Monetary Fund was responsible for AIDS" (Kenney, *Basic* [3rd ed.] 94).

Stevenson vowed that one way or another he would avoid being teamed with Fairchild in the election. None of his alternatives were suitable, and he ended by giving up the Democratic nomination and forming a third party, which was called Solidarity! Some pointed out that even the party name demonstrated Stevenson's political ineptness, evocative as it was of communist Poland.

The result was predictable. Stevenson lost to Thompson by almost four hundred thousand votes. The Democrats made no effort to win votes for their pair for governor and lieutenant governor, but the other Democrats on the statewide ballot won smashing victories. That suggests that if the Fairchild incident had not occurred, Stevenson would have had a chance to win. As it was, it was an ignominious defeat and a sorry ending to an Illinois political dynasty that had endured for over one hundred years.

Adlai Stevenson went back to Chicago to his law practice, and on weekends to his farm. His law firm was Mayer, Brown and Platt, since 1958. He spoke of it in 1998 as "Bill Daley's law firm." Bill Daley is Mayor Daley's brother.

In his law career, Stevenson began to build up an "Asian practice." From that base, he became a player in the field of merchant banking. Eventually, he organized a company called SC&M Investment Management. His interest was in Asian economic and investment policy—a way for him to relate to foreign policy matters without the struggle of running for and holding office.

He referred to his one-thousand-acre farm in 1998 as "marginally profitable." He was fattening cattle there and planting three hundred acres in corn each year. Asked to compare it to his father's seventy-acre farm home in Libertyville, he spoke of the latter as "not really a farm. It was one of our many unsuccessful attempts to convince the Illinois voters that we were really farmers" (Natale and Mackey, "Adlai" 10). The sheep kept there had as their primary purpose to keep the grass cut.

Asked if he missed the political spotlight, he said "no." He did miss the kind of politics he had started in as a young man, but not the kind he left behind in 1986. "Politics has been commercialized; issues . . . trivialized; the financial requirements are astronomical. . . . I wish I could say that I missed politics. I wish I could say I regretted my children were not in politics, but I don't" (Natale and Mackey, "Adlai" 10).

When 2002 came, however, his son Warwick surfaced as a candidate for the Illinois House of Representatives in the newly shaped Eighty-ninth District in the northwest corner of the state—generally considered to be Republican in its views. At forty, his work experience had been as a public school teacher and principal. Adlai Stevenson said, "When he decided to run, we were pleased" (Conklin 2:1). Old ways die hard. Adlai was not involved in Warwick's campaign, although Warwick's mother was. But it was not enough in this case, and Warwick was beaten by a wide margin.

After an in-depth interview of Stevenson by Joe Natale and Bruce Mackey for the *Springfield Business Journal* in 1998, the reporters concluded that he was intelligent, thoughtful, and sensitive. He voiced seemingly sensible ideas of the need for businesses in the United States to internationalize to a greater degree. He stressed the need for reform in education, in structure and financing. He held the media to be at fault for paying too little attention to international news. He felt that attention to the foreign media and the Internet is essential for one to be fully informed.

In response to a question, he said that he "had a lot of fun in Springfield when his father was governor," especially one summer when he worked as a newspaper reporter. His best political years were as state treasurer. That was the "old politics" he liked. The fact that it was a patronage system was also to his liking; it allowed him to "bring in a lot of good people"—and, one might add, quickly to be rid of the bad.

Stevenson said that he had gotten out of the Senate in 1980 because it had changed greatly during the decade he served there. The impact of Vietnam and Watergate was largely responsible. He knew that either Jimmy Carter or Ronald Reagan would be elected president that November, and he did not see much good happening under either one.

He wanted to run for governor partly, he realized, because his father had been governor but also because of the good experience he had had as state treasurer. He did not think he had lost to Governor Thompson, in spite of the vote count, nor could he believe he had won. The race was very close, and it will never be known who really deserved the office, for there was no recount.

Stevenson chose carefully the court to which his motion for a recount had been taken. It was the Illinois Supreme Court, which had four Democrats and three Republicans sitting. He thought he had the partisan edge there to get the recount he wanted.

The vote was four to three, as Stevenson expected, but not in the direction he had hoped. The recount statute was found unconstitutional, on grounds that the attorneys arguing against recount had not even raised. According to Stevenson, "[O]ne of the Democrats strayed. It is a fact I [passed one of the Democrat's sons] over for federal judge. It's a fact that the judge's son was receiving a fair amount of legal business for his law firm from the State of Illinois" (Natale and Mackey, "Stevenson" 10).

When he was asked whether he thought he would have won in 1982 if there had been a recount, he said "yeah." Four years later, when he felt compelled to leave the Democratic ticket for governor because a LaRouchite had been nominated in the primary for lieutenant governor to run with him, he ran virtually as an independent but still got 40 percent of the vote. He thought he would have been elected governor in 1986 if the Democratic slate had been kept intact with him on it.

As it was, he reflected on that campaign. "What a way to go, running . . . no money . . . Solidarity Party . . . hopeless contest . . . you knew you couldn't win. It was hell" (Natale and Mackey, "Stevenson" 12). He placed the blame on party leaders for the LaRouchite upset of the Democratic slate, which forced him off the ballot. They would not place the name of the party's slated candidate for lieutenant governor on sample ballots unless they were reimbursed for doing so. They were not, and disorder followed.

The last question Stevenson was asked in this series of two in-depth interviews was, "What question am I glad these guys did not ask?" His answer is revealing:

> It makes me think. The goddam wimp issue [he had been called a "wimp" in the 1982 campaign and the suggestion clung to him]. I had enlisted, volunteered for combat in Korea, became a tank platoon commander in the Marines in Korea, and was running against a draft avoider, who collected antiques, and I was the wimp. And maybe I was. When I think what they did to Clinton and what other candidates have done with similar issues, and I felt that this was just beneath me. I had his draft records, his medical exam. He pleaded asthma . . . you know, pollen count. What I could have done to, at least, to have defused that issue. It still makes me angry. It did stick. I thought I was being honorable and decent and right, not to reply at that kind of level. Then I kept kicking myself for not really calling a spade a spade. (Natale and Mackey, "Stevenson" 12)

Adlai Stevenson III has moved beyond the political world in which his three immediate male forebears spent so much of their lives, and in which he made a considerable investment of his time and energy. Now he functions in the world of international finance and seems much more comfortable there. His views on the politics of our time seem sound and persuasive.

Perhaps we should listen to him more as time goes on.

18 ★ "Al the Pal" and the "Cheshire Cat"

Illinois set new standards for its senators during the years from 1948 to 1985, first with the Democrat-Republican pair of Douglas and Dirksen, who served together from 1951 to 1967, and then with the same sort of pairing of Stevenson and Percy from 1970 to 1980. A division of the two senators between the two major parties seemed appropriate for a state in which the parties were evenly balanced.

It is provocative to ask, Could the quality of those Senate years and their bipartisan nature be continued?

Alan John Dixon (1980–93)

When Adlai Stevenson chose not to seek reelection in 1980, it was a natural progression for the man who then was Illinois secretary of state to file his intent to become a candidate. The man was Alan Dixon, who had a long record of public service, most of it in the Illinois legislature, extending back almost to a time before he was old enough to vote. If there ever was a natural-born officeholder in the fashion of Shelby Cullom, it was Alan Dixon.

He was born in Belleville, Illinois, on July 7, 1927, and attended the University of Illinois, where he was awarded a B.S. degree. In 1949, when he was twenty-two, he received a law degree from Washington University in St. Louis. At once he began a law practice in Belleville and almost as quickly was elected a police magistrate, or local judge. He became an assistant state's attorney in 1950. It seems that he was intent on a career in politics from the beginning of his entry into the world of work.

In 1950, Dixon was elected as a Democrat to the Illinois House of Representatives, with the backing of the Al Fields political organization of East St. Louis. After the Chicago Democrats, it was the strongest political structure in the state. Dixon served in the House for six terms, until 1963. He was elected to the Illinois Senate in 1962.

Dixon and his friend and fellow-Democrat Paul Simon went to the Illinois Senate from the House at the same time, from adjoining districts. They have been playing "political tag" for most of the last half century. Dixon was the first of the two in the House, in 1951, and Simon joined him there four years later. Simon was the first of the two to be elected to the Congress, in 1974, and Dixon followed him to Washington in 1980. At that time, one writer referred to the two as "the boy wonders of Illinois politics." After a decade in the U.S. House, Simon joined his friend in the Senate in 1985. With Shelby Cullom, Dixon and Simon are the record holders for Illinois in longevity in public office.

Dixon was in the state Senate for nine years and was the minority whip in 1964 and 1970. In the latter year, he was elected state treasurer, following Adlai Stevenson to that office, and served in that capacity for six years. In 1976, he was elected secretary of state and was in that office when it became known in 1979 that Stevenson was bowing out of the Senate picture. Literally within hours of Stevenson's announcement, Dixon released his own, stating his intention to enter the primary for that seat (Hartley, "Dixon").

There was substantial opposition in his own party to Dixon running for the Senate. The governor was Republican Jim Thompson, and the secretary of state's office was the Democrat's principal patronage haven. If Dixon were to leave it in midterm, Thompson would almost certainly appoint a Republican in his place. The Republican would than have the advantage of running as an incumbent when the term ended.

Dixon could almost certainly have had another term or terms if he had continued as secretary of state. For him to leave that office opened up the certainty of an appointed Republican taking his place, and the probability that a Republican would win it in the next election. Concern was also expressed over the fact that Dixon had no experience with national and international issues.

The worst fears of the Democrats were realized. Soon after Dixon was elected to the Senate, with 56 percent of the vote, Senator Stevenson resigned, and Senator-elect Dixon was appointed to take his place for the few days remaining in Stevenson's term. In that way, he gained seniority over any other senator first elected in 1980.

Governor Thompson had obligingly appointed the Democrat Dixon to the balance of Stevenson's term, because it was in the state's interest for its junior senator to have an advantage in seniority. In any case, Thompson had the office of secretary of state to fill by appointment, and he rewarded his director of legislative relations, Jim Edgar, by elevating him to that post, setting him on the road to election as secretary of state for two terms, before he became governor in 1991.

When Dixon left the secretary of state's office, leaving it open to be filled by appointment by a Republican, there was a considerable turnover in personnel. Dixon had earned a good deal of hard feelings for himself within his party but had no trouble winning the Senate seat in 1980, nor again six years later, when his margin of victory was almost two to one against a weak conservative candidate, Judy Koehler.

There is no doubt that Alan Dixon was a consummate politician. His jovial ways caused him sometimes to be referred to as "Al the Pal." Persons visiting the offices of members of Congress from Illinois often found the warmest reception and the most personal attention from the officeholder himself, in Dixon's suite.

At the start of his second term in the Senate in 1987, Dixon was known as an "insider," a pragmatist who concentrated on bringing good things to Illinois. One observer characterized him as a "senator from Illinois," rather than a "United States senator." The difference is significant.

"I'm right where I want to be," Dixon said as his second term began. He had just been made chairman of the Armed Services Subcommittee, which was in charge of oversight of 40 percent of the three hundred billion dollar defense budget. Spending of that kind was important in Illinois (Collin, *Power* 3).

He was also on the Banking and the Small Business Committees. In the latter, he headed a subcommittee on government contracting. He had given up membership on the Agriculture Committee because of a Senate rule against service on the part of any senator on more than two major committees, without a special waiver. In view of the importance of agriculture in the Illinois economy, that choice on Dixon's part raised some eyebrows. But he felt he could do more good for the state on the other committees.

Dixon had also become one of four deputy whips in the majority party in the Senate, a sign that he was on his way up in his party's hierarchy. As his second term drew to a close in 1991, he had every reason to look forward to an easy victory at the polls and six more years of upward mobility in Senate ranks. But that was not to be.

The Senate primary contest became complicated late in 1991 when, in addition to the incumbent Dixon, a wealthy Chicago lawyer named Albert F. Hofeld and the Cook County recorder of deeds, Carol Moseley-Braun, threw their hats into the ring. Dixon was losing strength in some quarters because of his support of Clarence Thomas for appointment to the U.S. Supreme Court, in spite of the negative testimony of Professor Anita Hill on sexual harassment charges.

Hofeld had an almost unlimited supply of his own money to use in campaigning. It was clear that he would be able to win a significant number of votes. Moseley-Braun, in addition to the elective county office she was then holding, was a veteran of several years service in the Illinois House of Representatives. She was also the possessor of an engaging smile that caused some to think and speak of her as a "Cheshire cat."

Moseley-Braun was politically astute enough to realize that two white men, one the incumbent and the other with a good deal of money to spend, were going to divide a certain number of votes and that she, as an African American woman, just might be able to walk in between them and take the nomination, even if by less than a majority vote. And that is just what happened.

Moseley-Braun got the nod with 38.3 percent of the ballots cast on the Democratic side. Dixon was second with 34.6 percent. The unbelievable had happened—"Al the Pal" had gone down in defeat for the first time in over forty years of running for public office.

One must hark back to 1986, when the LaRouchite Mark Fairchild took the Democratic nomination for lieutenant governor and, in so doing, blew Adlai Stevenson's chances of becoming governor out of the water, to recall a primary election that so shocked the Illinois political community. An earlier shocker had been the nomination in the Democratic primary of Jane Byrne for mayor of Chicago.

There was nothing left for Alan Dixon to do but mark time until his term ended the following January. Once out of office, he returned to Belleville. In 1994 and 1995, he chaired by appointment the important Defense Base Closure and Realignment Commission. One of the military facilities under the commission's scrutiny was Scott Air Base, literally in Belleville's backyard. It remained open. Other longtime and important military facilities in Illinois, such as Chanute Field near Rantoul, and Fort Sheridan on the shore of Lake Michigan, were not so favored.

Carol Moseley-Braun (1993–99)

Carol Moseley-Braun was born in Chicago on August 16, 1947. She graduated from the University of Illinois at Chicago and attended the prestigious University of Chicago Law School on a scholarship, where she was awarded the doctor of jurisprudence degree in 1972. She served five terms in the Illinois House of Representatives and, in 1990, was elected Cook County recorder of deeds.

Following her surprising victory in the Democratic primary in 1992, before Moseley-Braun could take her place as the first woman to be elected to the U.S. Senate from Illinois, and the first African American female senator, she had to win the general election in November. Fortunately for her, the Republicans had put up a "throw-away" candidate, since before the surprising primary election outcome, they had entertained little hope of beating Alan Dixon, whom they assumed would be the primary winner and candidate for a third term. The primary purpose of a throw-away candidate is not to win but to force the opponent to spend money on his or her campaign, money that otherwise could be used for other party candidates.

With that assumption, the Republicans had settled on Richard S. Williamson, a wealthy young lawyer with an Ivy League background, who had a law office in Chicago and a home in the suburbs. He had credentials, since he had been a part of the Reagan administration and had held a diplomatic post in the United Nations.

Williamson was of the conservative type who seem able at winning Republican Senate primaries but not at coming out ahead in the general election. No one else wanted to run, and Williamson got 100 percent of his party's vote in the Republican primary.

He was a novice at the kind of big-league politics that Moseley-Braun had mastered during her schooling in the Springfield and Cook County political wars. Even so, her campaign was in many ways a disaster. It seemed poorly organized, and her campaign manager, a native of South Africa named Kgosie Matthews, ran things with an iron hand and a manner that seemed intended to alienate many of her supporters.

The scheduling of her time was badly done. To make matters worse, she had problems with legal ramifications over a sum of money that was credited as belonging to her mother, but that had been divided among Moseley-Braun and her siblings. Her mother was in a nursing home on Medicaid, the welfare program for medical care. Eventually, all that got straightened out, but it left a bad taste in many mouths.

There were rumors about her having a costly apartment at Lake Point Tower and a new Jeep, paid for out of campaign funds. Matthews, who briefly was her fiancé, was thought by some staffers to be wasting money and other resources. One friend of the candidate called him a Rasputin. There were allegations of sexual harassment of staffers. But no one would go public with the charges.

Some felt that Moseley-Braun covered up for him, and that also hurt her in the public mind. On election night, flush with victory, she had referred to Matthews as "my knight in shining armor" (James 21). By 1995, he was spending time in Africa and was described as only "a friend" (Collin, "Power" 15).

Even with all those problems, Moseley-Braun managed to win the general election, taking 53.6 percent of the vote in her contest with Williamson. If the Republicans had put up one of their heavy hitters, such as Jim Thompson, Jim Edgar, or George Ryan, it is likely that they would have won the seat. As it was, Williamson, the throw-away, did quite well for the kind of candidate he was originally intended to be.

Matthews seemed to cause more difficulty on election night when Moseley-Braun went on the platform at the McCormick Hotel ballroom to make a victory speech. She was accompanied only by her fifteen-year-old son Matthew, a student at a Catholic high school in Chicago.

Her entire family, mother and siblings, had wished to be there with her. So had several other high-ranking Democratic officeholders. But Matthews said "no," and Moseley-Braun and her son went on the stage alone (James 18).

Almost at once, Moseley-Braun got in more difficulty with the public when, instead of arriving in Washington to begin learning her way around, setting up an office, and angling for preferred committee assignments, she and Matthews went to Africa. Early on, she had several disputes with Senator Jesse Helms that seemed to cast her as an African American symbol rather than a working senator.

Eventually, she began to gain a feel for being a senator. Her experience in legislative and Cook County politics in Illinois had prepared her to be skillful in negotiation and parliamentary procedure. By the end of her first two years in the Senate, Senator Paul Simon, also from Illinois, felt able to say of Moseley-Braun, "[S]he's doing well on the job here . . . but she has a public relations problem in Illinois" (Collin, "Power" 15).

One-time Senate majority leader George Mitchell of Maine said of Moseley-Braun, "She really is a serious legislator. She is very well-prepared. She's persuasive." Republican Senator Orrin Hatch of Utah, who was on the Judiciary Committee with Moseley-Braun, said that she was "the best politician" in her class of new senators. That class included Diane Feinstein and Barbara Boxer of California and Ben Nighthorse-Campbell of Colorado, all veterans of the political wars.

Senator Edward Kennedy, who was impressed by her persistence in getting funding for a new school rehabilitation program, said, "She did better than most old timers. . . . Behind that wonderful smile is a will of steel." Majority leader Bob Dole said of her, "She just fits right in. She's one of our colleagues" (Collin, "Power" 15).

Things seemed to be going well with Moseley-Braun during her first two years in the Senate, even though it appeared that she had recurring troubles in managing her staff, a repetition of difficulty during her campaign in 1992. Her success in becoming a real player in Senate affairs seemed to be heightened when, at the beginning of 1995, she gained a seat on the important Finance Committee. She served there with such heavyweights as Bill Bradley and Jay Rockefeller.

But even that accomplishment, as with so many events in Moseley-Braun's political career, seemed to have its "flip," or negative, side. Grumblings were heard that she had been too aggressive in seeking the seat on Finance, and that she had gained it by double-dealing. She had made it clear to both Senator Tom Daschle and Senator Christopher Dodd, who were contending for the post of Democratic Party leader, that her vote could be had for an appointment to Finance, which she longed to have.

When hands were counted, Moseley-Braun held the deciding vote. It went to Daschle, who than gave up his seat on Finance and appointed her to fill it. Some said she had promised to support Dodd. He held no ill will over the matter. As time passed, the criticism of her died away.

Moseley-Braun's next misadventure got her into difficulty not only with the voters at home but also with the U.S. Department of State. Only days before she was to act as vice chairwoman of the Democratic national convention, which was held in 1996 in Chicago, she faced a rising tide of criticism over a visit she had then recently made to Nigeria.

The news media called it a "free lance" visit. It had taken place without notice to the State Department, and even in the face of sanctions that the department had applied to Nigeria, where General Sani Abacha held power as a "ruthless dictator," according to some observers. Moseley-Braun expressed a fondness for the political chief's wife, and for him, that columnist Mike Royko characterized as "weird."

Other troubles piled up for Moseley-Braun in 1996. Her campaign spending in 1992 had been investigated over and over. She was cleared of any personal wrongdoing, but charges of improper spending, poor accounting practices, and a continuing debt of half a million dollars continued to haunt her. Her former campaign manager—not Matthews—sued in 1996 for two hundred thousand dollars in unpaid salary.

All of this made Moseley-Braun appear to be highly vulnerable as Democrats looked toward the election in 1998, when her seat in the Senate would be at stake. Downstate leaders called for her to step aside, and Democrats everywhere in the state were nervous over her impact on the whole ticket.

Some of her problems seemed to fade away with the coming of the primary election campaign early in 1998. She was intent on retaining office and won the primary with little difficulty. When the Republicans chose conservative Peter Fitzgerald to oppose her, the odds seemed better that she would prevail at the polls in November.

Her campaign was clouded when charges were made that her sister had used her job with the state as a base for fund-raising for Moseley-Braun. That revived thoughts of earlier missteps, and when the votes were all counted, Fitzgerald led by an eyelash, with 50.3 percent of the total number and a winning margin of less than a hundred thousand.

Moseley-Braun vowed never again to run for public office. That assertion has to be taken with a grain of salt, since it is the sort of thing a wounded loser is likely to say in the pain of the moment.

For the time, however, she and any criticism that might have clung to her to darken her party's chances in the presidential election in 2000 were safely stored away in far-off New Zealand. She journeyed there early in that year, to take up her post as ambassador, by appointment of President Clinton, with the approval of her former colleagues in the Senate. The vote there to confirm her appointment comprised ninety-eight "ayes."

It is likely that we will continue to hear from Carol Moseley-Braun as a political figure seeking elective office. Her performance in the Senate was of good quality, according to colleagues; it was the missteps of personal behavior that brought about her defeat—those are defects for which the public has short memory. On the other hand, her personal assets and political skills will likely continue to be refined, as during diplomatic service abroad. That service was short lived, however, since President Bush named her replacement.

When Moseley-Braun came to the campus of Southern Illinois University to speak in December 1999, shortly before departing for New Zealand, her former Senate colleague Paul Simon said in introducing her, "[S]he speaks from conviction."

The talk that followed, and her answer to questions from her large and friendly audience, indicated that she was a believer in free trade while sensitive to the problems of child labor, the environment, labor rights, and human dignity that the rise of manufacturing in emerging nations might bring.

She emphasized the importance of quality education accessible to all and regretted the "nineteenth-century" system we have of funding it in Illinois. She believes that it creates disparity of opportunity and that some other method, perhaps on the model of the interstate highway system, with predominantly federal funding, might serve us better.

Asked for advice for women seeking careers in politics, she counseled, "Learn about government first" and stress principle above personality. Her talk was part of a series titled "What I Have Learned and Would Like to Pass Along." In it she pointed out that the individual person *can* make a difference and used the struggle for civil rights as an illustration.

Even in New Zealand, Ambassador Moseley-Braun was not long in becoming the object of accusations of impropriety. The deputy chief of mission there, a career diplomat, made various charges against her. One was that she had improperly accepted free lodging at a luxury hotel for herself, her son, and a friend, where the charges for each room were $895 a day. Eventually, she made reimbursement for those facilities.

The Department of State moved quickly to investigate the matter. It made no finding of any impropriety and so informed the ambassador. It recalled the deputy chief to Washington for reassignment.

Little was heard from Moseley-Braun until early in 2003, when she began to speak of seeking to recover in the 2004 elections the Senate seat she had lost to Peter Fitzgerald. Soon talk began of her entering the rather large field of persons intending to seek the Democratic presidential nomination. Although there was no feeling that she might be successful in winning the nomination, some felt that a primary campaign by Moseley-Braun would draw African Americans, and especially African American women, into election year activity on behalf of the Democratic Party.

She organized an exploratory committee and on February 18 formally announced her intention to enter the presidential primary. Visits to three states—Iowa, New Hampshire, and South Carolina—were planned. She styles herself a peace candidate and a budget deficit hawk. She is also opposed to the death penalty.

One member of Moseley-Braun's committee, former U.S. Senator Paul Simon, observed that he "encouraged her to run, although her chances are thin, because I think she will contribute to the national dialogue. She will be a bit of a Harry Truman in the race and speak candidly" (*Tribune*, February 14, 2003, 6:1).

Columnist Clarence Page cut closer to the bone when he observed that "party insiders see Moseley-Braun as their Great Black Hope to stop the rise of the Rev. Al Sharpton as a major player in the presidential sweepstakes.

As such, her candidacy, like that of Sharpton, is a symptom of deeper problems in today's Democratic Party. The current lineup of Democratic presidential candidates has a big, wide charisma gap when it comes to energizing the party's base of black and liberal-progressive wings.

Her winnability is, to put it mildly, challenged. But as an old joke goes about what one man said to the other as they were outrunning a bear, "I don't have to outrun the bear. I only have to outrun you!" To earn the gratitude of party moderates, Moseley-Braun only has to outrun Sharpton, or, at least, to make enough of a dent in his vote that one of their rising stars won't be embarrassed. (Page)

Only a few days after her announcement, the candidate made it known that she was dropping the hyphen from her name and becoming Carol Mosely Braun all over again. During her time in state and county government, that had been her name. When she went to the Senate in 1993, she added the hyphen. One result was in alphabetical roll calls, in voting or expressing opinions in committee, her name would fall in the middle instead of among the first. For a freshman legislator, that might have seemed to be an advantage.

Dropping the hyphen, the candidate offered, would make things simpler for the news media. By that reasoning, her action of ten years earlier complicated the matter. A sociologist at Pennsylvania State University who has studied the use of maiden and married names observed that "we make assumptions about people who have hyphenated last names. We assume they have a whole feminist bent. That's not always good in politics" (*Tribune*, March 4, 2003, 6:10).

In any case, office seeking by Carol Moseley Braun is hardly over.

19 ★ A Moralist in Politics

Paul Simon (1985–97)

Paul Simon is one of the most durable figures in Illinois political history. With forty years of service as lieutenant governor and in the state legislature and Congress, he held elective office longer than all but two other U.S. senators in the state's history. (Shelby Cullom was in office for fifty-one years and Alan Dixon for forty-two.)

During those forty years, Simon's service paralleled that of seven different Illinois governors and nine U.S. presidents. Over more than four decades, he ran successfully for office fifteen times—not counting primary elections—and lost only once—in the 1972 Democratic primary for governor.

Statistics do not do justice to the Simon story, however. From his first term as a member of the Illinois House of Representatives to his last days in the Senate, Simon built and maintained a reputation for competence, honesty, and independence. These attributes kept him from the inner circle of legislative leadership, but they established him as an effective public servant known for his principles.

U.S. Representative Henry Hyde, an Illinois conservative who served with Simon in Springfield and in Washington, D.C., addressed Simon's reputation in comments in the *Washington Post* in

1987: "You can't help but like the guy. He first of all is a decent, fine gentleman. He is thoughtful, conscientious and honest" (Peterson 14).

Simon worked within the Democratic Party as a social liberal and a fiscal moderate, not always in step with party leadership and often confounding critics. His advocacy of an open, accountable, pay-as-you-go government, and his concern for social conditions, all familiar to Illinois constituents, received national attention in 1988 during his quest for the Democratic presidential nomination.

Much of Simon's appeal to a friendly press and approving statewide constituency was his appearance as more than a professional officeholder, which of course, he was. He also worked as a weekly newspaper owner and editor and earned a reputation as courageous under fire.

Simon is the author of more than a dozen books, ranging from scholarly nonfiction about Abraham Lincoln to setting out his ideas on national issues such as literacy, hunger, and morality. For his entire time in public office, he personally wrote a weekly newspaper column, a practice he resumed in 2000, writing for the *Chicago Sun-Times*. Rather than identify himself as a politician, he usually stated his profession as "writer."

There always was a strong moralistic tone to his interest in matters of public policy. He came by that sensitivity naturally, with parents who served abroad as Lutheran missionaries. For his occasional righteous outlook on issues, he was kidded by colleagues, enemies, and admirers, who called him "Reverend" and "the Deacon." He accepted the comments with good grace.

At times, Simon could be as pragmatic a politician as could be found in all of Illinois. Getting elected fourteen times required building a steady, dependable, voter base. As a result, he remained true to the interests of labor and of blacks, and he put a high priority on constituent service.

Politically, he usually did what was necessary to get elected and reelected. He campaigned across Illinois with Paul Powell in 1968, although he often was at odds with the Vienna native, who was running then for Illinois secretary of state. Simon accepted the blessing of Chicago Mayor Richard J. Daley, after he had openly criticized the mayor as an autocratic party leader.

Inclined to turn the other cheek in slam-bang political fights, he aggressively attacked Senator Charles H. Percy in their contest in 1984. As often is the case of elected officials who serve many years, Simon was not always easy to pigeonhole.

Paul Simon was born on November 29, 1928, soon after his parents returned from missionary work in China and settled in Eugene, Oregon. The Simon family lived modestly, and its home life featured a respect for Christianity and hard work.

At sixteen, Paul began studies at the University of Oregon, concentrating on journalism. When his parents soon moved to Highland, Illinois, he transferred to Dana College, a Lutheran school in Blair, Nebraska. When he was nineteen, and approaching graduation, he had an opportunity in Illinois that did much to shape his later life.

Citizens of Troy, a community of twelve hundred in southwestern Illinois, were about to lose their weekly newspaper due to its owner's illness. Through Simon's father, town leaders contacted the teenager and offered to finance the purchase of the paper. The Troy Lions Club loaned him thirty-six hundred dollars and pledged its support. Simon dreamed of becoming another Walter Lippman, one of the most highly respected newspaper columnists of that time. He never went back to college.

Corruption permeated local government in the late 1940s and early 1950s, and hoodlums ran unchecked, in Madison County. Troy was east of the county's population centers in Alton, Granite City, and Edwardsville, but the voice of the *Troy Tribune* soon was heard in protest of corrupt conditions. Simon took on the sheriff and the state's attorney, whom he believed were taking payoffs. He clashed with the Democratic political bosses in the county and caught the eye of outsiders.

In 1950, Simon helped persuade Governor Adlai Stevenson to conduct a series of state police raids on gambling establishments in southern Illinois. When U.S. Senator Estes Kefauver of Tennessee brought his investigation of organized crime to St. Louis, Simon was asked to testify about conditions in Madison County. His crusade was interrupted from 1951 to 1953 for a stint in the U.S. Army, but he returned to newspapering and another challenge.

Anxious to take his reform ideas to the state legislature, Simon ran as a Democrat for the state House of Representatives from his home district in Madison County in 1954. He succeeded at the ballot box over entrenched party regulars whom he accused of lining their pockets by taking advantage of their public offices.

Simon continued as owner and editor of the *Troy Tribune* and eventually owned fourteen weekly newspapers, in his own name or jointly with others, in southern Illinois. One of his partners in that business was Belleville attorney Alan Dixon, who already had begun his own lengthy service in office with election to the state House of Representatives in 1950.

The two, whose homes were not far apart, took almost parallel paths in Democratic politics and became lasting friends and associates. With differing styles, and differing opinions on many issues, they served together in the state House and Senate for a considerable period of time, and again in the U.S. Senate from 1985 to 1993. They sold their newspaper interests in 1966.

The behavior of many colleagues in the legislature, especially when it came to conflict of interest and outright corruption, appalled Simon when he first went to Springfield. This feeling led him to prepare an as-told-to article, which appeared in 1964 in *Harper's* magazine entitled "The Illinois Legislature: A Study in Corruption."

Outraged legislators bestowed on Simon a "Benedict Arnold Award." When challenged to produce hard evidence, he declined to do so. Even so, the bombshell article prevented him from gaining any positions of special responsibility in the legislature.

Simon had alienated too many of his House and Senate colleagues ever to be on the inside track in leadership, but nevertheless he was an active legislator. He sponsored forty-six pieces of legislation that were enacted, including the state's first "open meetings" law. Good government organizations gave him their highest awards.

Service in the legislature changed Simon's life in another way as well. Seated not far from him on the Democratic side of the aisle in 1957 was Jeanne Hurley, an attorney from Wilmette, one of the few women to serve in the legislature at that time. They were married on April 21, 1960, and Jeanne retired from elective office the following year, eventually to raise two children, Sheila and Martin.

She did not retire from public affairs, however, and became significant in the further success of her husband. She campaigned vigorously for him and pursued her own interests in public policy until her death early in 2000 from a brain tumor.

In 1962, Simon was elected to the state Senate. Four years later, he was successful in seeking a second term. His career advanced a step in 1968, when the state Democratic organization slated him to run for lieutenant governor with the incumbent governor, Samuel

Shapiro of Kankakee. Shapiro had become governor from his post as lieutenant governor when Otto Kerner resigned late in his second term to become a federal judge.

In one of the quirks of Illinois political history, and a unique event, Simon won his contest while his running mate Shapiro lost to Republican Richard Ogilvie. It was not until after the constitution of 1970 was adopted that the candidates for governor and lieutenant governor of each political party were required to run as a team and the voters limited to casting a single vote for the preferred pair. It is probable that the constitution was changed largely because of the split of the two offices between the two major parties in 1968, although a more general desire to shorten the ballot also played a part.

The post of lieutenant governor had been a burial ground for political ambitions ever since Illinois became a state. That might have been Simon's fate but for the fact that he decided not to let it happen. He formed the role of ombudsman and held meetings across the state with citizens to hear their complaints and concerns about government. To keep from being pushed aside by other ambitious politicians, he also maintained a high profile with the media, a task that his work as a newspaper editor had helped him master. Soon he was being talked about as a possible Democratic candidate for governor in 1972.

As late as the end of 1971, the consensus among politicians and media across Illinois was that Simon and Ogilvie would battle it out for governor. Barely visible on the political horizon as a primary election foe for Simon was Daniel Walker, a renegade Democrat who had never held elective public office. He was a corporate attorney who had dreams of one day being president of the United States.

Walker gained much public attention by walking the length and breadth of Illinois during the primary campaign. He criticized Mayor Daley as a tyrant, an attitude that was popular downstate, everywhere except in Chicago. By implication, and then explicitly, he extended the criticism to Simon on the ground that he was the mayor's choice for the gubernatorial nomination.

In his battle with Walker, a letter that Simon had written to the *Edwardsville Intelligencer* in 1960 came back to haunt him. He had written, "Whether it is the mayor of Chicago, the mayor of Troy or the mayor of your hometown, I believe that no man should have the power to say who a party is to nominate. Something is very wrong with democracy when that happens" (Dowling B6). Walker made hay of that appearance of hypocrisy on Simon's part.

Simon took victory over Walker in the primary election for granted; he rarely struck back when his opponent attacked. He also made several tactical errors in his campaign, including a statement that an income tax might be necessary if the state eliminated local personal property taxes and the state sales taxes on food and drugs. Walker accused Simon of calling for a tax increase. Incorrect as that charge was, it hung over the Simon campaign like a dark cloud.

The outcome of the Democratic primary in 1972 was the lowest point of Simon's political career. He lost the nomination for governor to Walker by forty thousand votes in one of the notable upsets of Illinois political history. Walker went on to defeat Ogilvie, who was running for a second term, in an equally close general election.

Paul Simon was left, out of office, to contemplate his next step in public life. After a short time lecturing at Harvard, he taught journalism at Sangamon State University at Springfield, in the early days of what has become a distinguished graduate program in public affairs reporting.

Then Simon announced his intention to seek the congressional seat representing deep southern Illinois in 1974. Opponents called him a "carpetbagger" because he moved his home into the district just days before filing for the primary election. The way had been cleared for him by the retirement of longtime Democratic Congressman Kenneth Grey of West Frankfort.

Making his home in Carbondale, Simon campaigned throughout the district and won the seat in 1974. In those days, it contained most of deep southern Illinois and was not divided down the middle of the region as it is today, a change introduced by a Democratic-controlled legislature in 1981 to make the district safer for Simon and the Democratic candidates who would follow him. It was a gerrymander that drew howls of protest from many southern Illinois citizens, including many Democrats.

In 1975, Paul Simon began a decade-long tour of duty in the U.S. House of Representatives. There were no significant departures there from his approach to public policy. He addressed favorite social issues, specialized in concerns of higher education, and maintained an involvement in fiscal affairs. Safe as his Illinois district seemed to be for his continued reelection, he chafed under House rules that limited debate. He wanted greater opportunity to take the floor and speak on a wide range of issues. There was only one place he could do that—the Senate.

The first rumbles that Simon might challenge Senator Percy began in 1977. He decided against such a contest in 1978, and Percy went on to win a third term in a tight and tense battle with Democrat Alex Seith. When Percy's number came up for another term in 1984, Simon decided to make a run at the incumbent.

Percy was under heavy fire from the start of the campaign. First he faced a stiff primary challenge from conservative Congressman Thomas Corcoran. Percy won that contest but carried scars from it into the general election battle with Simon, who defeated four other Democrats in the primary. The struggle was costly to both candidates, and unpleasant, and Simon finally won in an upset with a slim 50.1 percent of the vote, and a margin of just less than ninety thousand.

Simon's wish to become a senator had come true. He took up where he had left off in the House on social questions and carried forward a fight for a balanced budget amendment to the Constitution, which continued until he left the Senate.

Hardly had he warmed his seat in the new chamber, however, when another unpredicted circumstance influenced his career. After just two years as a senator, he decided to contend for the 1988 Democratic presidential nomination.

When Simon entered that race in the spring of 1987, other Democratic contenders included U.S. Senators Gary Hart, Albert Gore Jr., and Joseph Biden; Governors Michael Dukakis (the eventual winner) and Bruce Babbitt; U.S. Representative Richard Gebhardt; and the Reverend Jesse Jackson. Simon was entering a distinguished field.

It probably was as large as it was because in that year President Ronald Reagan's second term was coming to an end. Thus, there would not be an incumbent in the general election. No doubt Simon reasoned that the winner in 1988 would be another two-term president and that he would not have as good a chance again.

Simon said in his announcement, "I seek the presidency not because I want to live in a large white house or because I want to hear the band playing 'Hail to the Chief' or I want to hear the applause of the crowds. I seek the presidency because of the force for good that office can become."

His candidacy generated derision among the media and the public. Jon Margolis wrote in the *Chicago Tribune,* "Most people probably will have these two reactions: Laughter and wonder what Simon is smoking." While there always remained a doubt among party leaders and the media, the impression that Simon could not win eventually softened. His finest hour was in the Iowa caucus primary, where he finished second to Gebhardt. Its format was suited to his personal style of campaigning.

Simon remained competitive until after the Wisconsin primary, when he folded his campaign. It had been an absorbing experience for him, one that he eventually made the subject of one of his books.

After recovering from the punishing effects of a presidential campaign, Simon faced a reelection effort toward a second Senate term, in 1990. Republicans viewed him as vulnerable, given his slim margin of victory six years earlier, and the number of controversial votes he had cast in the Senate. Congresswoman Lynn Martin of Rockford, a high profile Republican, took up the challenge to unseat Simon.

Martin did well at fund-raising and kept an attack going on Simon's voting record and his general approach to public policy. Still, on election day, he won with 65.1 percent of the vote, a margin of almost a million. It is likely that his search after the presidential nomination two years earlier had raised his standing in the eyes of many voters. That may have been the major purpose of that candidacy.

In 1994, Paul and Jeanne Simon took a long, hard look at whether they wanted to face a third campaign for reelection to the Senate. Writing in his autobiography, he says he ran out of enthusiasm for many of the chores of public office, although not for the substantive work of the Senate.

He had little stomach for raising the millions of dollars necessary for a campaign at the Senate level. In the end, he and Jeanne decided that he would not seek reelection. Congressman Richard Durbin, a protégé of Simon, sought the position in 1996 and won over his Republican rival.

A look back at Simon's four decades in the public limelight reveals that he was never a power in the legislative bodies he served, that he never held a leadership position above that of subcommittee chair. There is no piece of historic legislation that bears his name. But the record also shows that he was often a key player in the realm of ideas and the solutions to problems in Illinois and nationally.

At age sixty-seven, in 1997, and free of elective public life, Simon never gave a thought to retiring. He had offers from numerous nonprofit organizations and universities. After careful consideration, he accepted an offer from Southern Illinois University at Carbondale, which allowed him to return to Illinois, to his home in the village of Makanda, and to work with issues that had concerned him for a lifetime.

With the help of Mike Lawrence, who had been Illinois Republican Governor Jim Edgar's press secretary, he organized the SIU Public Policy Institute and became its director. He also taught classes in political science and journalism. His impact on the campus and the local, national, and international communities was soon evident and was profound.

The institute allowed Simon to draw on forty years of national and regional experiences and contacts in exploring solutions to perplexing public problems. He brought to Illinois and to Southern Illinois University people with ideas and influence to discuss new approaches to old issues.

In the course of preparing this chapter, Mr. Simon was asked to summarize the sort of symposia he felt had made a difference during the brief lifetime of the Public Policy Institute. His reply was so succinct and telling we will use it here.

> Looking at Social Security with Alan Simpson, Jack Danforth and David Pryor was important; we're the only public policy institute in the world that looked at Rwanda and the lessons to be learned at Rwanda; our session on mental health in the prisons has resulted in eight states now reviewing what they're doing in this field; a session we did on foreign language in the elementary schools is causing at least a few ripples around the nation. Some of these, like the one on mental health in our prisons, result in concrete action fairly quickly, even though eight states is a long way from 50 states moving on the problem. But its a concrete start.

While Paul Simon is at home in Illinois, his reach is international in scope. Early in 2001, he led a group of thirty persons from Southern Illinois University to Cuba, for study of the economy and culture of that island nation. Cuba's president, Fidel Castro, spent six hours with the group. No doubt further work concerning the problem of U.S. relations with Cuba will appear on the agenda of Simon's and SIU's Public Policy Institute.

Following the death of his wife early in 2000, Paul Simon was married in the spring of 2001 to Patricia Derge, whose late husband had been president of Southern Illinois University during the 1970s.

20 ★ The Incumbents

Richard J. Durbin (1997–)

Much like the descendants of a dynasty, those Democrats who followed in the "Paul H. Douglas seat" in the U.S. Senate from Illinois have carried the indelible philosophical imprint of a political family. After Douglas, there was Senator Paul Simon, an open admirer of Douglas. Richard Durbin, who served briefly in Douglas's office and considers Paul Simon his mentor, was the third to fill those shoes.

Taken together these three liberal Democrats extend from 1948 to the present in the Senate, except for the three terms served by Republican Charles Percy. In 1984, Simon gained a measure of "family" revenge by defeating Percy, who had gained senatorial office by beating Douglas.

Under the political microscope, Douglas, Simon, and Durbin share many approaches to public policy. On social issues, they fall clearly in the liberal segment. Fiscally, and on a myriad of other issues, they take independent courses that do not always jibe with views of the Democratic Party.

Durbin, the "third generation" of this ideological family, has distinctive characteristics. He is a native of southern Illinois, born on November 21, 1944, in East St. Louis. The other two came to Illinois from other states as young men. Durbin attended Catholic schools in East St. Louis, received a bachelor's degree from Georgetown University, and was graduated from the Georgetown Law School. Neither Douglas nor Simon was Catholic, nor a lawyer. Douglas was a professor of economics, and Simon, who did not graduate from college, was a journalist and writer.

Out of law school, Durbin joined Lieutenant Governor Simon's staff in Springfield. From 1972 to 1978, he was a state Senate staff member on the Democratic side, and from 1978 to 1982, he was on the faculty at the Southern Illinois University School of Medicine. He ran for office twice and lost during those years.

Durbin won election to the U.S. House of Representatives in 1982 from the Twentieth District, which included Springfield. He upset longtime Republican Representative Paul Findley. A turning point for Durbin was Findley's outspoken support of Arab interests in the Mideast. Jewish contributors provided large amounts of cash for Durbin's campaign.

By 1994, his constituents of central Illinois had reelected Durbin six times. However, the changing nature of the constituency caused him some problems. In 1994, he won over a weak Republican candidate with only 55 percent of the vote.

Durbin jumped at the chance to run for the Senate in 1996, after Paul Simon's decision not to run again, and he received Simon's wholehearted endorsement. He won the general election over trial lawyer and abortion opponent Al Salvi with 56 percent of the vote.

During his congressional career, Durbin has established himself as a Democratic partisan. He gravitated quickly to leadership positions in both the House and Senate and is considered one of the party's strongest advocates in public discourse. In the House, he rose to chairmanship of the Agriculture and Rural Development Subcommittee of the Appropriations Committee. In the Senate, soon after election, he was named an assistant floor leader for majority leader Tom Daschle.

One measure of Durbin's strong standing among Democrats in the Senate was his appointment by leadership to a seat on the powerful and influential Appropriations Committee in 1998. He was named to the Agriculture, Defense, District of Columbia, and Legislative Branch Subcommittees. Durbin is the first Illinois senator in twenty-five years to serve on the Appropriations Committee. His other committee assignments include Budget, Government Affairs, and the Select Committee on Ethics.

While Durbin has assiduously followed the liberal party line on antipoverty programs and social measures, he has set an independent course on other issues. In the House, he became known as a fierce opponent of tobacco interests. He led the fight for legislation banning smoking on most domestic commercial airplane flights. Durbin was fourteen years old when his chain-smoking father died of lung cancer, and he has continued his antitobacco fight in the Senate. His strong stand for gun control has been controversial in some parts of the state.

Durbin's favorite social issues in the Senate include more spending for secondary education, proposals for protecting the environment, food safety, and health care initiatives. One of the toughest issues for him has been abortion. A Catholic, he has struggled with the issue, and although opposed to abortion, he has backed federal abortion funding for poor women under certain circumstances, such as rape or incest.

The senator's liberal record in the House was a target of his Republican opponent Salvi in the 1996 campaign. Salvi presented a strong conservative approach to issues and attempted to label Durbin a free-spending liberal. This failed in large part because Durbin was able to point to his record of votes against a number of big-ticket expenditures during his House terms. However, given the nature of Illinois politics, Durbin can expect to hear that theme again.

During 2000, Durbin floated several trial balloons regarding the possibility that he might run for governor of Illinois in 2002 rather than seek reelection to the Senate. There was interest in his party and among the public as to that possibility. He seemed to be waiting to learn what role the elections in November would mean for his party when it came to organizing the Senate in 2001. He might have preferred a good chance at becoming governor over being part of a minority group in the Senate.

In December 2000, after the results of the elections of the previous month were finally in, it appeared that the Senate would be divided between the two parties fifty to fifty. Durbin must have been under considerable pressure from his party colleagues to go for reelection as the incumbent senator in 2002 rather than run for governor, in the interests of preserving equality or perhaps of becoming the majority. In mid-December, he announced that his decision was to remain in the Senate, presumably to seek reelection in 2002.

When Senator Jeffords abandoned the Republican Party for its rival in the Senate early in 2001, causing the Democrats to hold the majority, Durbin's decision to remain there rather than to run for governor appeared even more strongly to have been a wise move.

Meanwhile, Senator Durbin was employing the bargaining power at his disposal to gain choice committee assignments for himself. He was given a seat on the powerful Senate Judiciary Committee while being allowed to keep membership in two other "A list" groups. Judiciary is the body that reviews nominations by the president of Supreme Court justices and other federal judges. It also would give Durbin leverage in regard to the naming by the president of U.S. attorneys for Illinois.

In addition, Durbin was appointed to the Democratic Steering and Policy Committee while retaining his post as assistant floor manager. His brief dalliance with thoughts of running for governor of Illinois in 2002 had resulted in elevating his Senate role.

In fact, such successes seemed to be making him a little giddy, and it became known that he was dreaming of a possible run at the presidency in 2004. He was one of forty-two Democrats in the Senate who voted against the confirmation of John Ashcroft for attorney general. That was a vote that might have sprung from Durbin's deepest feelings. It also was one that preserved his good standing among labor unions, which muster both large memberships and "deep pockets" in times of presidential politics. He also opposed the nomination of Gale Norton as secretary of interior.

While his party was in the majority in the Senate in 2001 and 2002, Durbin exercised an increased role in its leadership, often appearing on television and issuing statements critical of Republican initiatives. It was clear that his public profile was strengthened as he prepared to run for reelection.

Durbin was opposed in 2002 by respected state legislator James B. Durkin, who mounted a strong campaign. He was bucking a definite Democratic tide across the state, partially due to Republican problems coming out of Governor George Ryan's two terms as secretary of state.

President Bush's strong stand against Iraq became a major campaign issue, climaxed by Durbin's Senate vote against the Iraq war resolution. One of twenty-one Democrats voting "no" on that issue, Durbin objected to the language in the resolution that gave the president broad authority to take military action against Iraq. On national public radio, after the vote, he said, "[H]istorically we have said it is not enough [to take military action] that you have a weapon that might hurt us. . . . It's not enough that you just possess those weapons" (Biographical Directory).

Republican Durkin said he would support the president's military initiatives. Although the issue became the essential focus of the campaign, Durbin's vote apparently did not impair his chances of winning. He swept the state in gaining reelection, with 60 percent of the vote and a majority in 78 of the state's 102 counties. In Cook County, he scored 70 percent and did well in the collar counties surrounding Cook where Republicans usually enjoy large majorities.

In winning reelection in 2002, Richard Durbin became the ninth person to be elected to a second Senate term since popular election was first employed in 1914. Given his talents and his position in the Democratic leadership in the Senate, there is little doubt that he will continue to be a force in state and national political matters for years to come.

Peter Gosselin Fitzgerald (1999–)

The junior senator from Illinois in 2003, Peter Fitzgerald, was a young man in a hurry. He had entertained political ambitions at least from college onward. He was just two years out of law school when he ran for a seat in the Illinois House of Representatives in 1988. He lost that battle to the incumbent in the Republican primary. Four years later, there was no incumbent running for reelection to the state Senate seat from his district. He went for it and prevailed.

In 1994, Fitzgerald challenged longtime Congressman Phil Crane in the Republican primary. Even though his bid failed, he earned some antagonism on the conservative side of the party. He was reelected to the state Senate in 1996, but even so, acquaintances there knew his sights were set on the national level. He saw his chance in 1998, with a faltering Senator Carol Moseley-Braun as the Democratic incumbent, and the insider's candidate on the Republican side a reluctant state Comptroller Loleta Didrickson. He challenged her in the primary and won and then unseated Moseley-Braun in November, but only by the narrowest of margins.

Peter G. Fitzgerald was born in Elgin, Illinois, on October 20, 1960. He was the youngest of five children. He grew up in subur-

ban Inverness and claims to have had an ordinary childhood, playing Little League baseball, receiving twenty-five cents a week allowance, and having chores to do such as cleaning the dog kennel.

His upbringing may have been ordinary in some respects but
was hardly so in others. His father had put together a string of
suburban banks forming a group called Bancorp. In 1994, he sold
Bancorp to a bank in Montreal for $246 million.

It is putting it mildly to say that young Peter enjoyed a privileged
background, no matter how many times he had to scoop out the
kennel and content himself with his quarter-a-week allowance. He
attended Catholic schools, and then a boarding school called Ports-
mouth Abbey. His college was Dartmouth, where he received a B.A.
degree cum laude on schedule. Next was the University of Michigan
Law School, after a year of study in Greece. He received the J.D.
degree in 1986. His tries for public office soon followed. Meanwhile
he was earning his living in and around the family's banking fortune.

A devoutly conservative Republican, Fitzgerald has been at odds
with the Republican establishment in Illinois since his first failed
attempt at public office. In 1998, he had to beat an established
Republican officeholder, state Comptroller Loleta Didrickson, in the
primary election on his way to the Senate. She had a background
of membership in the state legislature and was very much a member of the "good old boy" network in Springfield.

Didrickson had not wanted to run for the Senate, but the party
heads in Illinois felt that she would be a good counterbalance to
Senator Moseley-Braun as far as the women's vote was concerned.
In that way, the Republican statewide ticket would be strengthened,
they felt.

Two months before the March primary election, Didrickson
held a nearly thirty-point lead in the polls over the lesser known
Fitzgerald. He came out against abortion, gun control, and tax in-
creases, put up three million dollars of his own money for campaign
expenses, and blitzed the state with ads. Before the primary campaign ended, he had outspent his opponent by 7 million to 1.8
million dollars. Most of the seven million was his own money.

The gap between the two narrowed in February. Fitzgerald was
helped by an endorsement from conservative Congressman Henry
Hyde. Former Governor Jim Thompson, Governor Jim Edgar, and
gubernatorial candidate George Ryan favored Didrickson, as did
U.S. Senator Bob Dole, the Republican candidate for president in

1996. As primary day approached, the race had evened up, and when the vote was taken, Fitzgerald came out on top.

As he celebrated on primary election night, Fitzgerald labeled his campaign "the peoples' revolt" and declared that "the revolution has just begun." He continued his spending ways in the campaign against Moseley-Braun and took an early lead in the polls. By the time election day was at hand, his spending in the two campaigns was estimated at fifteen million dollars. His victory over Moseley-Braun was a narrow one.

Throughout his four years in the state Senate, Fitzgerald had continued to be critical of what he saw as "insiders' deals" in Springfield. The granting of gambling casino licenses and loans for hotel construction by the state were two of his favorite targets. He "demonized" William Cellini, Republican moneyman, and was critical of state Treasurer Judy Barr Topinka. He warred against what he saw as bloated, wasteful government. It is not difficult to understand why the Republican establishment looked upon Senator Fitzgerald with an unfriendly eye.

Fitzpatrick was still regarded as a Senate "freshman" when, late in the year 2000, he staged a two-day filibuster against federal funding for the building of a Lincoln library and museum in Springfield. His contention was that the fifty million dollars that was proposed as federal funding in aid of the library/museum project would be used as so much "pork" for political insiders if subject only to state rules of competitive bidding. He wished to interpose the more restrictive federal guidelines instead. "I believe that for a monument to Honest Abe, we need to make sure that we have an honest and ethical bidding process," Fitzgerald said (Long, "Divisive Fight").

Fitzgerald's effort at filibustering caught public attention, and inevitable comparison with the historic delays offered by Senators Strom Thurmond and Huey Long, and the fictional Senator Jefferson Smith of the motion picture *Mr. Smith Goes to Washington*. It also earned him considerable ill will on the part of congressional colleagues who did not look with favor on the Fitzgerald style. Representative Ray LaHood of Peoria said, "Peter is acting more like a senator from a high school class than a senator from Illinois. This is total immaturity on his part" (Pearson and Long).

One of Senator Fitzgerald's press aides replied that the senator "did what he thought was right, regardless of the political consequences. . . . He will continue to do what he can to protect the people of Illinois who trust and elected him" (Long). The senator himself addressed a lengthy letter to the editorial page of the *Chicago Tribune* setting out his point of view.

The flap over the Lincoln library funding was hardly over when Senator Fitzgerald found another crusade to follow. He had sought without much success to play a key role in George W. Bush's Illinois campaign for the presidency of the United States.

Instead Governor George Ryan served as Illinois chairman of the Bush campaign. In view of the public relations problems that the year 2000 brought to him, he was rather low key in his campaign efforts, and that lack was one factor in Bush losing the state by a considerable margin. Given the closeness of the presidential contest nationwide, that was a serious matter for Republican politicians. Perhaps Senator Fitzgerald had been correct in his view that he and not Ryan should have chaired the Bush campaign in Illinois.

With Bush in the Oval Office in January, Senator Fitzgerald launched a new crusade. This time it was for his exclusive right to determine, as the senior senator of the president's political party from Illinois, appointees to the three positions of U.S. attorney within the state. Since the U.S. attorney in each jurisdiction heads the prosecutorial process for criminal cases, those choices have enormous implications for a political system that Fitzgerald alleges is shot through with corruption.

Governor Ryan was understandably concerned about the driver's-licenses-for-bribes scandals that were under investigation at the time replacement of the U.S. attorneys was under way. Speaker of the House Dennis Hastert of Illinois claimed to have a share in the authority to select the new appointees. This clash within an already tension filled relationship between Senator Fitzgerald and the Republican power structure in Illinois, and in the Congress generally, did nothing to quiet the antagonism that had continued for at least a decade.

When Governor Ryan arrived in Washington, D.C., in January 2001 for the inauguration of President Bush, he tended to downplay the conflict between Senator Fitzgerald and mainstream Illinois Republicans. "I get along fine with Peter," he said. "I got a nice Christmas card from him" (*Tribune,* January 22, 2001, 1:7). Ryan also said, however, that he believed Speaker Hastert would carry more weight with the president than Fitzgerald would when it came to naming U.S. attorneys.

This was a delicate matter for the whole Senate. Senators tend to become upset when the time honored custom of having the dominant voice in certain appointments come from the Senate is threatened. The fifty to fifty division between Democrats and Republicans in the Senate made the voice and vote of every one of the fifty in each camp of vital importance to it.

In May 2001, Senator Fitzgerald announced that his choice for the U.S. attorney post in northern Illinois was Patrick J. Fitzgerald, an assistant federal prosecutor in New York City. The two were not related. Patrick Fitzgerald had gained prominence in prosecuting cases such as the 1993 bombing of the World Trade Center and U.S. embassies in Africa, as well as cases involving narcotics and organized crime. There was general agreement that he was well qualified for the Illinois position.

Senator Fitzgerald indicated that he had simply found the best person for the job. He stressed the fact that Patrick Fitzgerald could come to Illinois without any ties or associations that would make him less than fully equipped to function impartially.

Patrick Fitzgerald's parents had been immigrants from Ireland. He managed to find his way into a Jesuit high school, then Amherst College, and next the Harvard Law School. One of his associates in his later work as a prosecutor described him as "Eliot Ness with a Harvard law degree and a sense of humor" (O'Connor). Another said he simply was the best prosecutor in the United States.

Senator Fitzgerald promptly notified his Senate colleague Dick Durbin of his selection but pointedly refrained from doing the same for Speaker of the House Hastert. Fitzgerald voiced the opinion that it would be difficult for anyone to take exception with his choice. That seemed to be the case, for Patrick Fitzgerald was speedily nominated by the president and approved by the Senate. Before the summer of 2001 was over, he had arrived in Chicago to begin his work as U.S. attorney for northern Illinois.

Not long after his announcement of Patrick Fitzgerald's selection, Senator Fitzgerald made it known that his choice for U.S. attorney for central Illinois—with jurisdiction in Springfield—was another "outsider," Jan Paul Miller, then an assistant U.S. attorney in Maryland. The senator again said he wanted an "independent—not an insider. I want someone with no alliances, connections, someone not beholden to anybody. . . . He has no pre-existing connections here" (Long, "2d Outsider").

Apparently Senator Fitzgerald felt that it was less necessary to go outside the state in naming the U.S. attorney for southern Illinois. For that position, he chose Miriam Miquelon, a Chicago attorney noted for prosecuting political corruption cases. Perhaps the distance of that position from the seats of political power in Chicago and Springfield made the outsider's role less necessary, in Senator Fitzgerald's opinion, so far as southern Illinois was concerned. After lengthy delay seeming to come from the established political powers, Miquelon eventually was nominated and approved.

Patrick Fitzgerald had hardly warmed the U.S. attorney's chair in northern Illinois when, early in 2002, he began a prosecution that might end in far-reaching political shock waves. According to political analyst Dennis Byrne, writing in the *Chicago Tribune,* Fitzgerald

> delivered the biggest message to corrupt Chicago politicians, insiders, grafters and boodlers this town may have ever seen. Fitzgerald's first big indictment was of insurance executive Michael Segal for alleged insurance and mail fraud. Fitzgerald wasted no time in going after the biggest fish in town, to the shock and astonishment of just about everyone. Segal is not just the pal, but *the* pal, the top of the heap. His indictment makes the prosecution of Chicago aldermen look like the issuance of parking tickets. This is a hugely symbolic act; its effect will be like watching the bugs scurrying for cover after the rock has been lifted.

Byrne credited the fact that Senator Fitzgerald had funded his campaign for election largely with his own money—almost fifteen million dollars of it—for his independence of traditional donors. It remains to be seen what becomes of the Segal prosecution, and of other high-level indictments.

Only days before the Segal indictment, U.S. Attorney Fitzgerald had caused the records of the Illinois Gaming Commission relating to the proposed Emerald Casino to be subpoenaed, and F.B.I. officials had interviewed officials on the fifth floor of the Cook County Building about allegations of ghost payrolling. In February, additional records of the Gaming Commission were sought, and subpoenas were issued for city hall records about multimillion-dollar janitorial contracts given to the politically connected Duff family.

The greatest stir occurred early in April, with the indictment of Governor George Ryan's campaign committee, Citizens for Ryan, and two of its top officials, for corruption over a seven-year period.

The net of indictment seemed to be closing around the governor. U.S. Attorney Fitzgerald's

> steely promise that the investigation will continue "with vigor," has Springfield and Chicago pols in a tizzy over who'll be the feds' next corruption target. "Fitzgerald doesn't care about the political implications of all this," says a former federal prosecutor: "He's a street fighter. It's Marquess of Queensberry rules be damned." (*Tribune,* April 7, 2002, 8:1)

Late in 2002, Scott Fawell, who was chief of staff for Governor Ryan and earlier when Ryan was secretary of state, was indicted. Information filed by U.S. Attorney Fitzpatrick in the indictment indicated that the governor, during his campaign for that office, was present when Fawell ordered the shredding of material relating to the use of state employees, on state time, in Ryan's campaign. The net seemed to be tightening. The jury found Fawell guilty in March 2003.

It is difficult to imagine that if Loleta Didrickson, very much an insider, had been elected to the Senate in 1998 and in a position in 2001 to select the U.S. attorneys for Illinois, the current wave of indictments based on corruption in George Ryan's secretary of state's office would have occurred. In the battle against establishment corruption in Illinois public life, Peter Fitzgerald seems to be making a difference.

In spite of the voice of dissent that Senator Fitzgerald had become, he fared rather well in 2001 in committee assignments. He requested and was given a seat on the powerful Commerce, Science, and Transportation Committee. He also learned that he could continue on the Agriculture and Small Business Committees.

Ideologically speaking, Senator Fitzgerald has been slowly moving toward the center of the spectrum. If he runs for the Senate in 2004, he knows his chances of being elected will be better if he is viewed as a moderate (Sweet 19). It will be interesting to observe the role that Senator Fitzgerald chooses to play during the balance of his first term in the Senate. Some characterize him as principled, intelligent, and prepared. Others see him as arrogant, rude, and overly ambitious. In either case, the voting public in Illinois is likely to have still more chances to endorse or oppose him at the polls.

After an initial coolness brought about by Senator Durbin's ardent support of Carol Moseley-Braun in 1998, he and Senator Fitzgerald seemed to find a basis for harmonious interaction in a Senate almost equally balanced between the two major parties. By mid-2001, Durbin was able to say, "We trust one another." Fitzgerald agreed, saying, "He's never breached a confidence. We work well together" (Zuckman 16).

One observer found the "chemistry" between Durbin and Fitzgerald to be "terrific," in spite of the fact that they are "political opposites." She quoted Durbin as saying, "I get along well with Peter Fitzgerald, and we have had a good working relationship . . . to the amazement of both of us, and I want it to continue" (Sweet 17).

Continuing a custom begun by Senator Simon in 1985, Senators Durbin and Fitzgerald met for a time with visitors from Illinois once a week while the Senate was in session. Those sessions began at 8:30 A.M. on Thursday, with coffee and doughnuts. Often, and especially in the spring when students visit Washington, there were hundreds of their constituents in attendance.

Each of the two senators listened to the other propound on the issues of the moment. The two treated each other with respect, even though usually they differ on issues.

Late in 2001, however, their affection for one another went into decline. Durbin was attempting to incorporate an agreement between Mayor Daley and Governor Ryan concerning the expansion of O'Hare Airport into another piece of "likely to pass" legislation. Fitzgerald led a near-filibuster that stopped the bill in its tracks. Durbin claimed that he had had an agreement with his counterpart that no such delay would occur. Fitzgerald denied that his action was a filibuster, saying that it simply was honest debate.

The *Chicago Tribune* came down hard on Fitzgerald editorially, for halting the furtherance of much needed improvement of O'Hare. It charged the senator with disregarding the great economic advantages that would flow to the area and its people if the airport were enlarged and otherwise improved (December 8, 2001). Fitzgerald countered, in dueling press conferences held in Chicago, that the O'Hare expansion would cause the destruction of "thousands" of homes in the area, rather than hundreds, and would mean an end to the hope of many for a new airport at Peotone (December 10, 11, 2001)).

Fitzgerald is often at odds with the leaders of his party, in Washington as well as in Springfield. Durbin is within the leadership of his and seldom deviates from its line. He has been mentioned as one who could become minority or majority leader. To date, no one has viewed Peter Fitzgerald in that light.

It is probable that he did not endear himself to the leader of his party in the White House when in February 2002, he addressed Enron's former chief executive Kenneth Lay during a hearing of the Senate's Commerce Committee. Fitzgerald said:

> Mr. Lay, I've concluded that you're perhaps the most accomplished confidence man since Charles Ponzi. I'd say you were a carnival barker, except that might not be fair to carnival barkers. A carny will at least tell you up front that he's running a shell game. You, Mr. Lay, were running what purported to be the seventh largest company in America. (Neikirk)

The Republican debacle in Illinois in November 2002, in the face of the party's success across the nation, will have the effect of clearing away much of the longtime leadership that brought the Illinois G.O.P. to its present sorry state. As new leadership emerges, with State Treasurer Judy Baar Topinka becoming the party's state chairman, there is no doubt that Senator Peter Fitzgerald has gained equal prominence.

To a public disgusted with the sleaze, cronyism, and corruption that has long flourished in Springfield, Senator Fitzgerald stands as a beacon of hope. Even so, conservative elements in his party continue to see him as a threat, as one who shuns becoming a part of the "good old boy" network.

There was talk in conservative Republican circles late in 2002 of seeking an opponent for Senator Fitzpatrick in the 2004 primary election. Experience suggested that if that were done and Fitzpatrick were beaten, the party would lose the seat in the general election. As his first term in the Senate heads toward conclusion in 2004, we can expect to see lively campaigns for his position in both March and November.

Early in January 2003, Carol Moseley-Braun, whom Senator Fitzgerald had defeated in 1998, expressed some interest in running again for the office in 2004. It is probable that her party threw cold water on her ambitions along that line, feeling that with her record while in the Senate, she would have little chance of beating Senator Fitzgerald. The Democratic Party had other rising stars to groom for the Senate contest, such as state Comptroller Dan Hynes, Cook County Treasurer Maria Pappas, and state Senator Barack Obama.

Obama announced in mid-January 2003 that he intended to file for the Democratic primary for the Fitzgerald seat. A lawyer and a state senator, Obama was reputed to be of keen intelligence. Moseley-Braun was lured away into other pastures by the suggestion that she make a run for the Democratic nomination for president of the United States. Hardly a serious contender, the hope was that she could offer an alternative to Al Sharpton to Black voters and help energize them for participation in the general election. Party officials probably breathed easier with her out of the Senate race.

Barack Obama's formal announcement came early in February 2003. It is likely that he will have at least one strong opponent, Dan Hynes, in the Democratic primary. In a race having several candidates, anything can happen.

> "Four years ago, Peter Fitzgerald bought himself a Senate seat, and he's betrayed Illinois ever since," said Obama, referring to Fitzgerald's heavy personal spending on his 1998 campaign. "But we are here to take it back on behalf of the people of Illinois." (Pearson and Chase)

Later in February, Fitzgerald made it known that he had not asked any of the Republican leaders in the state to back him in his bid for reelection in 2004. He felt that he faced the stiffest contest of any of the Senate Republicans who would be before the voters. At that time, there had been no specific opponent surfacing to enter the primary election against Fitzgerald. However, neither Speaker of the House Dennis Hastert nor State Treasurer and Republican Party Chairperson Judy Baar Topinka had endorsed the incumbent.

Fitzgerald claimed to have the support of President Bush and Senate Majority Leader Bill Frist. That appeared to be the case in March 2003, even though Fitzgerald had embarrassed the president by statements reporting a conversation with him aboard Air Force One enroute to Washington following the president's speech in Chicago about the economy.

"I have personally talked with the president about this," Fitzgerald said,

> and if we had intelligence on where [Saddam Hussein] is now, and we had a clear shot to assassinate him, we would probably do that.

President Bush would probably sign an executive order repealing the executive order put in place by President Ford that forbade the assassination of foreign leaders. (*Tribune,* March 3, 2003, 1:1)

The president's press secretary was hit with a barrage of questions the next day. President Bush, he noted, did not recall making that observation. The president's support for Fitzgerald for the upcoming campaign remained unchanged.

As for endorsements from Illinois Republicans, Fitzgerald said that "there's a price to pay for independence and that price is the wariness of the established order." He claimed to be "an independent voice" in a "machine state" (*Tribune,* February 19, 2003).

Many of his supporters were taken by surprise when Fitzgerald announced, on April 15, that he did not intend to run for a second term in 2004. He admitted a lack of "fire in my belly" and felt that a campaign would require more of his own money and time from his family than he wished to expend.

Regarded as the weakest of the Republican senators whose terms were ending, Fitzgerald has been under some pressure to withdraw. There was no clear consensus among party leaders about a replacement. Former attorney general Jim Ryan, who had lost a contest for governor in 2002, was best known of those being spoken of as possible candidates for the Republican primary, with the exception of former governor Jim Edgar (Pearson, "Fitzgerald").

21 ★ Conclusion

We were not fully aware, when we began this study, of the full breadth of insight it would afford us of the place that Illinois has had in the history of the U.S. Senate. Looking at the political lives of all the senators from Illinois has informed us as to the major issues that have come and gone on both the state and national scenes since statehood was gained in 1818.

The number of our subjects of study—forty-seven—has been large enough to allow us to generalize and small enough to be manageable. In the space that follows, we wish to share with you certain observations that we believe have application to other political systems.

Almost all of the early political leaders in Illinois—and that includes judges and governors as well as U.S. senators—were born, grew to adulthood, and were educated in a more eastern state of earlier settlement. Illinois simply did not have enough talented and trained persons among its early populations to staff those positions.

That condition persisted until after the Civil War. Examples are Senators Stephen A. Douglas and Lyman Trumbull. Both were from New England. Douglas was prominent in the Senate and a leading figure in the controversy over the extension of slavery, during the decade immediately preceding the Civil War. Trumbull served with distinction in the Senate throughout that conflict.

We believe that this observation has implications for other developing and emerging political cultures. Early on, it may be necessary for them to do as the new state of Illinois did and draw upon, for their political leaders, persons born and educated in other milieus. And that need may persist, as it did in Illinois, for half a century or more, depending on the speed of political and general cultural development.

Another area in which we observed worthwhile generalizations was that relating to the method of choosing U.S. senators. Throughout the nineteenth century, the general rule was for that selection to be made by the state legislature. That manner of choice produced some good senators from Illinois—notably Stephen Douglas, Trumbull, and John Palmer—and also a number that at best could be called average. No doubt the same was true in other states.

Choice by the legislature also proved in Illinois often to be enormously time consuming. As time went on and legislative bodies met for longer periods, it was not unusual in Illinois for the bargaining and balloting over a position in the Senate to be extended over two to four months, with little else accomplished during that time.

Perhaps the worst example of the product of legislative choice in Illinois was William Lorimer. He was a last-minute compromise after dozens of ballots had been taken. He was a political boss of dubious reputation who eventually was expelled from the Senate because of corrupt practices having to do with his selection. The example of Lorimer, coming when it did, may have been the final impetus for the ratification of the Seventeenth Amendment to the U.S. Constitution, which mandated the popular election of senators.

We also observed that the Seventeenth Amendment, while it was implemented promptly in Illinois, did not seem to have much effect until two decades had gone by. The last two United State senators chosen by the legislature in Illinois were also later sent to the Senate by popular vote in that state, one by immediate reelection and the other after a decade had gone by.

While the quality of senators from Illinois did not seem to improve noticeably with popular election during the first two decades of its use, there was the gain that no longer were great quantities of precious legislative time taken up, though the players in the political process that had been making the choices—party leaders, political bosses, legislative leaders, and the media—seemed still to be in control so far as choosing senators was concerned. It seems that the public was slow in developing an awareness of the new tool of democracy that had been thrust into its hands by the Seventeenth Amendment.

Finally, a change in that situation seemed to be at hand. It is evidenced by the election of Scott W. Lucas in 1938 and C. Wayland Brooks in 1940. Neither would have been the choice of the legislature that was sitting at the time of his election. Each represented a wave of popular feeling that was dominant at the moment.

Lucas eventually became the majority leader of his party in the Senate. That was a position of power that no earlier senator from Illinois had achieved. Brooks was a leading example of opposition to the ideologies that were advanced by Presidents Roosevelt and Truman. There is no doubt that he truly represented many Illinois voters.

Brooks and Lucas were followed by a succession of senators, from both parties, of high national reputation—Paul Douglas, Everett Dirksen, Charles Percy, Adlai Stevenson, and Paul Simon—which suggests strongly that election by the people is clearly superior to choice by the legislature. It would be interesting to learn if there has been a similar experience in other states.

It seems desirable to call attention again to figure 2, in the preface. It clearly indicates that even though popular election of a U.S. senator was first employed in Illinois in 1914, it did not seem to cause much change in the quality of the persons who were sent to the Senate or to the duration of their tenure, until nearly a quarter of a century had gone by.

Then, with the election of Scott Lucas in 1938 and "Curly" Brooks in 1940, the voters seemed at last to comprehend the tool of democracy they had at hand. Since that time, the period of service for each senator has noticeably lengthened—except for Ralph Tyler Smith, who was not elected but appointed by the governor following the death in office of Everett Dirksen—and the quality on the whole greatly improved.

Longer tenure after 1940 was due in part to the superior quality of the persons who were sent to the Senate by the voters. It is probable, too, that the "incumbent advantage" weighed more heavily in the system of popular election than it did when selection was by the legislature. Prior to the Seventeenth Amendment, a change in the majority party in the legislature inevitably meant that when the senatorial term ended, a new face would appear in the nation's capital.

When Illinois became a state, almost all of its citizens were found in its southern quarter. Consequently, its U.S. senators were residents of that region. As settlement was extended into the central prairie lands, we began to find that the communities from which senators were chosen were often located there. As Chicago grew after the Civil War, it too began to be productive of persons placed in the Senate, either by the General Assembly or, after 1913, by the voters.

The geographic distribution of our subjects of study, as determined by their place of residence when they were first selected, through time, is shown in figure 3. The impact of their longevity in the Senate is measured by the number of years each served. Presenting this data graphically was accomplished by dividing the total time involved (1818 to 1998) into four equal segments, and marking off a map of the state of Illinois into four sectors equal in length on a south to north axis.

This process created a matrix of sixteen cells, resulting from having four segments on the time line, the x axis, and four sectors on the spatial line, the y axis. Each person sent to the Senate could then be placed in one of the sixteen cells of this figure, as determined by the year of selection or election, and by the place of residence when initially chosen. Then, to add precision to the mix, each senator was assigned a number equal to the number of years served. For Frank Smith, elected but never seated, that number was one. For all others, each year served counted as one.

For the persons in each cell, the tenure numbers assigned to each were totaled, giving a total count for the cell. For the entire matrix, the correlation between time and location of representation in the state is 0.56. When location is regressed against time, the estimated equation is $y = 1.15 + 0.60x$ with an R^2 of 0.314, where y equals location and x equals time.

It is apparent from figure 3 that as time went on, the southern one quarter of the state, with the exception of the election of Paul Simon, became progressively less likely to produce a senator, while the most northern tier became progressively more likely to do so. Since power follows the office, we can assume that all other things being equal the passage of time has seen power in the Senate being exercised in behalf of more northern, rather than more southern,

Illinois, from south (bottom) to north (top), in miles	1818 to 1863		1863 to 1908		1908 to 1953		1953 to 1998	
400			Farwell	6	Lorimer	2	Douglas	18
			Mason	6	Lewis	14	Percy	18
			Hopkins	6	Brooks	8	Stevenson	10
				18	McCormick	6	Moseley-	6
					Deneen	6	Braun	
					Slattery	1	Fitzgerald	4
						37		56
300	Browning	2	Oglesby	6	Sherman	8	Dirksen	18
			Davis	6	McKinley	6	Durbin	6
			Cullom	30	Dieterich	6		24
				42	F. Smith	1		
						21		
200	Semple	4	Richardson	2	Lucas	12	R. Smith	1
	S. Douglas	14	Yates	6			Dixon	13
	Trumbull	18	Palmer	6				14
		36		14				
100	Thomas	11	Logan	13	Glenn	4	Simon	12
	Edwards	6						
	McLean	2						
	Baker	1						
	Kane	11						
	McRoberts	2						
	Breeze	6						
	Ewing	2						
	Shields	6						
	Robinson	11						
	Young	6						
		64						

Fig. 3. The Distribution of Senate Tenure, by Time and Region

interests. There has been much variation from that tendency, of course, as determined by the natures of the individuals involved, and from issue to issue. Still, the region from which one comes does make a difference.

Illinois is seen as a "swing state" in which the two major political parties are sufficiently balanced to allow each one a fair chance of victory in the election of U.S. presidents and U.S. senators. From the time line of figure 2, in the preface, it can be noted that as of-ten as not, since popular election became the rule, the two seats in the Senate for Illinois have been divided between a Republican and a Democrat.

Taking into consideration the odd numbered years—in which Senate terms ordinarily begin—from 1919 to 1999, the two Senate seats for Illinois were divided between the two major political par-ties 50 percent of the time. There were two Democrats in those po-sitions for 30 percent and two Republicans for 20 percent of the time.

The most persistent dominance occurred for the Republicans during the 1920s and for the Democrats in the 1930s and the late 1980s and 1990s. Those periods should come as no surprise to anyone familiar with the way the political winds of the twentieth century were blowing in Illinois.

From 1941 to 1984—nearly half a century—there were only three of the nineteen odd-numbered years taken into account in which one party held both seats—the Democrats in 1949, with Douglas and Lucas, and the Republicans in 1967 and 1969, with Dirksen and Percy.

That must be considered a remarkable display of the fact that much more often than not Illinois is truly a state in which both major political parties are capable of presenting and electing wor-thy candidates for the U.S. Senate. Its reputation as a swing state is thereby enforced.

To present those divisions graphically, figure 4 is offered here. It shows clearly the alternations of party victory and defeat. In each case, the losing percentage is very nearly a mirror image of the winning percentage. There is seldom a third party vote that reaches as much as 5 percent of the total.

Thus, it is not necessary to plot the percentage of votes of both major political parties. In each case, the one is basically the mirror image of the other. To show both graphically leads to an unduly complex figure. In figure 4, the arbitrary choice was to show only the Republican vote, based on the fact that the early years of the election of senators by popular vote was a time of Republican domi-nance. The Democratic vote in each case can be visualized as the mirror image of the Republican.

Figure 4 shows that the Republicans were dominant in the 1920s, the Democrats in the 1930s. During the period from 1940 to 1980, the two parties alternated in winning Senate contests, usually within

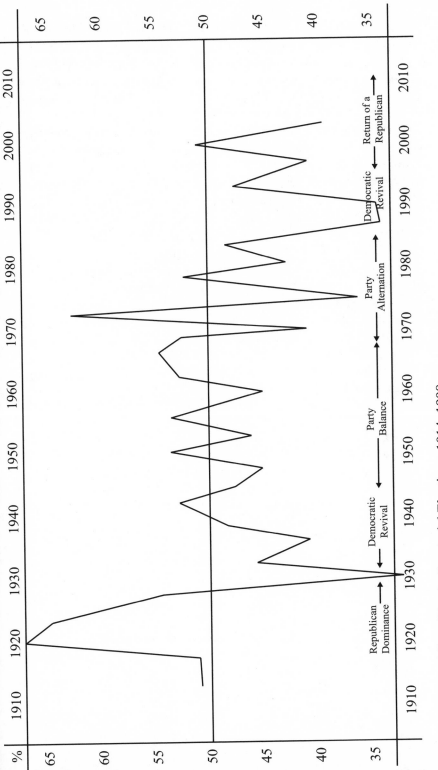

Fig. 4. The Republican Vote in Senatorial Elections, 1914–1998

the range of 45 to 55 percent. That suggests these facts: The parties were quite evenly balanced during that time, neither was able to field a strong candidate in election after election, and the voters were capable of going for a favored candidate rather than a straight party vote in sufficient numbers to decide the contest. Again, the image of Illinois as a swing state is reinforced.

The Democratic Party held both Illinois Senate seats in the 1980s and 1990s until Peter Fitzgerald narrowly defeated Carol Moseley-Braun in 1998. During that period, the Republican Party suffered its worst defeats in Senate elections since 1930 when, in 1986 and 1990, it offered the voters, in turn, a female candidate, both candidates notably conservative figures. The Republicans might win with a middle-of-the-road Charles Percy, when they could not with a right-leaning Judy Koehler or Lynn Martin.

Contests for the Senate seat are affected by the unique strengths of candidates and by the political climate surrounding their personalities and state and national issues. Thus, those contests do not invariably follow the lead of the contest for the presidency in the years in which that election occurs.

It is the hope of the authors that studies such as this will take place in other states. It will be interesting to see if conclusions there will be similar to those expressed above.

★ BIBLIOGRAPHY
★ INDEX

BIBLIOGRAPHY

Allen, Howard, and Vince Lacey. *Illinois Elections, 1818–1990.* Carbondale: Southern Illinois UP.

Allinson, May. "The Government of Illinois, 1790–1799." *I.S.H.S. Transactions,* 1907, 277–92.

Alvord, Clarence W. *The Illinois Country, 1673–1818.* Urbana: U of Illinois P, 1987.

Angle, Paul M. *Bloody Williamson.* New York: Knopf, 1952.

Barnhart, Bill, and Gene Schlickman. *Kerner: The Conflict of Intangible Rights.* Urbana: U of Illinois P, 1999.

Baxter, Maurice G. *Orville H. Browning: Lincoln's Friend and Critic.* Bloomington: Indiana UP, 1957.

Berry, Daniel. "Forgotten Statesmen of Illinois: Hon. John M. Robinson." *I.S.H.S. Journal,* vol. 7, 1905, 77–81.

Biles, Roger. *Big City Boss in Depression and War: Mayor Edward J. Kelly of Chicago.* De Kalb: Northern Illinois UP, 1984.

———. *Crusading Liberal: Paul H. Douglas of Illinois.* De Kalb: Northern Illinois UP, 2002.

———. *Richard J. Daley: Politics, Race, and the Governing of Chicago.* De Kalb: Northern Illinois UP, 1995.

Biographical Directory of the U.S. Congress. <http://bioguide.congress. gov/scripts>.

Boylan, Rose J. *Metro-East Journal,* May 9, 1963.

Bright, John. *Hizzoner Big Bill Thompson: An Idyll of Chicago.* New York: Cape and Smith, 1930.

Buck, Solon J. *Illinois in 1918.* Urbana: U of Illinois P, 1967.

Burton, William L. "James Semple, Prairie Entrepreneur." *Illinois Historical Journal,* no. 2, 1987, 66–84.

Byrne, Dennis. *Chicago Tribune,* February 14, 2002, 1:8.

Caro, Robert A. *Master of the Senate.* New York: Knopf, 2002.

Casey, Robert J., and W. A. S. Douglas. *The Midwesterner: The Story of Dwight Green.* Chicago: Wilcox and Follett, 1948.

Clayton, John, comp. *The Illinois Fact Book and Historical Almanac, 1673–1968.* Carbondale: Southern Illinois UP, 1970.

Cole, Arthur C. *The Era of the Civil War, 1848–1870.* Urbana: U. of Illinois P.

Collin, Dorothy. "Illinois Odd Couple Chase Two Agendas in the Senate." *Chicago Tribune,* February 15, 1987.

———. "Power and Glory." *Chicago Tribune Magazine,* April 16, 1995.

Conklin, Mike. "Family Matters." *Chicago Tribune,* October 29, 2002.

Converse, Henry A. "The Life and Services of Shelby M. Cullom." Proceedings of the I.S.H.S., 1914, 55–79.

Dallek, Robert. *Flawed Giant: Lyndon Johnson and His Times, 1961–1973.* New York: Oxford, 1998.

Davis, James E. *Frontier Illinois.* Bloomington: Indiana UP, 1998.

Deason, Brian S. *Eye of the Storm: A Political Biography of U.S. Senator Scott W. Lucas of Illinois.* Unpublished doctoral dissertation, S.I.U.C., 2000.

Dictionary of American Biography. New York: Scribner's, 1964.

Dirksen, Louella, with Norma Lee Browning. *The Honorable Mr. Marigold.* New York: Doubleday, 1972.

Douglas, Paul H. *In the Fullness of Time: The Memoirs of Paul H. Douglas.* New York: Harcourt Brace, 1968.

Dowling, John. "'Rev.' Simon Planted Political Roots." *Journal-American,* December 13, 1987.

Dunn, J. P., Jr. *Indiana: A Redemption from Slavery.* Boston: Houghton Mifflin, 1888.

Ford, Thomas. *A History of Illinois from Its Commencement as a State in 1818 to 1847.* Ed. by Milo Quaife, 2 vols. Chicago: Lakeside, 1945.

Furlong, W. B. "The Son Also Rises." *Chicago,* June 1979, 116, 174–78.

Goodwin, Doris K. *Lyndon Johnson and the American Dream.* New York: Harper and Row, 1976.

Gottfried, Alex. *Boss Cermak of Chicago: A Study of Political Leadership.* Seattle: U of Washington P, 1962.

Hansen, Stephen, and Paul Nygard. "Stephen A. Douglas, the Know-Nothings, and the Democratic Party in Illinois, 1954–58." *Illinois Historical Journal,* 1994, 109–30.

Harrison, Carter H. *Stormy Years.* New York: Bobbs-Merrill, 1935.

Hartley, Robert E. "Adlai for President?" *Southern Illinoisan,* October 26, 1975.

———. "The Boy Wonders Are Back Together." *Illinois Times,* May 8–14, 1981.

———. *Charles H. Percy: A Political Perspective.* Chicago: Rand McNally, 1975.

———. "Dixon Has No Record on Affairs Outside of State." *Decatur Herald and Review,* April 8, 1979.

———. "Middle Ground Not Radical." *Decatur Herald and Review,* February 25, 1973.

Holt, Robert D. "The Political Career of William A. Richardson." *Journal of the Illinois State Historical Society,* 1993, 222–69.

Horner, Harlan H. "Lincoln Rebukes a Senator." *Journal of the Illinois State Historical Society,* 1951, 103–19.

Howard, Robert P. *Illinois: A History of the Prairie State.* Grand Rapids: Eerdmans, 1972.

———. *Mostly Good and Competent Men: Illinois Governors 1818 to 1988.* Springfield: *Illinois Issues,* Sangamon State University, and the Illinois State Historical Society, 1988.

Hulsey, Byron C. *Everett Dirksen and His Presidents.* Lawrence: U. of Kansas P, 2000.

Hutchenson, William T. *Lowden of Illinois: The Life of Frank O. Lowden.* 2 vols. Chicago: U of Chicago P, 1957.

Isikoff, Michael. "Percy Says He Learned Lessons." *Decatur Herald and Review,* November 10, 1978.

James, Frank. "Welcome to the Club." *Chicago Tribune Magazine,* December 6, 1992.

Jensen, Richard J. *Illinois: A Bicentennial History.* New York: Norton, 1978.

Johannsen, Robert W. *The Frontier, the Union, and Stephen A. Douglas.* Urbana: U of Illinois P, 1989.

———. *Stephen A. Douglas.* New York: Oxford UP, 1973.

Jones, James P. *Black Jack: John A. Logan and Southern Illinois in the Civil War Era.* Carbondale: Southern Illinois UP, 1982.

———. "John A. Logan, Freshman in Congress." *Journal of the Illinois State Historical Society,* 1963, 36–60.

———. *John A. Logan, Stalwart Republican from Illinois.* Tallahassee: Florida State UP, 1982.

Kaiser, Robert G. "Stevenson Hints He Might Seek the Presidency." *Washington Post,* February 9, 1979, A:8.

Keiser, John. *Building for the Centuries: Illinois, 1865 to 1898.* Urbana: U of Illinois P, 1977.

Kelly, Harry. "Adlai after Daley." *Chicago Tribune,* February 13, 1977, 1:12.

Kennedy, John F. *Profiles in Courage.* New York: Harper, 1964.

Kenney, David. *Basic Illinois Government.* 1st ed. and 3rd ed. Carbondale: Southern Illinois UP, 1970, 1991.

———. *A Political Passage: The Career of Stratton of Illinois.* Carbondale: Southern Illinois UP, 1990.

Kimball, E. L. "Richard Yates: His Record as Civil War Governor of Illinois." *I.S.H.S. Journal,* vol. 23, 1930, 2.

King, Willard L. *Lincoln's Manager, David Davis.* Cambridge: Harvard UP, 1960.

Krenkel, John H., ed. *Richard Yates, Civil War Governor.* Danville: Interstate, 1966.

Littlewood, Thomas B. *Horner of Illinois.* Evanston: Northwestern UP, 1969.

Long, Ray. "Divisive Fight about Library." *Chicago Tribune,* October 10, 2000, 1:1.

———. "2d Outsider Backed for U.S. Prosecutor." *Chicago Tribune,* August 15, 2001.

MacNeil, Neil. *Dirksen.* New York: World, 1970.

Margolis, Jon. *Chicago Tribune,* April 14, 1987, 15:1.

Martin, John B. *Adlai Stevenson of Illinois: The Life of Adlai E. Stevenson.* Garden City: Doubleday, 1976.

McCulloch, David. *Truman.* New York: Simon, 1992.

McFeely, William S. *Grant: A Biography.* New York: Norton, 1981.

McPherson, Michael. "Charles Percy: A Power in the Senate, but Will He Play in Peoria?" *Washington Post Magazine,* October 25, 1981.

Miller, Kristie. "Ruth Hanna McCormick and the Senatorial Election of 1930." *Illinois Historical Journal,* 1988, 191–210.

Milton, George F. "Douglas' Place in American History." *I.S.H.S. Journal,* 1934, 323–48.

Morton, Richard A. *Justice and Humanity: Edward F. Dunne, Illinois Progressive.* Carbondale: Southern Illinois UP, 1997.

Myers, James. *The Astonishing Saber Duel of Abraham Lincoln.* Springfield: Lincoln-Herndon, 1968.

Natale, Joe, and Bruce Mackey. "Adlai Stevenson Talks about Family, Business." *Springfield Business Journal,* August 1998.

———. "Stevenson Remembers Campaigns for Governor." *Springfield Business Journal,* September 1998.

Neikirk, William. "Senators Pummel Silent Lay." *Chicago Tribune,* February 13, 2002.

Neilson, James W. *Shelby M. Cullom: Prairie State Republican.* Urbana: U of Illinois P, 1962.

Nevins, Allan. *Adams.* Urbana: U of Illinois P, 1968.

———. "Stephen A. Douglas: His Weaknesses and His Greatness." *I.S.H.S. Journal,* 1963, 121–38.

Northrup, Jack. "Richard Yates: A Personal Glimpse of the Illinois Soldiers' Friend." *I.S.H.S. Journal,* 1963, 121–38.

O'Connor, Matt. "Fitzgerald Taps an Outsider for U.S. Attorney." *Chicago Tribune,* May 14, 2001, 1:4.

Page, Clarence. "Democrats Facing Dilemma in Party." *Chicago Tribune,* February 3, 2003, 2:11.

Palmer, George T. *A Conscientious Turncoat: The Story of John M. Palmer 1817–1900.* New Haven: Yale UP, 1941.

Pease, Theodore C. *The Frontier State, 1818–1848.* Urbana: U of Illinois P, 1987.

———. *The Story of Illinois.* Chicago: U of Chicago P, 1965.

Pearson, Rick. "Fitzgerald Not Going to Pursue Re-election." *Chicago Tribune,* April 15, 2003, 1:1.

Pearson, Rick, and John Chase. "Legislator in Race to Unseat Fitzgerald." *Chicago Tribune,* February 5, 2003.

Pearson, Rick, and Ray Long. "Library Spat Hints at Trouble." *Chicago Tribune,* September 30, 2000, 1:3.

Pensoneau, Taylor. *Governor Richard Ogilvie: In the Interest of the State.* Carbondale: Southern Illinois UP, 1997.

Percy, Charles H. Letter to Fletcher Farrar, April 13, 1981.

Peterson, Bill. "Another Midwesterner." *Washington Post* (Weekly Edition), December 7, 1987, 14.

Plummer, Mark A. *Lincoln's Rail Splitter: Governor Richard J. Oglesby.* Urbana: U of Illinois P, 2001.

Quatannens, Jo Anne M. *Senators of the United States: A Historical Bibliography, 1789–1995.* Washington: GPO, 1995.

Reynolds, John. *The Pioneer History of Illinois.* Belleville: N. A. Randall, 1852.

Rose, Don. "The Politics of Adlai Stevenson." *Chicago Sun-Times,* April 8, 1979, 8, 10–11.

Royko, Mike. "Adlai Serves Up Justice." *Chicago Daily News,* February 11, 1979.

Sandburg, Carl. *Abraham Lincoln War Years,* vol. 1. New York: Scribner's, 1939.

Schapsmeier, Edward L. "Dirksen and Douglas of Illinois: The Pragmatist and the Professor as Contemporaries in the United States Senate." *I.S.H.S. Journal,* 1990, 75–84.

Schapsmeier, Edward L., and Frederick H. Schapsmeier. *Dirksen of Illinois: Senatorial Statesman.* Urbana: U of Illinois P, 1985.

———. "Paul H. Douglas: From Pacifist to Soldier-Statesman." *I.S.H.S. Journal,* 1974, 307–23.

Schmidt, John R. *The Mayor Who Cleaned Up Chicago: A Political Biography of William E. Dever.* De Kalb: Northern Illinois UP, 1989.

Simon, Paul M. *P.S.: The Autobiography of Paul Simon.* Chicago: Bonus, 1999.

———. *Winners and Losers: The 1988 Race for the Presidency.* New York: Continuum, 1989.

Smith, Richard M. *The Colonel: The Life and Legend of Robert R. McCormick, 1880–1955.* Boston: Houghton, 1997.

Snyder, J. F. "Forgotten Statesmen of Illinois: Hon. Jesse Burgess Thomas." *I.S.H.S. Transactions,* 1904, 514–23.

Sparks, Edwin E., ed. *The Lincoln-Douglas Debates of 1858.* Vol. 1, Lincoln Series, Collections of the I.S.H.L. Springfield: I.S.H.L., 1908.

Stevens, Frank E. "Life of Douglas." *I.S.H.S. Journal,* vol. 16, 1923, 293–94, 393.

Suppiger, Joseph E. "Amity to Enmity: Ninian Edwards and Jesse B. Thomas." *I.S.H.S. Journal,* 1974, 201–11.

Sweet, Lynn. "Senator Peter Fitzgerald." *Illinois Issues,* March 2001.

Tarr, Joel A. *A Study in Boss Politics: William Lorimer of Chicago.* Urbana: U of Illinois P, 1971.

Tingley, Donald E. *The Structuring of a State: The History of Illinois, 1899 to 1928.* Urbana: U of Illinois P, 1980.

Warren, James. "Simon-Percy Senate Duel." *Chicago Tribune,* October 14, 1984.

Weaver, Warren, Jr. "Stevenson Says He May Oppose Carter." *New York Times,* February 9, 1979, A19:2, 3.

Wendt, Lloyd. *Chicago Tribune: The Rise of a Great American Newspaper.* Chicago: Rand McNally, 1979.

Zuckman, Jill. "Across the Great Divide." *Chicago Tribune Magazine,* April 22, 2001.

INDEX

David Kenney is a professor emeritus of political science at Southern Illinois University Carbondale. In 1969–1970, he was an elected member of the Sixth Illinois Constitutional Convention. He is the author of *Roll Call, Making a Modern Constitution, Basic Illinois Government,* and *A Political Passage,* which is a biography of former Illinois governor William G. Stratton. From 1977 to 1984, Kenney was a member of the governor's cabinet in Illinois as the director of the Department of Conservation. In 1984–1985, he was the founding director of the Illinois State Historic Preservation Agency.

Robert E. Hartley is the author of *Charles H. Percy: A Political Perspective, Big Jim Thompson of Illinois* (which received a 1980 Award of Merit from the Illinois State Historical Society), *Paul Powell of Illinois: A Lifelong Democrat,* and *Lewis and Clark in the Illinois Country: The Little-Told Story.* He has written and presented articles on Illinois history programs of the Illinois State Historical Society and the Illinois Historic Preservation Agency. He was a reporter and an editor on the *Metro-East Journal* (serving the Illinois counties of St. Clair and Madison), the managing editor of the *Decatur* (Illinois) *Herald* and the *Sunday Herald and Review,* and the editor of the *Decatur Herald and Review* and the Lindsay-Schaub group of newspapers. In 1979, Hartley became executive editor of the *Toledo* (Ohio) *Blade* and later publisher of the *Journal-American* in Bellevue, Washington.